The Real X-Men

The Heroic Story of the
Underwater War
1942–1945

Robert Lyman

Quercus

First published in Great Britain in 2015 by

Quercus Publishing Ltd
Carmelite House
50 Victoria Embankment
London EC4Y 0DZ

An Hachette UK company

A CIP catalogue record for this book is available
from the British Library

HB ISBN 978 1 78429 993 4
Ebook ISBN 978 1 78429 113 6

10 9 8 7 6 5 4 3 2 1

Text designed and typeset by Hewer Text UK Ltd, Edinburgh
Printed and bound in Great Britain by Clays Ltd. St Ives plc

Also by Robert Lyman

Slim, Master of War
First Victory
Iraq, 1941
The Generals
The Longest Siege
Japan's Last Bid for Victory
Kohima, 1944
Operation Suicide
Into the Jaws of Death
Bill Slim
The Jail Busters

www.robertlyman.com

This book is dedicated to the memory of Philip and Isla Brownless, who passed away within three months of each other in 2014; and to those gallant Charioteers and X-Men described here, who paid the ultimate sacrifice during operations against their country's enemies between 1942 and 1945.

Let your thoughts dwell day by day on your country's true greatness, and when you realise her grandeur, remember it is a heritage won for you by dauntless men who knew their duty, and who did it. In the hour of trial – the one thing they feared was dishonour – they failed not their motherland, but laid their gallant lives at her feet. In one great host did they give themselves to death: but each one, man by man, has won imperishable praise. Each one has won a glorious grave – not that sepulchre of earth wherein they lie, but the everlasting tomb of remembrance that will live on the lips, that will blossom in the deeds of their countrymen the world over.

For the whole earth is the sepulchre of heroes; monuments may rise, and tablets be set up to them in their own land, but on the far-off shores, there is an abiding memorial that no pen or chisel has traced; it is graven, not on stone or brass, but on the living heart of humanity.

Take these men for your example. Like them, remember that prosperity and true happiness can only be for the free, and that freedom is the possession of those alone who have the courage to defend it.

Pericles, c. 430 BC

Contents

Abbreviations and Glossary

AB	Able Seaman
Abaft/aft	Towards the rear (stern) of a vessel
AEDU	Admiralty Experimental Diving Unit
ASDIC	An active sound-detection device on ships, to detect submarines
A/S	Anti-submarine
A/T	Anti-torpedo
BAD	British Admiralty Detachment, Washington
Benzedrine	An early amphetamine tablet, used as an artificial stimulant
CGC	Conspicuous Gallantry Cross
C-in-C	Commander-in-Chief
CO	Commanding Officer
COMINCH	Commander-in-Chief, United States Fleet
COPP	Combined Operations Pilotage Parties
CPO	Chief Petty Officer
DSC	Distinguished Service Cross
DSEA	Davis Submarine Escape Apparatus
DSO	Distinguished Service Order
ERA	Engine Room Artificer
Heads	Naval slang for lavatory
MGB	Motor Gun Boat
MSC	Motorised Submersible Canoe (the 'Sleeping Beauty')
MTB	Motor Torpedo Boat

Pompey   Naval slang for Portsmouth

Q ship   A decoy vessel, designed to catch U-boats by
            deception

RAF   Royal Air Force

RNVR   Royal Naval Volunteer Reserve

SLC   *Siluri a Lenta Corsa*; Italian 'Slow Speed Torpedoes',
            also known as *Maiali* ('pigs')

SOE   Special Operations Executive

SUE   Submarine Underwater Explosives, a means of signal-
            ling to X-craft, and known as 'Suzies'

XE-craft   X-craft specially designed for use in the Far East

Preface

Between 1942 and 1945 the Royal Navy engaged in a type of warfare so secret that very few people knew about it at the time, and few have heard about it since. It was extraordinarily tough work, and demanded unusually high standards of personal courage, physical fitness, determination, training and leadership from those engaged; not merely to get through training, but to survive a live operation against the enemy. It was concerned with using tiny sub-surface craft to take the war to the enemy. There were four main types. The first were manned torpedoes – known in the British Service as 'Chariots' – designed to sink enemy shipping in its harbours. This was an ingenious idea borrowed from the Italians, who demonstrated its effectiveness in a spectacular attack against the Royal Navy in Alexandria harbour in December 1941. The second were three- and four-man 30-ton mini-, or 'midget', submarines, known as X-craft, which were designed in the first place to take on the mighty German battleship *Tirpitz* in 1943, but whose use extended to other strategic targets in the Far East in 1945. Mini-submarines were an idea that had long been in consideration by navies around the globe, but which was applied with success by only a few. The Japanese experimented with this concept, but no other belligerent during the Second World War developed it as thoroughly, or enjoyed as much success with it, as the Royal Navy. The third were the Special Operations Executive's (SOE) single-man submersible craft, known as the 'Welman', and the fourth were Motorised Submersible Canoes (MSCs).

Both the Welman and the MSC were ingenious ideas which reached stages of development that allowed them to be considered for deployment against the enemy, although the Welman (in an attack against Bergen, Norway) and the MLC, in a disastrous raid against Japanese-held Singapore in 1944 (Operation *Rimau*), saw limited operational service. The numbers of men and women involved in the successful deployment of these weapons were tiny, but a measure of the demands made on the men who crewed these contrary and often dangerous devices, and of their success on operations against German, Italian and Japanese targets, can be seen in the extraordinary number of men awarded medals for gallantry: sixty-eight.

The two-man teams who operated the Chariots, and the four-man crews who operated the X-craft, were a breed apart. The courage required to sit astride 600 pounds of high explosive in a cold, dark and claustrophobic underwater environment, at a time when little was known about the effect of oxygen on the body at more than two atmospheres (rudimentary oxygen rebreathers were worn); or to sit cramped within a 30-ton submersible coffin across many hundreds of miles of hostile ocean, to enter a heavily guarded enemy harbour and then to exit the craft to lay anti-ship ('limpet') mines on the hull of an enemy vessel, called for men to whom the otherwise largely devalued title of 'hero' can properly be given. They willingly took on the challenge of mastering entirely new skills in an often hostile natural environment, pushing the boundaries of physiological science, military technique and human endurance as they strove to carry out their missions and to defeat their enemy.

What the British achieved in the field of submersible manned torpedoes originated inside Italy's *Regia Marina* (Royal Navy), and it is to the Italian pioneers of this innovative method of warfare that full credit must go for creating and mastering the concept. The

British rapidly learned the lessons the Italians taught them, and in turn conquered the intricacies of this new form of warfare. The Royal Navy was enabled to do this by the quality of its men: a mixture of professional sailors and part-timers from across the Commonwealth – Britons, Australians, Canadians, New Zealanders and South Africans – mobilised for the duration of the war; together with conscripts and volunteers whose military service would end – they hoped – at the cessation of hostilities, when they could return to their peacetime civilian occupations. It is for reasons of authenticity, therefore, that this account is built, where available, on the direct reminiscences, records, logbooks and reports of some of the brave men involved.

This is not a story of high strategy. It undertakes no detailed account of the technology associated with this innovative branch of warfare, or the tactics required for mounting a successful attack. Nor does it follow the mini-submarine ventures of the Axis countries, with the obvious exception of the Italian *Maiale*, the forerunner of the British Chariot. It offers, instead, selected tales of the extraordinary achievements of small, well-trained and committed groups of men – most of them teenagers – who faced immense dangers and overwhelming odds to bring their nation's enemies to heel. Never did they doubt whether their role – tiny amidst all the noise of the big ships and the heavy battalions – made them somehow less significant than those fighting the battles that made it into the press. As Pericles explained, they were content to do *their* duty. Many did this to the death, paying the ultimate sacrifice. They, and those who survived to carry the flame of their achievements to a new generation, achieved, as Pericles rightly asserts, 'imperishable praise'.

ONE

Sea Swine

It was a warm, clear, humid night. Off the coast of Alexandria the Mediterranean lapped unhurriedly against the darkened coast. Light from a bright moon glistened on the surface of the sea, making up in part for the fact that during these years of war the Ras-el-Tin lighthouse no longer routinely threw its warning rays out to sea, but switched on only to guide returning British warships to the safety of the port. It was perhaps the only sign that this tranquil place was at war. On 18 December 1941 the war in Europe had been raging for over two years. The Italians under Mussolini had thrown in their lot with Hitler in mid-1940. Eleven days earlier the Japanese had announced their entry to the war in spectacular fashion, with simultaneous surprise assaults on Thailand, Malaya, Borneo, Hawaii, Hong Kong and the Philippines.

The Mediterranean had witnessed a desperate struggle for naval supremacy, which demonstrated that, for the first time in two hundred years, it could not be described as a British lake. Alexandria was the home in the eastern Mediterranean of the Royal Navy's Mediterranean Fleet, but it had recently been severely weakened by a series of devastating losses. The remnants of this fleet, now reduced to two battleships – HMS *Queen Elizabeth* and HMS *Valiant* – both veterans of the First World War, were now hemmed in within the security of the harbour chain and the anti-submarine nets of Alexandria harbour. The C-in-C of the Mediterranean Fleet, Admiral Andrew Browne Cunningham

1

(known universally in the Royal Navy as 'ABC'), whose flagship the *Queen Elizabeth* was, had warned London at the beginning of the month that he was worried about losing any more of his capital ships. 'I must keep them rather in cotton wool as it won't do to get another put out of action,' he told Sir Dudley Pound, the ailing First Lord of the Admiralty.

Cunningham's fears for his few remaining battleships had been prompted by a run of devastating losses suffered as German and Italian pressure against the North African shore increased. This included the sinking off Gibraltar on 13 November 1941 of the Navy's only modern aircraft carrier, HMS *Ark Royal*, sent to the bottom after a strike by a single torpedo from Kapitänleutnant Friedrich Guggenberger's *U-81*. Then, on 25 November, off Sidi Barrani, three torpedoes fired at close range from Leutnant Hans-Diedrich Freiherr von Tiesenhausen's *U-331* at HMS *Barham* sank the veteran battleship and took with it the lives of 841 men in a single extraordinary explosion – captured by a Pathé cameraman on board HMS *Valiant*. (The moment that violent death came to many hundreds of men can still be viewed, at the click of a button, on YouTube.) The Royal Navy had twice as many warships as the *Kriegsmarine* and *Regia Marina* combined, but of course these were spread thinly across the globe, attempting to meet and curb a host of threats to its security interests.

The *Queen Elizabeth* and *Valiant* were now all Cunningham had left to counter the threat posed to his lines of communication across the Mediterranean – which stretched from Gibraltar to the Suez Canal, as well as to Egypt, Malta and the entire seaboard of Cyrenaica – by the more powerful Italian fleet which now amounted to five battleships, two of them new. If this wasn't bad enough, a week later came the humiliating loss, off the eastern coast of the Malay Peninsula, of the mighty HMS *Prince of Wales* and the battle cruiser HMS *Repulse*. The two capital ships of Force Z, weakened by the absence of its accompanying aircraft carrier HMS *Indomitable*, which had been forced to remain in the United States undergoing repairs, had been sent to the bottom of the South China Sea together with 835 men after a sustained attack by Japanese torpedo bombers. The shock waves of this humiliation coursed through the Royal Navy and the Admiralty and thundered against the stone steps of 10 Downing Street. Nineteen forty-one was wartime Britain's *annus horribilis*, perhaps the worst in its modern history and the closest it came to defeat in a war that now coiled its destructive tentacles around the globe.

That night, underneath the surface of the gently undulating ocean just over a nautical mile off Ras-el-Tin, Lieutenant Luigi Durand de la Penne and Petty Officer Emilio Bianchi, together with four colleagues (Captain Antonio Marceglia, Petty Officer/diver Spartaco Schergat, Captain Vincenzo Martellotta and Petty Officer/diver Mario Marino) from a top-secret assault squadron of the *Regia Marina* – the Decima Flottiglia Mezzi d'Assalto (MAS), or 10th Light Assault Vehicle Flotilla: often abbreviated to Decima MAS or Decima Flottiglia – prepared to disembark from the submarine *Scirè*. Unaware perhaps of the imperatives of grand strategy, or of the full extent of the Royal Navy's predicament, but imbued nevertheless with determination to do honour to Italian martial pride, the world's first commando frogmen prepared to launch an assault – unique in the annals of modern warfare – against the remaining capital ships of the British Mediterranean Fleet. De la Penne and his comrades were certain only of one thing: they represented Italy's David against Britain's Goliath, and they would do their duty.

Was it a coincidence that Cunningham had that very night sent a signal to his fleet that 'attacks on Alexandria harbour by air, boat or human torpedo might be expected in calm weather'? Recent attempts against British shipping in Gibraltar had spread the alarm amongst the British fleet. In his memoirs Cunningham noted:

Besides the boom and the net defence at the harbour entrance, each battleship was surrounded by a floated net as a protection against torpedoes, human or otherwise. Arrangements were also made for patrolling boats to drop small explosive charges at the harbour entrance at regular intervals.

The war clouds threatening Europe in 1939 prompted the establishment in Italy of a unit designed to translate the *Maiale* concept into operational reality. This became, in 1941, the 10th Flotilla, commanded by Commander Vittorio Moccagatta. The 10th Flotilla had two ways of taking its particular style of warfare to its enemy, the Royal Navy, long dominant in the Mediterranean. The first was with a 2-ton wooden motorboat packed with explosives, which the unfortunate operator was expected to bring into close proximity with the target, before aiming the vessel at the enemy hull and ejecting himself into the water at high speed before impact (thus hopefully to survive the resulting explosion). Despite the crudity of the concept, the method enjoyed some success, with the sinking off Souda Bay on Crete on 26 March 1941 of the heavy cruiser HMS *York* and three other vessels. The second was the human torpedo, known officially as '*siluri a lenta corsa*' (slow-speed torpedoes), or SLC.

The SLC was the product of the collaboration in 1935 between two engineers in the *Regia Marina*'s submarine service, Sub Lieutenants Elios Toschi and Teseo Tesei. They knew, from Italy's experience in the First World War, that a manned torpedo was not only technically feasible but could reap sizeable rewards in combat, relative to its puny size. At 6.30 a.m. on 1 November 1918, a mere ten days from the end of the First World War, two enterprising *Regia Marina* sailors, Sub Lieutenant Raffaele Paolucci and Major Raffaele Rossetti, took a standard 22-foot-long torpedo, which they called the 'Leech', made a number of simple modifications (such as designing a detachable warhead) that allowed it to be operated manually by two operators sitting or lying astride it as it travelled to its target under compressed air at 1 mile per hour, and steered it into Pula harbour, Croatia. There they sank the

4

20,000-ton ex-Austrian battleship *Viribus Unitis*, after detaching the charge and fixing it by ropes to the vessel's hull. The original plan was to do this by magnetic clamps, but the hull had been so seldom cleaned that it was covered in barnacles, which prevented the magnets attaching successfully. Unknown to the Italians, the vessel had only days earlier changed ownership from the Austro-Hungarian Empire, which was sliding into the dust of history, into what would, later that year, become the newly independent state of Yugoslavia. But its sinking demonstrated the principle that a small, manned, unarmoured submersible, exploiting nothing more than the underwater environment, stealth and the audacity of its operators, could reap an outcome that far outweighed its size.

Seventeen years later Toschi and Tesei took the idea a step further to design a considerably more elegant submersible vessel that could enter enemy harbours unobserved, there to sink capital ships with an explosive charge incorporated in the body of the vessel. By January 1936 they had successfully demonstrated the design of their 'slow-speed torpedo' to the Naval High Command. Powered by batteries, the vessel was designed to carry two operators submerged for up to twelve hours at a speed of 3 knots. Dressed in specially designed rubberised suits, the men sat astride the 22-foot machine as if they were riding a horse. The idea was that it would travel just below the surface for its approach journey, with the operators' heads just above the water. It could then submerge to the limit for human diving – estimated at the time, and before anyone fully comprehended the physiology of oxygen poisoning, to be a maximum depth of 120 feet – for the final approach, with the operators using British-designed oxygen rebreather sets.

Manufactured under licence by Pirelli, these Siebe Gorman devices, originally designed to assist submariners to escape from their sunken craft, had enjoyed a growing use amongst sports divers in France and Italy during the 1930s, as well as offering – to the Italians at least – considerable military possibilities. Before the advent of the rebreather, diving could only be conducted using hoses that pumped compressed air down long tubes to the harnessed diver. Now, with an oxygen rebreather, frogmen – as they became known in the British press during the war – could, within the limits provided by the amount of oxygen carried, and the still unknown medical science associated with prolonged oxygen use, enable underwater swimmers to remain submerged for the entire duration of an attack. Unlike compressed-air sets, rebreathers did not release any telltale bubbles from the divers, likely to alert an enemy to their presence. Other items of equipment, such as flippers (or 'fins') and masks, had become a standard part of the sports-diving community on the French and Italian Riviera in the same decade.

The 660-pound main charge was detachable from the front of the vessel: the operators had merely to fix it to a rope hung underneath the hull. The ubiquitous bilge keels on a ship's hull – long strips of metal welded to each side of the vessel and designed to prevent excessive rolling – provided a useful platform on which to clamp both ends of the line. It was during the early days of learning to master these underwater beasts that Tesei described one that had just sunk under him as a 'pig'. The name stuck, and in Italian service they were henceforth always known as *Maiali*.

The men selected to become *Maiale* frogmen were to prove some of the toughest in the *Regia Marina*, subject to thorough selection and extensive training. Not only did they need to be physically strong, but also capable swimmers, able to withstand the psychological pressures of prolonged immersion under water. They were trained to travel up to 6 miles in their submersible vessels from their escort submarine, cut through anti-submarine nets, and place the heavy charge underneath their target. The approach was described by one Italian 'pilot' (or Number 1) as follows:

You approach, at 'observation level', to within about 30 metres of the target ... You take a compass bearing, then you flood the diving-tank and the water closes over your head. Everything is cold, dark and silent. Now you are deep enough; you close the flooding valve, put the motor into low gear and slide onwards. It gets suddenly darker; you know that you are underneath the ship. You shut off the motor and open the valve for pushing the water out of the diving tanks. As you rise, you lift a hand above your head. You wonder whether it will touch smooth plates or knife-edged barnacles, which will play the devil with your fingers, or, worse still, tear your rubber overall and let the sea seep through.

Now you have found the hull. You push the torpedo back, so that your assistant can catch hold of the bilge keel, a couple of hands' breadths wide . . . You feel a thump on the shoulder; your assistant has found the bilge [keel] and is fixing a clamp on it. Two thumps on the shoulder: the clamp is in position. Now you go ahead to get at the bilge keel on the other side. Your assistant is paying out a line from one side to the other. He fixes the second clamp. And now back again, pulling oneself along by the line stretched under the hull, as far as the centre of the ship. While you clutch the rope with your hands, holding the torpedo between your legs, your second leaves his seat and passes you till he reaches the warhead in front. In the darkness you know that he is fasten-ing the warhead to the rope stretched under the ship between the bilge keels. Now he has detached the head; the firing clock that will cause the 330 kg of the charge to explode in two and a half hours begins to measure off the seconds . . . Now you may think of escape.

Within two months of Italy's declaration of war against Britain, the assault units, both surface and sub-surface, of what was to become the 10th Flotilla went aggressively in search of the Royal Navy – despite the relatively primitive design of the SLC and the fact that the *Regia Marina* boasted probably no more than a dozen of the machines. They understood that it would be difficult for the *Regia Marina* to destroy the British Mediterranean battle fleet in an open fight and therefore, in addition to conventional strategies, it would need also to pursue a 'war of the flea': striking the British where they were most vulnerable, and at times and places where they were least expected. This included mining, submarine warfare and attacks on enemy harbours. The concept was that of the short, sharp offensive strike that would deal death and destruction in unexpected places and in unexpected ways, and by so doing sap the morale of an enemy who still provided a significant threat to Italian dreams of being able to dominate their own naval backyard.

Attacking the foe in his harbour, a place where perhaps he felt safest, was a stratagem whose virtues the British were to demonstrate to the Italians' considerable cost at Taranto in December 1940. In this engagement the *Regia Marina* lost half of its capital ships in a single night, the result of a devastating attack by seventeen obsolescent Swordfish 'Stringbag' torpedo bombers of the Fleet Air Arm. But from the very outset of the war Italian ingenuity and bravery did not make up for their failure to come up with a strategy suited to exploiting their tactical successes. Italian technical achievements, doggedness and standards of personal training, small-unit leadership and courage were exemplary. Alas for the Axis Powers, they were not coordinated with other operations, nor ever part of a coherent naval or military plan to defeat the British. And for this reason individual successes failed to deliver any more than a short-lived advantage. Worse, they were intimately bound up with concepts of national honour and military pride that should have had no place in the attitudes of men whose single-minded purpose should have been the defeat of their enemy, not the glory of Italian arms.

Tesei's operational concept was built around the idea of the *Maiale* as the tip of an offensive spear able to destroy the enemy in an overwhelming pre-emptive strike. The chief British bases in the Mediterranean were Gibraltar and Alexandria, and the eyes of the 10th Flotilla were on both. An attack on Alexandria was designed to be an Italian version of the Japanese strike on Pearl Harbor, maiming the Royal Navy in the Mediterranean. The first attempt to deliver this plan came in September 1940, when eight *Maiali* carried aboard two submarines – *Gondar* and *Scirè* – set sail for Alexandria and Gibraltar respectively to strike a simultaneous and decisive blow against British naval hegemony in the Mediterranean. The day after *Gondar* left La Spezia for Alexandria, *Scirè*, commanded by Commander Junio Valerio Borghese, headed for Gibraltar with three human torpedoes. Unfortunately, when he arrived he found the cupboard bare: the British battleships HMSs *Renown*, *Ark Royal* and *Sheffield* were away in the Atlantic searching for the *Bismarck*. It might have worked, if Italian intelligence had been superior.

Exactly a month later, Borghese returned, but was again frustrated. A technical failure with their Pirelli rebreathers prevented one team from getting close to their target, and the sudden sinking of a *Maiale* ended another mission. The third vessel lost steerage only a few hundred feet from the hull of the Queen Elizabeth-class battleship HMS *Barham*. The two crewmen – Gino Birindelli and Damos Paccagnini – attempted to drag the heavy and unresponsive vessel – a 'pig' indeed – but had to give up in exhaustion. Rather foolishly, they set the fuse on the warhead even though they had not reached and would not reach their target, so that when it exploded harmlessly a few hours later it simply advertised to the British that they needed to be wary of a new threat against their capital ships. The first two crews (including Teseo Tesei) managed to scuttle their two *Maiali* and escape through Spain with the help of an Italian secret agent, although Birindelli and Paccagnini became prisoners of war. With days, however, one of the two scuttled pigs was washed onto the Spanish shore, where it was photographed by the British.

Some of the Italian equipment and parts of the SLCs were recovered and returned to the UK. For the first time, the Royal Navy could see what they were up against. Nevertheless, there is no evidence that anyone in the Royal Navy acted upon this discovery, except to initiate defensive procedures across the Mediterranean ports that included the regular dropping of charges into the sea to counter the threat of frogmen. After all, the SLC had not yet demonstrated that it could cause the British any harm.

One of the lessons of these failures was the development of the idea of the assault swimmer in the Italian service, who formed themselves into what became the 'Gamma' unit. This concept involved not the self-destruction of the *Maiale* by means of its main warhead, but the use of the pig to transport assault swimmers to a target, at which point they would attach small limpet mines to the underside of an enemy ship's hull. They would then swim to safety and be collected by their escorting pig and be far away before the detonation of their charges.

But the strategy of the flea had its attendant weaknesses, one of which was the danger of compromise during the extended submarine journey to the target area. On 22 August 1940, whilst en route to attack the two British battleships which, in addition to HMS *Eagle*, were believed to be in Alexandria, the third submarine in the flotilla, the *Iride* (carrying four human torpedoes and five two-man crews, including men who would make their names in Italian SLC operations, such as Gino Birindelli; Damos Paccagnini, Teseo Tesei, Luigi de la Penne and Elios Toschi), accompanied by two support vessels, paused to carry out final arrangements in the Bay of Bomba. However, the little flotilla had been spotted the day before by a British Blenheim flying an aerial reconnaissance flight along the coast to Tobruk, and it was there, the following day, that three of HMS *Eagle*'s 'Stringbags' led by Captain Oliver Patch, Royal Marines, found them. The Stringbags – flying from a desert airfield at Maaten Bagush, the headquarters of the Royal Air Force in the Western Desert – had only just arrived in Egypt from Cyprus, for the express purpose of attacking Italian shipping. One of the pilots, Royal Marine Lieutenant John Welham, described how Ollie Patch's torpedo, dropped from a height of 30 feet and at a

10

distance of 300 yards, struck the *Iride* amidships, destroying it in a single huge explosion and 'leaving only a small fraction of the stern above the surface'. Welham went for the second vessel, a motor torpedo boat that had brought the SLCs to the area to rendezvous with the *Iride*:

> The destroyer [*sic*] opened fire with pom-poms, multi-machine guns and 0.5-ins. The fire was accurate and at 3,000 yards my aircraft was struck by a 0.5-in bullet . . . At a range of about 500 yards I dropped my torpedo . . . Three seconds later my torpedo exploded . . . just forward of amidships. The ship was left blazing furiously. Four minutes later there was a further large explosion which caused smoke to rise to a height of 300 feet.

Both the *Iride* and the torpedo boat *Calipso* were sunk. Neither Ollie Patch nor John Welham had any idea of just how significant their intervention had been in preventing an SLC attack against Alexandria, believing that their attack was a minor part of a general strategy of interdiction along the enemy coast.

A month later, a second attempt to strike at Alexandria also failed, in much the same way. The submarine *Gondar*, commanded by Lieutenant Francesco Brunetti and carrying three human torpedoes and four two-man crews, was attacked by the Australian destroyer HMAS *Stuart* close to Alexandria on 29 September. The following day the crew were forced to scuttle the submarine, and all, including the 10th Flotilla frogmen – among whom was one of the two inventors of the Italian submersible, Lieutenant Commander Elios Toschi – were captured. But again there is no evidence that the British understood at the time the nature of the threat to their naval supremacy that these operations posed. Both *Iride* and *Gondar* were seen merely as predatory submarines on patrol. Britain, in common with other 'big gun' navies of the time, had a tendency to belittle and disregard underwater innovation as somehow unworthy of true seamen: a little too piratical perhaps.

Each time an attack in these early days failed, however, the men of the *Regia Marina*'s submarine service, together with the 10th Flotilla, worked hard to understand the causes of failure, to remedy faults in equipment or tactics, and press on with their offensive plans.

Indeed, repeated failures to strike a successful blow against the British seemed only to spur the 10th Flotilla to greater effort. In May 1941 a further attempt to attack Gibraltar failed for want of suitable targets, and on 26 July a brave assault on the harbour defences of the British bastion at Malta was defeated with considerable loss. The British, possibly warned by Ultra and equipped with radar, could see the oncoming Italian force long before it arrived, and the big guns of the defences held their fire before unleashing a devastating salvo at close range. None of the raiders – surface or sub-surface – were able to press home their attacks. Fifteen commandos were killed, including Moccagatta and Teseo Tesei. Eighteen became prisoners of war.

In the aftermath of this disaster Borghese was promoted from being commander of the *Scirè* to running all sub-surface operations. Borghese concentrated on developing the work of piloted torpedoes. He knew that he needed operational success to re-establish the morale of his submariners, and to demonstrate the viability of the piloted torpedoes. A small successful operation would give them the authority they needed to proceed with a more substantial task.

I took advantage of the summer season, which was unsuitable for piloted torpedo operations owing to the shortness of the nights and the length of the hours of daylight, though favourable, on account of the mildness of the temperature of the sea, to intensive and prolonged training . . . The object was to put them in a condition to overcome the difficulties which had in the previous operations, especially the last one against Gibraltar, prevented successful action.

It was now that the *Maiale* achieved its first operational success, after more than a year of trying, and the loss in combat of many of the originators of the concept. On 10 September 1941 the *Scirè* left La Spezia once more, carrying three SLCs. The plan was that they would meet up with the eight SLC frogmen at Cadiz in neutral Spain, where an Italian freighter, the *Fulgor*, would provide cover during their night-time rendezvous. On 16 September Borghese sailed quietly through the Strait of Gibraltar, before spending the whole of the next day on the seabed off Cadiz, waiting for nightfall. After successfully collecting the crews and, according to Borghese's report, enjoying 'a hot bath, fresh victuals, bananas and brandy' on the *Fulgor*, the *Scirè* was under way in the darkness of the following morning. By 19 September it had reached Algeciras Bay. The primary targets for the SLC were the capital ships of the Royal Navy's Force H – such as the aircraft carrier HMS *Ark Royal* and the battleship HMS *Nelson*. This required breaching the harbour defences, which was no easy task with British vigilance at an all-time high. Borghese recalled hearing, in the deeply submerged *Scirè*, the dull thuds of the half-hourly detonations from the guard boats on the surface above, designed specifically to counter the threat of enemy frogmen. If the SLCs could not penetrate the harbour they were to attack less prestigious cargo vessels in the Gibraltar roads.

The teams set off just after midnight on the morning of 20 September. Following the problems experienced on the previous mission, they wore improved Pirelli breathing apparatus. It was only a matter of days before their targets – unbeknown to the Italians – would be responsible for escorting the largest-ever British convoy to the besieged island of Malta.

Lieutenant Vesco, tasked with the destruction of HMS *Nelson*, struggled to break through the British defences and enter the harbour. Defences had been substantially improved since the British had realised that a new type of underwater threat existed against their vulnerable warships in harbour. Anti-submarine nets and regular surface patrols, together with underwater searches using divers, were extensively deployed. Vesco's report described what happened next:

> Surface approach was normal, though impeded by wind and high seas. I removed my mask at intervals, so as to see with the naked eye, but on each occasion only for a few seconds, because, even when I was stationary, the waves breaking over my face were a great nuisance especially to my eyes. After an emergency submersion to evade discovery by a patrol boat on duty I sighted the entrance to the harbour. I was about 300 metres from the defences and slowed down so as to prevent my being heard by hydrophones and in order to have time to find out about the manoeuvres of a boat which was shuttling, with her lights on, in front of the entrance . . . I set a bee-line course and submerged to the greatest possible depth, proceeding at low speed to prevent the phosphorescence of my wake from being detected from the surface.
>
> At about 3.15 a.m. I got down to a depth of about 26 metres, just grazing the bottom, which was hard and smooth, and did not interfere in any way with my progress. At about 3.30, at a depth of 15 metres, I heard and felt against the cask of the 'pig' and against my own body three consecutive underwater explosions. As everything continued to function normally I decided to go on. At 3.40 I was at a depth of 13 metres when I heard two further explosions, slightly more subdued than the previous ones, but of greater volume.

Unable to get through without risking his craft, he decided to attack a secondary target, one of the merchantmen sitting in the roads, which were considerably less well protected than those within the harbour.

> At four a.m. I started to look for the most important target. A boat with its lights dimmed was moving about among the steamers. At

14

last I sighted a vessel with a long, slender outline, lying low in the water and therefore heavily laden; I guessed her to be about 3 or 4 thousand tons displacement. I made my approach . . . I submerged deeply beneath the ship, stopped and came up, exhausting the tanks, till I reached the hull. I managed to do this unseen and unheard, but owing to damage to my breathing set I could not avoid swallowing water containing soda-lime, which caused painful burning to my mouth and throat.*

Surfacing, Vesco changed his breathing set before submerging again, successfully setting the warhead. Returning to the parent submarine was considered too difficult for the frogman and too dangerous for the waiting submarine, and the Italian policy was that frogmen must swim to shore to escape, trusting to their luck to get away. With Spain so close, the plan in this instance was for the men to make for its coast. It was a tough swim. When they finally gained the shore they were detained by Spanish soldiers but were able to see the explosion that ripped apart the 48-year-old, 2,444-ton *Fiona Shell*.

The second SLC, commanded by Lieutenant Catalano, likewise struggled to enter the heavily guarded harbour. After spending two hours attempting to dodge a patrol boat they also decided to attack a freighter in the Gibraltar Roads. Rejecting a requisitioned Italian vessel, he and his diver chose another:

The work proceeded in first-rate style, owing to the splendid conduct, both in skill and in enterprise, of my second operator [Giannoni]. At 5.16 a.m. I set the fuses of the warhead. We left at high speed and I sank the 'pig' in 5 metres of water, after setting the fuses of her self-destructor charges: by that time it was 5.55

---

* The soda-lime concoction was in fact a British-designed invention – by Siebe Gorman – called Protosorb. The soda-lime absorbed the carbon dioxide created when a diver exhaled.

a.m. I surfaced with Giannoni; after removing our breathing sets and sinking them, we swam to the shore, landing at 7.15 a.m. At 9.16 a violent explosion took place at the stem of the motor ship I had attacked; a column of water rose to about 30 metres. The motor ship settled slowly by the stem, the entire structure of her bows emerging from the water. Four powerful tugs came to her assistance and towed her ashore, with considerable trouble, at a point opposite the neutral zone. I afterwards found out her name; she was the armed British motor ship *Durham*, of 10,900 tons.

The third SLC was under the command of Lieutenant Lioria Visintini. This 'pig', after playing cat-and-mouse with two patrol boats, managed to slip between them and through the anti-submarine nets to place the warhead underneath a large tanker. The fuses set at 4.40 a.m., Visintini retraced their steps, sank their vessel and swam safely to the Spanish shore. At 8.43 a.m. they heard an explosion in the harbour. Their victim was the *Denbydale*, a Royal Fleet Auxiliary fuel tanker of 17,000 tons, which was badly damaged, with a broken back. The six frogmen had all returned safely to shore, and each saw or heard the results of their efforts. Borghese was jubilant, as he had every reason to be. 'At last, after so many disappointments,' he later wrote, 'we had a positive result, though not of the importance we had desired. It was the first success of the piloted torpedoes; three vessels, including a large naval tanker and amounting in all to 30,000 tons, had been sunk.'

But disaster then struck. Desperate for positive publicity, and ignoring the need to retain operational security around the means by which they had achieved these successes, the Italian Propaganda Ministry loudly trumpeted:

Assault craft of the Royal Navy have succeeded in penetrating the Roads and the Grand Harbour of Gibraltar, where they sank a 10,000-ton tanker and a 6,000-ton merchant ship loaded with munitions. A 12,000-ton merchant ship loaded with war material was hurled against the rocky outcrop by the force of the explosions and can be regarded as lost.

Until this point in time the British had little understanding of what was attacking them, and how. Vice Admiral Sir James Somerville, commander of Force H, reported:

> A breathing apparatus, picked up in the Commercial anchorage, where an oil hulk, the *Fiona Shell* had been sunk, and SS *Durham* damaged, indicated that the probable cause was attack by two-man submarines.

Even though details remained sparse, the cat was now out of the bag, and both Gibraltar and Alexandria were placed on high alert.

TWO

Cavities in the Lion's Mouth

In the early morning of 19 December 1941, lying on his bunk in the bowels of HMS *Queen Elizabeth*, Midshipman Tom Dowling awoke to a Tannoy announcement from the Captain warning that 'midget enemy submarines were supposed to have got into the harbour'. Another midshipman, Frank Wade, recalled being awoken at 4 a.m. 'by the alarm rattlers buzzing us to action stations and a bugler blowing the alarm'. He went up to his station on the bridge. Seaman A. J. Wilkins was a:

gunner on board HMS *Queen Elizabeth*, stationed at gunnery control. At about 2 a.m. the news was given that enemy under-water vehicles had entered the port while the barriers were open to let our own ships into the harbour. So the alarm was given – the entire ship's crew had to clear the lower decks and go onto the upper decks. I was serving above by the anti-aircraft guns some two hours later when the order was given to return to the lower decks because everything was now all right.

Tom Dowling later wrote in his midshipman's journal: 'This seemed like a dream. Later through the length of the night we heard smaller and greater explosions – which we accepted as being depth charges. The last and greatest explosion caused us junior midshipmen to jump out of our hammocks and run round in small circles.' On the bridge of the *Queen Elizabeth*

Frank Wade heard 'the low rumbling underwater explosion and the quarterdeck was thrown upwards about six inches, maybe more. I bent my legs and threw out my arms to keep my balance as the huge ship lurched beneath me. A blast of thick smoke and flame shot out the funnel. Then the ship seemed to settle rapidly.' Down below, Wilkins was astonished at the power of the explosion:

The explosion was so terrific that the lights went out at once and the mess decks were completely flooded. The ship was in total darkness, the men sought shelter and we had to find our way out of the ship in order to reach the upper decks. I managed to do so, and when I arrived above I saw that the bow of the *Valiant* had sunk and that the *Queen Elizabeth* was still sinking because its armour-plating had been ripped off.

Admiral Cunningham related the events of the evening in his memoirs:

At about 4 a.m. on December 19th I was called in my cabin on board the *Queen Elizabeth* with the news that two Italians had been found clinging to the bow buoy of the *Valiant*. They had been taken on board and interrogated; but had vouchsafed nothing and had been sent ashore under arrest. I at once ordered them to be brought back to the *Valiant* and confined in one of the forward compartments well below the waterline. The boats of all ships were also called away to drop small charges around them, while the ships' companies were turned out of their hammocks below and chain bottom-lines were dragged along the ships' bottoms.

Just before 6 a.m., when I was on the quarter-deck of the *Queen Elizabeth*, there was a violent explosion under the stern of the tanker *Sagona*, lying close to the *Queen Elizabeth* with the *Jervis* alongside. Both the tanker and the destroyer were badly damaged, the *Sagona* being badly holed aft with her rudder and screws damaged. The *Jervis*'s injuries were to keep her in dock for a month.

About twenty minutes later I saw another heavy explosion under the *Valiant*'s fore turret, and four minutes after that, when I was right aft in the *Queen Elizabeth* by the ensign staff, I felt a dull thud and was tossed about five feet into the air by the whip of the ship and was lucky not to come down sprawling. I saw a great cloud of black smoke shoot up the funnel and from immediately in front of it, and knew at once that the ship was badly damaged. The *Valiant* was already down by the bows. The *Queen Elizabeth* took a heavy list to starboard. Three of our boiler-rooms were flooded, and we were unable to raise steam. Our list was compensated by flooding the opposite compartments; but with some thousands of tons of water in the ship the *Queen Elizabeth* was very low in the water. We brought a submarine alongside each side to provide power, and in twenty-four hours were able to provide power for ourselves; but there was a hole about forty feet square under the two foremost boiler-rooms and the ship was out of action.

Cunningham's fears of an attack on Alexandria harbour, following the suspicious attacks on the Gibraltar roads, had been well founded. The British Mediterranean Fleet had lost its two remaining battleships and, at a stroke, British naval power in the region was crippled. It was the worst possible outcome for Britain. Despite previous failures, the attack entirely vindicated the deliberate strategy adopted by the *Regia Marina* to challenge British big-gun superiority with a weapon as small and simple – albeit ingenious in its design, and courageously deployed – as a manned torpedo.

The raid had begun fifteen days before and 1,600 nautical miles away, at twilight on 3 December 1941, when Borghese's *Scirè* slipped quietly from the 10th Flotilla's home base at La Spezia. It had three manned torpedoes secreted within specially designed garages built on the submarine's deck, and was en route for the Greek island of Leros. There, on 12 December, they were joined by the three crews, six commando frogmen of the 10th Flotilla, who had flown in, together with four reserves.

The 10th Flotilla had, by this stage of the war, learned some painful lessons. One was to ensure that its operations were subject to the utmost secrecy; for this reason the *Scirè* arrived quietly in Leros under cover of urgent repairs, and her frogmen – all volunteers, and led by Luigi de la Penne, a veteran of the previous mission to Gibraltar – travelled clandestinely. During their time on Leros they were hidden on a freighter outside the harbour, only being united with the submarine under cover of darkness on the night of departure. Another hard-learned lesson was that thorough preparation paid great dividends. Borghese and his colleagues became obsessive in their planning for the greatest raid of all, especially given the two previous failures, building on their success in September against Gibraltar. Reconnaissance photographs of Alexandria were taken by German aircraft, braving Egypt's fighter defences, to ensure that their intended targets were in the harbour when the *Scirè* arrived with her cargo. Borghese supervised relentless training, at night and in conditions similar to those that the frogmen would find when they launched their attack (no one, of course, not even the submarine crew, knew their destination, which remained a closely guarded secret).

This was the 10th Flotilla's third attempt against Alexandria. The previous two had both ended in discovery, failure and death. Borghese recalled:

This kind of operation, if it were to have any decent chance of success, had to be thought out to the last detail; the whole of an extensive organisation had to be got ready; there were a thousand details to be studied and put into practice: from the collection of

21

hydrographic and meteorological data to intelligence as to enemy vigilance; from the taking of aerial photographs of the harbour to the arrangement of safe and extremely rapid channels of radio liaison with the submarine, so that the latter could be informed, immediately before the operators were dropped, as to the number and disposition of units on the night of the operation; from the determination of suitable ciphers to getting materials ready for action; from composition of the series of operational orders to the training of operators so as to bring them to the maximum of physical efficiency by the pre-arranged day; from the study of navigation and the best routes of approach for the submarine and those for the forcing of the harbour by the pilots, to research on new devices for causing the enemy maximum damage should the occasion arise; in a word, the proceedings were exactly the opposite of what the phrase 'assault craft' might be supposed to mean; there was to be nothing in the nature of making a dash, nothing was to be left to chance, all impulsiveness was to be held in check; on the contrary, everything was to be coolly calculated and every technical and ingenious resource was to be exploited to the fullest extent possible.

With the weather prospects good, Borghese planned to slip away unnoticed from Leros on the night of 14 December. He would proceed to a position about a mile off Alexandria, travelling submerged during the day under battery power and on the surface by night by diesel, in order to refresh the air supply in the boat and to recharge his batteries. No risks were to be run of the enemy observing his movements during the journey – such as halts on the surface in daylight – to avoid suffering the fate of both *Iride* and *Gondar* the previous year. As a diversion, Axis aircraft would bomb the harbour on the night of the attack, forcing defenders to safety underground or to look up into the sky, rather than at the surface of the harbour.

Once released from the submarine, each of the six human

torpedoes would have to find a way to break through the submarine net at the harbour mouth and thereafter make his way undetected to their targets in the inner harbour. They would then clamp
their charges to the bilge keels of each ship. One end of a rope or
chain would be clamped to one side of the vessel, and the other
would be attached to the bilge keel on the opposite side. The charge
would be hung underneath, and the timer set. Afterwards, they
would release a number of floating incendiary devices designed to
ignite water-borne oil discharged from their targets, in the hope
that this would cause a secondary conflagration, and maximise the
damage caused by the initial explosions. As was the case in
Gibraltar, once the crews had left the submarine they would have
to swim to shore: from there to make their way along the coast to
Rosetta, some 35 miles east, at the mouth of the Nile. If they were
successful in securing a boat, the submarine *Zaffiro* had been
instructed to patrol 10 miles off the coast for two days after the
raid. If they failed to make this rendezvous, they were on their
own.

In truth, the men knew that making it back to the *Zaffiro* was a
forlorn hope. The reality was that, if they survived the attack, the
best they could hope for was to hide amongst the Egyptian popula-
tion: the worst was that they would find themselves prisoners of
war. In the Italian concept of operations, even with the provision of
the *Zaffiro*, the operators, like their 'pigs', were dispensable. It was
simply too dangerous to risk allowing the *Scirè* to await their return
off the coast of Egypt on the night of the attack: the British would
be after them like a swarm of angry hornets. They were one-shot
weapons, with one-shot crews.

Borghese's plan went exactly as he had intended. The *Scirè*, with
the pilots aboard, left Leros early on the morning of the 14th.
Borghese was confident enough to send a signal to Ernesto Forza,
the commanding officer of the 10th Flotilla: 'Departing at Dawn.
Foresee cavities developing in Lion's mouth.' *Scirè* proceeded without incident and complete secrecy. There is no evidence that British

intelligence – in Bletchley Park or elsewhere – had any inkling of her voyage. Extreme precautions were taken to mask her noise from listening hydrophones.

The defences of Alexandria port were formidable. Minefields, detector cables, observation positions and anti-submarine nets protected the port in layers a considerable distance out to sea. It would be a challenge just to get the *Scirè* close to the entrance, let alone to dispatch the pigs successfully. And the pigs would still have to make their way through the final anti-submarine barrier beyond which lay their targets. A heavy storm at sea on 16 December delayed the submarine's arrival by twenty-four hours, but confirmation by radio signal that the two British battleships were in harbour raised spirits measurably. Then, at 6.40 p.m. on 18 December the submarine came to a rest at a depth of 15 metres, about 1.3 miles off Alexandria. When darkness had fallen, Borghese gently raised his boat so that only the top of the conning tower sat above the gently undulating surface of the sea. Opening the hatch, he made a visual sighting of prominent buildings on the shoreline, and recorded with some pleasure that, after sixteen hours at sea, they had arrived at exactly the point they had planned. The deck 'garages', in which the 'pigs' were enclosed, remained underwater. The frogmen climbed out of the conning tower wearing their new Pirelli rebreather sets and began the task of submerging, opening the garage doors and readying each of the pigs. One by one, de la Penne and Bianchi, Marceglia and Schergat, Martellotta and Marino launched their vessels, rose slowly to the surface and, with only their heads showing above the darkened sea, made their way silently towards the harbour.

Conditions were perfect. The sea was beautifully calm, and the moon shone brightly enough for the crews to make their way towards the coast using visual cues. So smoothly did the approach go that when some 500 metres from the darkened Ras-el-Tin lighthouse, they stopped together for a brief meal of combat rations before making their way to the entrance to the mole, which reached out into the sea at the western end of the harbour. Men – sentries probably – could be heard talking. Beyond the pier, on the seaward side of the steel chain that blocked the entrance to the harbour – underneath which lay the anti-submarine nets – the men could see a motor launch slowly patrolling the barrier. It was periodically dropping explosives into the water as a precaution against precisely the threat that the British Navy now unknowingly faced. 'These charges were rather a nuisance to us,' Luigi de la Penne was later to observe wryly. He was also facing a challenge of a different sort. His suit was leaking, cold seawater slowly chilling his body to the point that, before long, he would be unable to continue. They were close enough to the underwater explosions for Captain Antonio Marceglia to feel violent shock waves hitting the casing of his pig, and to feel the contractions of his leg muscles.

But fortune favoured the brave. As the three crews lay off the pier at about 1 a.m., attempting to work out how they might get past, a clanking of chain not far away indicated the sudden and almost silent arrival from seaward of three British destroyers. It transpired that they were returning from operations against the Italians in the Gulf of Sirte. Miraculously, guide lights were switched on, and the harbour chain and its hanging steel-mesh nets pulled back to allow the vessels access. Without a second thought, all three pigs powered in behind the enemy vessels, the gates drawing closed behind them. It had been easy! Each *Maiale* now sought out its individual target. Lieutenant Luigi de la Penne was to attack HMS *Valiant*, Captain Marceglia the battleship *Queen Elizabeth*, while Captain Martellotta had been instructed to search for the aircraft carrier *Illustrious*, believed to be possibly in harbour – but if this was not found, to attack any of the large oil tankers known to be there.

De la Penne, together with Pilot Officer Bianchi, made for HMS *Valiant*, easily riding over the top of the anti-submarine nets that encircled the 32,000-ton battleship. The time was now

2.19 a.m. Suddenly de la Penne lost control of his vessel, and it sank to the bottom in about 45 feet of water. He was forced to let go as it plummeted to the depths. Diving to find it, he discovered that some wire had wrapped itself around the propeller. Looking around him, he could see no sign of Bianchi. He was entirely on his own.

Increasingly cold, due to the slow leak in his suit, de la Penne had to make a rapid decision. The success or otherwise of this operation was now in his hands, and his alone. Bianchi was nowhere to be seen. If he left the stricken SLC where it was, the 300 kg charge would explode harmlessly. To have any effect, he needed to somehow get the warhead under the nearby hull of the British battleship. Even though he would not be in a position to attach the charge to the bilge keel of the enemy vessel, where it could do most damage, an acceptable alternative would be to place the charge on the seabed directly under the ship's hull – HMS *Valiant* had a draught of 30 feet, allowing some 15 feet between the bottom of the enemy vessel and the harbour floor. The only way he could do so was by using brute strength – dragging the heavy warhead across the sea bottom, inch by inch, after detaching it from the now immovable pig. This was what he decided to do: it was exhausting and dangerous work. There was little knowledge at the time of the effect of oxygen on the blood at such depths, especially combined with severe physical exertion. But de la Penne somehow managed to drag the 300 kg warhead directly under *Valiant's* hull.

It took him about forty minutes. He set the timers to explode at exactly 6 a.m. local time. De la Penne then swam to the surface, discarded his face mask and rebreather set and, with no sign of Bianchi, began to swim to the shore. It was not long before a shout rang out from the ship, followed by some shots fired in his direction. De la Penne swam back to the mooring buoy at the front of the vessel, to await arrest. To his amazement he found Bianchi, who had blacked out underwater and, on coming to and finding himself on the surface, had hidden by the buoy to avoid raising the alarm before de la Penne had had a chance to prepare the device under the ship. As they lay in the water the British sentries on HMS *Valiant* laughed at them and made, according to de la Penne's report, many 'facetious remarks, believing that our operation had failed; they were talking contemptuously about Italians. I called Bianchi's attention to the probability that in a few hours they would have changed their minds . . .'

A motorboat eventually arrived to escort the wet and bedraggled men to a shed near the Ras-el-Tin lighthouse to be interrogated. When he was told of the arrests, Admiral Andrew Cunningham instructed that the men were to be brought back on board HMS *Valiant*, to be questioned by Captain Charles Morgan. The time was about 4 a.m. Refusing to answer his questions, they were placed in a forward hold, not far (unbeknown to Morgan) from where the charge was due to explode. Nevertheless, Morgan clearly hoped that, if an explosion was due to take place, the Italian frogmen would reveal its presence before it was due to go off. His supposition was correct. Luigi de la Penne's report, prepared after his release from a POW camp in 1943, told the story of the next few hours for himself and Bianchi:

When there were about ten minutes left before the explosion, I asked if I could speak to the commanding officer. I was taken aft, into his presence. I told him that in a few minutes his ship would blow up, that there was nothing he could do about it and that, if he wished, he could still get his crew into a place of safety. He again asked me where I had placed the charge and as I did not reply had me escorted back to the hold. As we went along I heard the loudspeakers giving orders to abandon ship, as the vessel had been attacked by Italians, and saw people running aft. When I was again in the hold I said to Bianchi, as I came down the ladder, that things had turned out badly and that it was all up with us, but that we could be content, since we had succeeded, in spite of everything, in bringing the operation to a successful conclusion.

Bianchi, however, did not answer me. I looked for him and could not find him. I supposed that the British, believing that I had confessed, had removed him. A few minutes passed (they were infernal ones for me: would the explosion take place?) and then it came. The vessel reared, with extreme violence. All the lights went out and the hold became filled with smoke. I was surrounded by shackles, which had been hanging from the ceiling and had now fallen. I was unhurt, except for pain in a knee, which had been grazed by one of the shackles in its fall. The vessel was listing to port. I opened one of the port-holes very near sea level, hoping to be able to get through it and escape. This proved to be impossible, as the port-hole was too small, and I gave up the idea: but I left the port open, hoping that through it more water would enter. I waited for a few moments. The hold was now illuminated by the light which entered through the port. I concluded that it would be rash to stay there any longer, noticing that the vessel was now lying on the bottom and continuing slowly to list to port. I climbed up the ladder and, finding the hatchway open, began to walk aft; there was no one about. But there were still many of the crew at the stern. They got up as I passed them; I went on till I reached the captain. At that moment he was engaged in giving orders for salvaging his ship. I asked him what he had done with my diver. He did not reply and the officer of the watch told me to be silent. The ship had now listed through 4–5 degrees and come to a standstill. I saw from a dock that it was a quarter past six. I went further aft, where a number of officers were standing, and began to watch the battleship *Queen Elizabeth*, which lay about 500 metres astern of us.

The crew of that battleship were standing in her bows. A few seconds passed and then the *Queen Elizabeth*, too, blew up. She rose a few inches out of the water and fragments of iron and other objects flew out of her funnel, mixed with oil which even reached the deck of the *Valiant*, splashing every one of us standing on her stern. An officer came up and asked me to tell him on my word of honour if there were any other charges under the ship. I made no reply and was then again taken back to the hold. After about a quarter of an hour I was escorted up to the officers' mess, where at last I could sit down, and where I found Bianchi. Shortly afterwards I was put aboard a motorboat, which took me back to Ras-el-Tin.

I noticed that the anchor, which had been hanging at the bows, was now underwater. During transit, an officer asked me whether we had got in through the gaps in the mole. At Ras-el-Tin we were locked in two cells and kept there until towards evening. I asked whether I could be given a little sunlight, as I was again very cold. A soldier came, felt my pulse and told me that I was perfectly all right.

Towards evening, we were put into a small lorry and transported therein to a prisoner of war camp in Alexandria. I found some Italians in the camp who had heard the explosions that morning. We lay down on the ground, without having had any food and, though we were soaked through, we slept till the following morning. I was taken to the infirmary for treatment of my knee injury and some Italian orderlies gave me an excellent dish of macaroni. The next morning I was removed to Cairo.

Marceglia and Schergat's story was similar. They too managed to find their way to their target – HMS *Queen Elizabeth* – and to clamp their warhead to a line attached to the two bilge keels, so that it hung about five feet below the hull of the ship. At 4.15 a.m. the task was complete, and the two men began to make good their escape. Marceglia takes up the story:

> We got astride our craft again: my diver made me urgent signs to surface, as he was just about all in. I pumped in air to surface; the craft only detached itself from the bottom with difficulty, then at last it started to rise, at first slowly, later more rapidly. So as not

to burst out of the water too suddenly, I had to exhaust;* the air bubbles attracted the attention of the watch aft. He switched on a searchlight and we surfaced right into its rays. We ducked down on the craft to make the target as small as possible and prevent our goggles from reflecting the light. Shortly afterwards, the searchlight was switched off; we started on our return, which took us past the bows of the ship; a man was walking up and down the fo'c'sle deck, I could see his cigarette glowing; everything was quiet aboard. We got out of the obstructed zone and, at last, took off our masks; it was very cold; I couldn't prevent my teeth chattering. We stopped again and began distributing our incendiaries after setting the fuses.

Sinking their pig, they managed to swim to an empty stretch of shore, and hide their suits and equipment under some rocks. All the crews had brought civilian outfits to wear in Egypt and, posing as interned French sailors, they sauntered out of the docks as nonchalantly as their fast-beating hearts allowed.

Vincenzo Martellotta and Marino, not finding any aircraft carrier, nevertheless sighted and targeted a large tanker, which turned out to be the *Sagona*. The physical strain of operating in this environment was beginning to tell on Martellotta, who was vomiting and could no longer keep the Pirelli mouthpiece between his lips. Because he was now unable to submerge, they compromised by attaching the device to the hull. While they were working to do this, another ship came alongside their target. It was a destroyer, HMS *Jervis*. This gave them the possibility of attacking two targets instead of one. The fuse was set successfully by 3.55 a.m.: they now distributed their incendiary devices.

The men managed to get to shore, after first sinking their 'pig'.

* i.e. to release air from the ballast tank, which rose to the surface in telltale bubbles.

Having destroying their suits and equipment, they attempted to make their way out of the port. Martellotta continues the account:

I set off with Marino to get clear of the harbour zone and enter the city: we were stopped at a control point and arrested by some Egyptian customs officials and police, who summoned a second lieutenant and six privates of the British Marines. We were taken to an office occupied by two lieutenants of the Egyptian police, who started cross-examining us. While I was answering the questions put to me in as evasive and vague a manner as I could, a British naval commander arrived and requested the senior of the two Egyptian officers to hand us over to the British. The Egyptian refused to do so in the absence of any authority from his government, pointing out that, as he had found us to be Italians from the documents we carried and Egypt was not at war with Italy, he would have to get special instructions.

The British commander, after obtaining the necessary authorisation from his admiral, made a personal application to the Egyptian government for the instructions required and succeeded in getting us handed over.

My waterproof watch was on the table with the other articles taken possession of and I never took my eyes off it. Shortly after 5.54 a.m., a violent explosion was heard, which shook the whole building. A few minutes later, as we were getting into a car to follow the British officer, a second explosion was heard, further away, and after the car had started a third. At the Ras-el-Tin naval headquarters we were briefly interrogated, courteously enough, and then dispatched to the concentration camp for prisoners of war at Cairo.

Marceglia and Schergat succeeded in making good their escape from the dockside, and remained at large for several more days. They managed to make their way to Rosetta on the evening of 20 December, but failed to find a boat with which to rendezvous with the *Zaffiro*, and were arrested three days later by the Egyptian police, who handed them over to the Royal Navy. So ended one of the most imaginative and daring operations of the war. All six Italian commandos were now prisoners of war, but with supreme courage and remarkable audacity they had succeeded in humbling Britannia, temporarily at least.

THREE

Chariots

With a handful of skilled men the 10th Flotilla had achieved what a squadron of battle cruisers would have struggled to do. In a moment, the naval situation in the eastern Mediterranean was dramatically shifted in Italy's favour. At the outbreak of the war, the Royal Navy could boast a two-to-one numerical superiority over the German and Italian navies combined, but her forces were stretched out between the British Isles, the Northern Atlantic, the Far East and the Mediterranean. The Fleet Air Arm was also weak: a handful of Swordfish Stringbags based on the two aircraft carriers – one in Gibraltar and the other in Alexandria – was supposed to provide air cover to the entire fleet. Now, that advantage had all but gone. The arrival in the Mediterranean of German U-boats in September 1941, followed by the transfer of II Fliegerkorps from the Eastern Front in December, together with the attack on Alexandria, combined to turn the tables on British naval supremacy, at least for the time being. Italy could now, as Borghese was to observe, 'resume, with practical immunity, supplies to the armies overseas and carry out transport of the German Afrika [Corps] to Libya, thus causing the defeat, a few months later, of the British Army, which was driven out of Cyrenaica'.

Although time was to demonstrate the short-lived nature of the advantage the Italians had gained, the nature of the attack, and the damage it caused, caused deep shock in the Admiralty. A news blackout meant that no hint of the disaster reached the press, and elaborate means were taken to hide the truth from the Italians. It is not hard to understand the impact the news of this loss would have had on Britain's enemies at a time of unparalleled bad news. The losses of HMS *Barham, Repulse, Prince of Wales, Valiant, Ark Royal* and *Queen Elizabeth* were closely guarded secrets. It wasn't until 23 April 1942 that Winston Churchill was able to announce them to a secret session of the House of Commons. Describing the attack on Alexandria, he commented in typical fashion:

> On the early morning of December 19 half a dozen Italians in unusual diving suits were captured floundering about in the harbour of Alexandria. Extreme precautions have been taken for some time past against the varieties of human torpedo or one-man submarine entering our harbours. Not only are nets and other obstructions used but underwater charges are exploded at frequent irregular intervals in the fairway. None the less these men had penetrated the harbour. Four hours later explosions occurred in the bottoms of the *Valiant* and the *Queen Elizabeth* produced by limpet bombs fixed with extraordinary courage and ingenuity, the effect of which was to blow large holes in the bottoms of both ships and to flood several compartments, thus putting them both out of action for many months. One ship will soon be ready again, the other is still in the floating dock at Alexandria, a constant target for enemy air attack. Thus we no longer had any battle squadron in the Mediterranean. *Barham* had gone and now *Valiant* and *Queen Elizabeth* were completely out of action.

Cunningham was horrified by this turn of events. With the other grievous losses to his fleet in recent weeks, this was the worst possible news. With typical understatement, ABC described the attack as 'very unpleasant'. 'It was a heavy blow,' he recalled in his memoirs. He wrote to the First Sea Lord, Sir Dudley Pound, a few days later:

We are having shock after shock out here. The damage to the battleships at this time is a disaster, and my chief concern is that it has added so much to your burdens and anxieties . . . The worst feature is we do not know how they penetrated the boom defence. The prisoners state they came in through the gate when it was opened for the destroyers to enter. This is certainly quite possible; but they must have been prepared to come under, through, or over the net. Charges were being dropped but do not seem to have deterred them, which lends colour to the suggestion that they came through when the gate was open . . . We are now getting concrete blocks on the bottom right across the entrance with a chevaux de frise on top up to a 40-foot depth and to the foot of the net. It is costing a lot; but we must have this harbour really secure . . . The last few days everyone has had the jitters, seeing objects swimming about at night and hearing movements on the ships' bottoms. That must stop.

Cunningham's memoirs reveal how little attention the Royal Navy had paid to the type of threat faced by the submersibles of the 10th Flotilla. There appeared to be a sense of a vague, undefined menace: but no more. Given the recovery of an SLC following the attack on Malta in July, their assessment of the danger their ships were in should have been far more precise than the position described by Cunningham:

For some time we had suspected that the Italians contemplated an attack on the battleships. We had information that they possessed some sort of submersible explosive motor-boat which could travel on the surface or under water, and was fitted with apparatus for lifting nets which enabled it to pass under the normal defences.

There was no excuse for such laziness. The cost was the loss of HMS *Queen Elizabeth* and HMS *Valiant*. Cunningham recorded that: 'The damage to HMS *Valiant* was, when investigated in dry dock, worse than expected, extending over about eighty feet including the keel. She would require at least two months for temporary repairs.' A subsequent Court of Inquiry found the defensive arrangements in the port to be wholly inadequate.

Cunningham, however, paid the Italians the respect they were due. 'One cannot but admire the cold-blooded bravery and enterprise of these Italians,' he wrote several years later. 'Everything had been carefully thought out and planned.' Midshipman Frank Wade, likewise, reappraised his attitude to the *Regia Marina*. 'All of us thought that the Italian navy was hopeless, inefficient, and even cowardly,' he wrote. 'However, we soon revised our opinions about their heroism and ingenuity.'

After thirty-nine hours under the surface of the Mediterranean following the attack, the *Scirè* at long last came to the surface; the darkness of the night hiding her exhausted crew from the attentions of any watching enemy, as she recharged her batteries and fresh salty air was pumped though the vessel. It provided an opportunity to receive coded signals from the *Supermarina* in Rome, one of which told them that aerial reconnaissance had indicated that two battleships had been hit. For the first time, major surface vessels of the enemy fleet had been struck by Italy's secret weapon: the lion felled by a mouse. The years of planning, training, failure and heartache had finally paid off. After diverting through Leros, on 29 December Borghese proudly brought the *Scirè* back to its home port of La Spezia, twenty-six days after setting out on the mission that proved a concept that had been six years in its gestation.

However, short-term tactical successes masked a fundamental problem with 10th Flotilla operations – namely the absence of any strategic intent other than the rather vague hope that, through these attacks, they might cause the Royal Navy a serious blow. The Decima Flottiglia was populated by extremely brave men, but most of them believed that courage was itself a strategy. The group around Tesei, for instance, believed in the moral effect of their operations, both among the Italian people at home and their enemies abroad. An attitude existed – misplaced as it turned out – that attacks by manned torpedoes would so demoralise enemy sailors by this demonstration of Italian ingenuity, courage and daring that British morale would plummet. Tesei argued that:

> Whether we sink any ships there or not does not matter. What does matter is that we prove able and willing to be blown up with our craft, under the very nose of the enemy. We will then have shown our sons and future generations of Italians at what sacrifice we follow our ideals, and at what price we reach for success!

In similar vein, Junio Borghese believed that repeated attacks gave rise to 'a feeling of insecurity . . . among the crews of enemy ships, even when moored in the interior of the harbours; this fact constituted in itself a success, as did also the expenditure of energy and ingenuity forced upon the enemy by his need to counteract this hidden threat . . .' But operations based on these concepts rarely survive sustained engagement with a determined, well-equipped, resourceful opponent. Alexandria provided only a short-lived advantage for the Axis powers in the Mediterranean, one that they failed to build on.

The successful use of the manned torpedo in combat was an Italian triumph. At a time when many British servicemen – such as those on HMS *Valiant* – made fun of Italian military expertise, the success of these highly trained men, equipped with ingenious devices like the SLC, provided food for thought. But, for the Royal Navy, the efforts of the 10th Flotilla at Gibraltar were at first viewed merely as an irritant, rather than representing a strategic threat. The failed assault against Malta in July seemed to have persuaded the Admiralty that the tiny Italian sub-surface vehicle posed no significant threat – given the ease with which the attack was repelled – and they did nothing to investigate its military possibilities. They made the mistake of confusing the SLC with the fast explosive boats used in the raid on Malta. By themselves, launched carefully and executed professionally, an SLC attack could have devastating consequences, as Alexandria dramatically proved.

It took an inordinately long time for London to realise that it could harness Italian inventiveness to its own advantage. The initial imperative had been to seek ways of improving harbour defences in Gibraltar, Malta and Alexandria. The question of how this invention could be used by the British against their enemies did not occur to them for several months after evidence of it had first been detected. On 18 January 1942, however, the prime minister sent a personal minute to General Hastings Ismay, for consideration by the Chiefs of Staff Committee:

> Please report what is being done to emulate the exploits of the Italians in Alexandria harbour and similar methods of this kind . . . Is there any reason why we should be incapable of the same kind of scientific aggressive action that the Italians have shown? One would have thought we should have been in the lead. Please state the exact position.

In the dying days of March 1942 the 45-year-old commanding officer of the Infantry Assault ship HMS *Prince Charles* left his vessel to be refurbished in the Thames near Tower Bridge and made his way to the headquarters of the Admiral, Submarines at Northways House on Finchley Road, London NW3. The New Zealander Captain William Fell (perhaps because of his relative slightness he was known to all his friends as 'Tiny') had joined the Royal Navy in 1915 and had served with submarines since 1918: but since the outbreak of war had spent his time on the surface, first with Q ships* and then in roles supporting

---

* A Q ship was a vessel designed to look innocent, thereby attracting a U-boat to attack her by surface fire, but in fact containing concealed guns enabling her to fire back on the enemy.

Combined Operations in Norway in 1940, and subsequently commando raids. Ordinary Seaman Sidney ('Butch') Woollcott, who was to serve with him throughout 1943 and 1944, described him as 'a legend among all who knew him'. Now he wanted to return to his first love: submarines. In London, as his memoirs attest, he 'found many old friends, ex-pupils and shipmates of peacetime days'. But he didn't intend his visit to be purely social. He wanted a job.

Fell happened to bump into George Roper, the Submarine Service HQ's chief of staff, who suggested, to Fell's delight, that 'Max would like to see you'. This was Rear-Admiral Sir Max Horton, Flag Officer Submarines. 'I had known Max for twenty-five years,' Fell later recalled:

and had once refused to go as his 3rd officer in submarine *M1*, and somehow managed to be tactful enough to escape his wrath. Sir Max was one of the truly great in the submarine world, but his reputation for ruthless discipline, and the ruthless removal of all who dared to stand in his way, led to many officers, senior as well as junior, taking good care not to cross his path. I had served under Sir Max on several occasions, but despite being on the mat* more than once, had always managed to survive.

'Hello, Fell! What mischief have you been up to?' was Horton's immediate response on seeing his visitor. According to Fell's recollection, Horton then asked, as if out of the blue: 'Would you like to come back to submarines?' 'I was struck dumb,' recorded Fell, 'as this miraculous question penetrated, and he was already growing impatient by the time I could stammer out, "Yes please, sir." "Well," said Max, "go away and build me a human torpedo. I will see about your appointment and relief in [HMS] *Prince Charles*."' Horton ordered him to start immediately and to report back on progress.

* 'On the mat' is slang for being 'carpeted', or told off.

He then went back to his desk and Fell stumbled out of the door. He had wanted to go back to submarines, but what in the world were human torpedoes?

George Roper filled Fell in on the detail, explaining the Italian attack on Alexandria and telling him that two of the enemy vessels had been recovered and were on their way to HMS *Dolphin*, the Royal Navy's submarine training centre at Fort Blockhouse, Gosport. Fell was responsible for attempting to replicate the Italian vessel and, in absolute secrecy, build British submersibles, crewed by British sailors, who could repeat the Italian success, this time on high-value Axis targets in their harbours. 'Max is in a hurry for this human torpedo,' Roper told him, 'and any red tape over your appointment and turn-over to your relief can wait.'

That night, Fell drove in his ancient and much repaired Austin Ten the 86 miles to the south coast, settling into a borrowed bunk with a glass of beer and a sandwich rustled up by the Officers' Mess steward, despite the lateness of the hour. Next morning he met the commander of the Fifth Submarine Flotilla, Captain Reggie Darke, DSO, RNVR, a famous submariner who had retired in 1939 but who had returned to the colours at the onset of war. Darke had been briefed by Roper the previous afternoon about Fell's imminent arrival. Together they pieced together what information they had. The Italian *Maiali* had not yet arrived, but photographs had, so they had enough to build a life-sized mock-up using what pieces of material they had lying around. Darke also told Fell that another famous submariner, Commander Geoffrey Sladen, DSO – who, as captain of HM Submarine *Trident*, had crippled the *Prinz Eugen* with torpedoes on 23 February 1942 (he also had three rugby caps for England) – was even then at Siebe Gorman's establishment at Tolworth. Sladen had been given the responsibility for designing a rubberised diving suit to enable a two-man crew to survive in cold northern waters, incorporating a rebreathing set based on the Davis Submarine Escape Apparatus (DSEA).

Together with the Chief Engineer at HMS *Dolphin*, Commander Stan Terry, Fell and Darke got to work with a drawing board and sketched out Britain's first human torpedo. They were to christen the contraption 'Cassidy'. Fell described their process of discovery:

> We began with a log of wood twenty feet long and twenty-three inches in diameter, rounded off at the fore end and tapered at the after end. To this log we fitted a two-gallon tank at each end and pipes and valves from these two tanks to a semi-rotary pump, so that either tank could be filled or emptied, or the contents of one transferred to the other. Amidships we fitted a third tank, which could be flooded from the sea or blown empty by a small bottle of compressed air. We then had our log lifted into the sea and, standing in waders beside it, we filled the tanks, at which point the log rolled over and remained floating upside-down. We now added a lead keel, and after much trial and error we produced a reasonably stable log that just floated when all three tanks were empty and sank when they were full. We then fitted a set of hydroplanes or diving rudders and a steering rudder, both operated from amidships by a joystick. Moving the stick fore and aft operated the hydroplanes and moving it sideways operated the rudder.

Stirrups for the crew completed the ensemble.

After a few days, Sladen turned up with his prototype diving suit – nicknamed the 'Clammy Death' by its operators. It was the first flexible diving suit of its kind in British service, and in its early versions was complicated and beset with problems. Sladen's idea was to create a one-piece suit that incorporated two eyepieces as well as the rebreathing equipment. A valve regulated the flow of oxygen from the DSEA oxygen cylinder into an airbag on the diver's chest, which was then fed by a tube into the diver's mouth. Exhaled air was fed back into the bag through a canister containing material that absorbed carbon dioxide. The future X-craft diver Australian Sub Lieutenant Max Shean recalled that the DSEA:

> comprised a rubber 'lung' worn on the chest. It had a mouthpiece at the top, a steel cylinder of oxygen below, and a canister of 'Protosorb' [containing a mixture of soda-lime] to remove carbon dioxide on exhalation, fixed in the middle. One also wore a nose clip to prevent oxygen escaping, and goggles. It took a little courage, once breathing from this bag of oxygen, to leap into the water and to breathe with head immersed, but it worked and soon everyone was doing it.

This 'rebreather' allowed divers to remain underwater without expelling to the surface the telltale air bubbles typical of compressed air exhalation, as in modern scuba equipment.

The first usable oxygen device had been patented in 1878 by the Englishman Henry Fleuss. It used an absorbent rope soaked in caustic potash to remove the carbon dioxide produced by breathing, although the risks of oxygen poisoning at depths over 30 feet were not fully understood until in 1942 extensive British testing was carried out as a result of the instructions to build a human torpedo. The most obvious military use for an oxygen rebreather set in the early days was to assist submariners escaping from a sunken vessel, and it was to this end that Fleuss and Robert Davis worked together to build a range of such equipment. This was further developed by Davis (now the managing director of the diving engineering firm Siebe Gorman) into his famous Davis Submarine Escape Equipment in 1927, using a French invention – oxylithe – to capture the carbon dioxide by-product of breathing. The DSEA was widely deployed by the Royal Navy before the Second World War, coming into service in time to save six lives in the loss of HMS *Poseidon* in the Far East in 1931.

The greatest drawback of the DSEA was its limited duration: a maximum of 60 minutes submerged was all that could be achieved, which of course was entirely inadequate for the tasks required of human torpedo crews. The orders which sent Fell to HMS *Dolphin* to design a British manned torpedo, and Sladen to Tolworth to design a new all-in-one diving suit, also included instructions to design a new oxygen rebreather apparatus – this time with a considerably extended underwater breathing duration. The specification called for six hours, with an operating depth of 90 feet.

The arrival of Sladen at *Dolphin* with his suit allowed rehearsals to be undertaken on Fell's log contraption, which had now been labelled a 'Chariot'. The experiments, which took place in the Admiralty Experimental Tank at Haslar, were designed to check that it could sink, achieve neutral buoyancy and then resurface satisfactorily. Once content with the fundamental seaworthiness of their design – copied of course from the two recovered *Maiali*, which had now reached them in Gosport – their next task was to ask the Admiralty to have a number of prototypes built. The company the Admiralty commissioned to do this was Stodhert and Pitts of Bath, an engineering firm whose normal peacetime fare was building cranes and bridges.

At the same time – May 1942 – Sladen and Fell began to solicit for recruits for work that was as yet undefined, and hence almost certainly dangerous. Searching for officers, they looked first amongst men of the RNVR undergoing training. 'We decided to call for volunteers,' Fell recalled, 'who had knowledge of small boats, for hazardous and arduous service.' Fell and Sladen travelled down to Brighton to make their pitch to a new batch of reserve officers in training. From a thousand men, two hundred showed an interest in volunteering for special submarine-related service (the exact details remained secret), although a mere eleven made it through the initial assessment. They then received a summons to join the 'Experimental Submarine Flotilla' at HMS *Dolphin*. They, and a similar number of ratings – recruited by the same means – arrived at Gosport in May. Fell was impressed with some of the early recruits, such as 'two magnificent Canadian sub-lieutenants called Chuck Bonnell and Al Morton' recruited by Geoffrey Sladen. A Welshman, 'Taffy' Evans, a submarine stoker petty officer, Cyril ('Jim') Warren, and Sergeant Don Craig of the Royal Engineers, who had mysteriously found himself in naval circles ever since Dunkirk, joined them from work they had been undertaking at Siebe Gorman.

While efforts continued at Tolworth to develop a suit, Fell began to train his men in Gosport. There were no manuals for this type of warfare, and he had yet to see a completed Chariot, even in proto-type: so he made it up. It made sense to start with the basics of diving: the standard modus operandi was fixed diving with helmets and compressed air. The men were connected by a rope and hose, through which compressed air was pumped to them from a boat on the surface. By this means the recruits were able to get used to working in the dark and cold of the underwater environment, dependent on an external source to survive.

It is rarely understood by outsiders just how alien this environ-ment is. There are massive mental hurdles associated with success-fully overcoming the challenge of working alone, deep under the surface of the sea, with limited means of visibility and communica-tion and only seconds available to recover if anything goes wrong. It is no surprise that so many men – in every other way strong, committed and courageous individuals – fell by the wayside when exposed to the rigours of diver training. Fell and Sladen also intro-duced the men to submarines, and they undertook a number of familiarisation journeys into the Channel. They also engaged in rigorous daily physical training. Once they had become thoroughly conversant with operating underwater at depths of up to 100 feet they were introduced to the DSEA, and the concept of oxygen rebreathing. Several of the recruits demonstrated that they were not suitable to this type of work, and were returned to their units, but a regular stream of new volunteers meant that numbers were maintained at around twenty.

So far the men had not been told the ultimate purpose of this training: most simply assumed that they would be involved with operating as divers from submarines against the enemy coast. In due course the men were informed, under conditions of great secrecy and despite the fact that none had yet seen even Fell's wooden mock-up, of the purpose of their existence. Their excitement and enthusiasm on hearing the news that they would soon have real machines to ride on was 'terrific', Fell recalled. 'From then on we had a devoted and inspired party, whose one idea was to get at the enemy.'

After about three weeks, a replica model of one of the prototype Chariots then under construction in Bath was delivered to HMS *Dolphin*, and the team under Fell took to using it on Horsea Lake. It had no means of self-propulsion, but could submerge and surface adequately enough by means of a hand pump, so they tied a rope to its bows and pulled it around the lake behind the diving boat. It gave the crews an opportunity to practise submerging and resurfacing, and to experience something of operating the vessel whilst clad in their Sladen suits. A buoy was attached to a crewman, which floated on the surface above the Chariot, alerting others to its precise location under water.

Max Shean considered dressing in a Sladen suit 'hard work':

The fabric was heavy and stiff. One entered down through the neck. Brass backing plates were placed as a collar inside and outside the suit, with bolts projecting up through it and clamping them together. Onto these, the helmet was lowered and secured with a twist. Heavy boots were laced in place and finally, when a man had started turning the air pump handle, the glass face piece was screwed into place. At this point the trainee, if he were at all susceptible to claustrophobia, would need all the self-control he could muster in order to remain calm.

An antiseptic lubricant was used to cleanse the mouthpiece after each use: Shean 'always felt that it was lubricated with the previous wearer's saliva'. The men called it 'gob'. Lieutenant Charles Andrew recalled that riding even the wooden Cassidy 'was novel, and good fun with pranks galore'. 'There was a good deal of joy and pleasure in moving through the dark water at a depth of say two to three fathoms, watching phosphorescence flow by.'

Officers and ratings worked together without any impediment of rank. Cyril Warren and Sub-Lieutenant James Benson ascribed this to 'Tiny' Fell, who 'had the gift of seeming to reduce the inevitable gap between officer and rating'. Likewise, 'Slasher' Sladen was larger than life, and was well liked. Warren and Benson described him as 'a whirlwind'.

> Whereas Fell appealed to a subordinate's sense of respect through his immense charm and understanding, Sladen's attraction was through his extraordinary capabilities. He had the genius of the quick decision, the unlimited energy, the great physical strength, and the outstanding ability at sport that the regular-serving naval rating looks for in the ideal officer.

Small-team camaraderie quickly built up among the party (which by 1 June comprised twenty-six officers and thirty-one naval ratings), exemplified by a story told by Butch Woollcott about another recruit:

> During training the divers wandered around the bottom at will, but they were attached to small blocks of wood by a line to their diving gear. The wooden blocks, which were numbered, acted as buoys and showed the position of each diver to the watchers in dinghies on the surface. I was plodding along in the darkness about forty feet down when suddenly I found that it became more and more difficult to make headway. I was getting rapidly exhausted with my efforts to move at all – so I decided to surface. When I arrived at the top, I found three chaps grinning all over their faces in a dinghy, one of them happily holding on

to my life-line. I'd been towing three husky men in a dinghy for about the last fifteen minutes – no wonder I found it a bit difficult.

One problem, however, began to raise its dangerous head during this initial training. This was the blackouts suffered by divers after prolonged exposure to oxygen at depth. Even in the otherwise benign environment of Horsea Lake outside Portsmouth, which was only 25 feet deep, danger lurked. All divers under training were routinely harnessed to a rope that was held by the safety boat above them. On one occasion during the early days of training a young officer recruit – Lieutenant P. C. A. Browning, RNVR – became detached from his safety line, held in the safety boat by Fell himself. His body was found several hours later. He had clearly undone his rope, in contravention of orders, an act considered only possible in the midst of the deliriums brought about by oxygen poisoning.

It seemed that, whatever precautions they took, danger and death lurked behind every corner. Tom Waldron describes how the unqualified success of the first demonstration of a human torpedo at Portsmouth before a crowd of senior officers in late June 1942 was preceded, unknown to the visitors, by one of the crew being 'pulled out of the water nearly unconscious at two o'clock that morning at the conclusion of the dress rehearsal'. Warren and Benson in fact described this as an accident that happened to Warren himself, inadvertently knocking open the oxygen valve on his DSEA apparatus and instantly sending him unconscious as a stream of pure oxygen hit his lungs. It was only the swift action of his No. 2, Chief Petty Officer Jack Passey, which saved his life. Browning's death reminded the Admiralty of the urgent need to study the science of oxygen use at depth, and a detailed programme of analysis, ultimately involving 1,000 test dives, was begun at the Tolworth works of Siebe Gorman. An appeal across the Navy called for volunteers to serve as guinea pigs in this testing programme.

47

FOUR

Oxygen Pete

Sidney 'Butch' Woollcott, a recent though bored and under-employed recruit to the Royal Navy, hoping to find his way onto a coppersmith's course to become an Engine Room Artificer (ERA), was kicking his heels in Portsmouth in July 1942 when he heard an advertisement for volunteers for 'special service' over the camp's loudspeaker system. As he had been waiting in Portsmouth since joining up in late March, it was a mixture of boredom and inquisitiveness that led him to tuck the cigarette he was rolling under the crown of his cap and wander over to the Police Office to record his name on the list. Several days later he was called to an initial weeding-out with about 100 other volunteers. 'Come on, you commandos!' the NCO bawled sarcastically. 'Fall in here!' About thirty survived this process, with all the non-swimmers eliminated. Two days later a stiff medical assessment reduced the number to about twenty, all of whom spent a further day across the harbour at HMS *Dolphin* being interviewed by Lieutenant Commander W. O. Shelford, RN.

'After taking my name,' Woollcott recalled, 'Shelford said: "Now, I'm looking for volunteers to enable me to find out valuable information." "Ah, espionage!" I thought. "Just up my street." Then he dashed all my hopes. "Information," he went on, "about diving apparatus, and underwater working. How do you feel about diving and underwater work?"' Woollcott admitted to being a good swimmer 'in a rugged, unpolished sort of way' and found himself admitted to Shelford's programme, along with about seventeen others.

Then back to barracks, to wait a few more days till we were once more called out. This time, with our kitbags and hammocks packed, we were drafted to HMS *Dolphin*, where for the first three days we received lectures on diving with oxygen breathing apparatus. As much knowledge was imparted to us as had already been discovered on the subject – which wasn't much in those days. Most of our instructors were Chief or Petty Officers, who were submarine coxswains who had specialised in this work, and had carried out the initial and most dangerous experiments with the embryo of the diving dress which we were to wear.

Shelford had been appointed to command the newly established Admiralty Experimental Diving Unit (AEDU), based at Siebe Gorman's Tolworth factory. His remit was to evaluate the safe limits for the use of pure oxygen under water, and a team of naval officers and divers, together with civilian scientists including Professors Sir Leonard Hill and J. B. S. Haldane, were tasked with defining the science for the first time around the limits of human exposure to oxygen at pressure. The work was of vital importance to guide operational decision-making in the future use of Chariots, although it was to have wider and more profound significance for oxygen rebreathing thereafter. Woollcott's memoirs describe the role of the first human guinea pigs:

We had our first dives at *Dolphin*. These were done in the fifteen-foot diving tank with the Davis submarine escape apparatus. After putting on the apparatus and receiving instructions by numbers in the correct way of loading the bottles, filling the bag with oxygen, emptying the bag of foul air, flushing our lungs with oxygen, and finally breathing from the bag, we were taken to the edge of the tank and shown how to use the apparatus in the water by one of the instructors. Then it was our turn. One by one, we climbed slowly down the ladder which went to the bottom of the tank, until only our heads were out of the water. Then, after a few last-minute instructions, we completely submerged ourselves, and waited with our heads just under the surface while the instructor had a good look for any tell-tale bubbles which would tell us if there were any leaks in our apparatus. Then the instructor patted us once on the head, and we broke surface again. He reported to us that everything was OK, and patted us twice on the head. We then submerged again and climbed down the ladder to the bottom of the tank.

It was then that some stout hearts failed for a brief spell. One or two of the volunteers registered great horror at the last moment at having to go down to the bottom. However, after a few reassuring words from the instructors, and a few more desperate efforts, everyone finally made the plunge, and we all mustered at the bottom of the tank. Personally, the whole thing had the opposite effect on me. I was thrilled to think that I could go for a good swim underwater without having to break surface to take in air . . .

I found it rather difficult to remain at the bottom when I first dived, and had a tendency to keep rising to the surface. I soon discovered the reason for my apparent lightness though. My breathing bag was blown up too hard with oxygen. I was able to remedy this by squeezing my bag and causing some of the oxygen to escape through the exhaust valve. By experimenting with filling the bag a little and squeezing a little, I soon attained a perfect trim which gave me neutral buoyancy, and enabled me to stay perfectly still in any position I liked, on the bottom, near the surface, or half-way between the two. I found I could alter my position simply by gently flapping my hands, just as a fish uses its fins.

There wasn't much room for us to move about in that confined circular space, about twelve feet in diameter, but we had great fun all the same. The instructor had us turning head over heels and doing other queer acrobatic tricks, just to get us used to the gear and give us confidence in it. We also did a mock escape from a replica of a submarine escape chamber built next to and connected with the diving chamber. This is the drill that all recruits to the submarine service have to go through.

We were told that the first symptom of oxygen poisoning was a twitching of the lips ('lips' as we afterwards called it), but that this could be got rid of by wriggling the lips round and round the mouthpiece of the breathing set. We were also told that, once we'd got rid of the 'lips' they would never occur again during that particular dive. Well – the 'lips' part was dead right, as far as being the first symptom, but as for getting rid of them never to have them return – well, that was a polite fiction. As I later found out to my dismay. We were also told that oxygen poisoning only attacked a diver at a depth of fifty feet or more. That, too, we later found out to be wrong. We did find out that one thing we had been told was quite right, however, and that was that we could be put into a state of unconsciousness by oxygen poisoning. Yes – the flaking-out part hit us very strongly. Luckily, none of us reached the dying stage, because that is what we were told would happen to us if we could not be brought to the surface very quickly after flaking out. I expect that was true too – because it was a near thing for us on several occasions.

When our initial dives in the tank and our lectures were completed, we spent the next fortnight diving with the Sladen Suit. This was done in a long, rectangular artificial lake at Horsea Island at the far end of Pompey [Portsmouth] Harbour. We were taken there every morning and brought back every evening by launch. There we put on the first models of the Sladen Suit, and rather rough-looking models they were, too. Actually, they were a light diving dress made of thin silk and rubber, with a headpiece made from the face piece of a service gas-mask, and rubber. The breathing apparatus was an improvement on the D.S.E.A. We carried a larger breathing bag on our chests connected to the face piece by a gas-mask breathing pipe, at the end of which was a rubber mouthpiece similar to that of the D.S.E.A. Instead of carrying one small oxygen cylinder under the bag, we carried two large cylinders strapped to our backs. It is perhaps interesting to note that these bottles were made in Germany, and were the oxygen bottles carried by German aircraft shot down over this country . . . They were made of some aluminium alloy, and were so light that when filled with oxygen they would float on the water. They were very strong too; we used to pump oxygen into them up to 2,400lb per square inch. When they came to us, they had not even been repainted, and still carried the German markings. We didn't wear frogman's flippers, but a pair of roughly made canvas diving boots, weighted with five pounds of lead each.

I could understand now why I had been asked if I had ever suffered from claustrophobia, because my first impression when wearing the suit was of being rather shut in, especially after the two circular eyepieces had been screwed in. This was the last operation in the dressing procedure, and I was then completely enclosed in the suit. My breathing, too, seemed constricted, but that was due to my own breath causing the Protosorb canister to warm up. The Protosorb was soda lime crystals carried in a metal perforated canister inside the breathing bag, for absorbing the carbon-dioxide gases in the exhaled breath returned back into the bag.

It is hard to describe the feeling I had when I got to the bottom of that lake. To look up and see the pale reflection of light from the sun faintly showing on the surface thirty feet above me, to see the grey-green water all around me, to see the clouds of mud rising at my every footstep, and to feel the great pressure of water on my legs and arms, gave me a great feeling of awe. I felt just a tiny speck in the centre of that lake, and this new world into which I had entered seemed enormous. And yet – there was also another feeling, a very pleasant feeling. I marvelled at the peace and quiet down here, and I felt that I was lord of all I surveyed. Here was I, completely cut off from the world of human beings except for a long, thin line attached to my shoulder harness, here in this big, new, peaceful world, where I can go where I like and do what I like.

At first, I found it rather hard to move around the bottom of the lake. I tried first to walk upright, but this was useless; as soon as I took one step, the resistance of the water in front of me caused me to rise a few feet off the bottom of the lake, and I came down again in exactly the same place. There was no future in that. I then tried leaning forward farther and farther, until I was almost lying flat. By doing this I presented a very small surface to the water, and so decreased the resistance. Then, by digging my toes in at each step and doing a sort of fin movement with my hands, I managed to get along pretty quickly.

After a very enjoyable time diving every day in Horsea Lake, all the volunteers finally became used to the gear and acquired perfect confidence in it. Our number had decreased to sixteen by now, two more having dropped out owing to sinus trouble, after making their first dip into thirty feet of water. The sixteen survivors were then sent to Messrs Siebe Gorman's factory, where the experimental job for which they were recruited really started in earnest.

The sixteen of us who arrived at Siebe's that August afternoon were a motley crew. There was one Petty Officer Physical Training Instructor (known as 'Clubs' in the Navy), one Leading-Seaman, three A.B.s [Able Seamen], three Ordinary-Seamen (of whom I was one), three Leading-Stokers, two Stokers, and three Cooks. We were all under the charge of a Warrant Gunner named Mr Crouch, who was an old diver, and a very pleasant person to know.

That morning we were allowed to wander around the factory a bit, inspecting the diving tanks and compression chambers which were used by the firm for testing the diving apparatus which they made, and watching the factory workers assembling the D.S.E.A. sets and fire-fighting equipment.

The diving experiments there were carried out in a two-storied building containing a cylindrical tank, twelve feet deep and twelve feet in diameter, another tank, twenty-five feet deep and six feet in diameter, a twelve-foot tank about six feet in diameter, several dry compression chambers, and an infamous affair known to us as 'The Pot'.

The Pot was a diabolical contraption, as we found out very shortly. It was a pressure tank, about twelve feet in depth and six feet in diameter, with the edges rounded off very much like one of Mr Churchill's famous hats. In the top, which protruded through a hole in the first floor, was an opening, oval in shape, about two feet six inches by two feet. The opening was sealed by a heavy, air-tight door, opening inwards, which was opened and shut by means of a twofold purchase. This door must have weighed about two hundredweight. The tank contained about eight feet of water. Pressure was built up in the remaining four feet of the tank by connecting four large compressed-air cylinders to a pipe leading into the top. By this means, pressure could be built up inside the tank equal to that which is met at great depths. Any depth up to 150 feet could be produced in this manner. A pressure gauge on the outside of the tank told us the depth of water that had been equalled inside.

Our first dive was made in the twenty-five-foot tank. We went down in pairs and stayed there for thirty minutes. We all completed this successfully, and by that time the first day's diving was over. The next day, we started diving in The Pot. This was where our troubles started. It was the intention of those in charge, who now included a Surgeon-Lieutenant [K.W. Donald], to send us down one by one to fifty feet for thirty minutes. The first diver to go into The Pot was Symington, a Leading-Seaman. In order to get into The Pot, the diver had a canvas harness put on him underneath his breathing apparatus. The harness was fitted with a big iron ring, into which was placed the hook of another twofold purchase, and in this manner the diver was hoisted into or out of the tank.

Symington went into The Pot, and everyone waited with apprehension. But the fellow who waited with the most apprehension was the next one due in. He sat on a chair at the other side of the room with his diving dress on, all except the headpiece. His apprehension increased considerably when, twenty-five minutes after Symington had entered The Pot, a sudden cry of 'Up, Up!' was heard, and all hands went to panic stations. Two unclipped the door of The Pot, two more stood by the diver-lifting tackle, another grabbed the air-pressure release valve, and with a terrific rush of air, the pressure in The Pot was lowered to zero. The door was opened, tackle lowered, the two lifters weighed-off on the tackle, and Symington was lifted slowly out of The Pot. He was unconscious. As he was gently lowered to the deck and his diving dress was stripped off, we all gathered round, wondering. He had flaked out from oxygen poisoning, after spending twenty-five minutes at fifty feet. He soon came round again, and apart from a terrific headache, he was OK.

The next chap down lasted only ten minutes, and he looked so bad when he surfaced that he was sent straight back to Portsmouth. His diving days were finished – and I guess he wasn't sorry either. After lunch, it was my turn. I began to wonder if I had been wise to eat such a heavy meal. I entered The Pot in the usual manner, and arrived safely at the bottom, without catching my chin on the edge of the opening, or the back of my head on the door. Above me, one of the instructors was seated on a wooden platform in that part of The Pot that was not filled with water. He wore a pair of waders up to his waist, as the space was so cramped that his legs had to dangle in the water. He held the other end of the life-line which was attached to my harness. He also wore a pair of head-phones and carried a microphone. He was connected to another instructor who was similarly equipped outside The Pot. In this way, my actions could be reported to the doctor and others interested, and a log could be kept.

When I had signalled that I was OK, the heavy steel door was slowly shut and clipped. This was a terrifying business in itself. When shut, the door was kept in position by two huge 'strongbacks' weighing about half a hundredweight each, through which passed two bolts of about one and a quarter inches diameter, and screwed down with a couple of immense nuts. Now, that door leaked a little, and to get it shut really tight we used to put a hefty spanner on the nuts and whack it home with a seven-pound hammer. Well, you can imagine what it sounded like to the diver inside. Each stroke of the hammer seemed to shatter my eardrums. I was reminded of the sound sometime later, when I experienced my first depth-charge attack in a submarine, and a couple of those 'ashcans' dropped a bit too close for comfort.

When the banging stopped, it was a horrible feeling too. There was dead silence for a few seconds – the last stroke of the hammer sounded like the clang of a cell door shut behind me. Then there was a sudden terrific hiss as the compressed air came rushing into The Pot. My rubber mouthpiece began to press in on my face. I allowed some oxygen to trickle through the side of my mouth, which blew the rubber out again to the proper position. Then I found that my bag had been flattened by the increased pressure, and my breathing was getting weak through lack of oxygen. I blew it out again by giving myself a 'guff' of oxygen, by opening the bypass valve on my bottles for a fraction of a second. Then my ears started to pain. I tried to clear them by swallowing. This didn't work, so I pressed my nose against the inside of my face piece and blew down it. That did the trick. As the pressure became greater, I had to go through these actions again and again. Suddenly, the hissing stopped – I was at fifty feet. Dead silence reigned again. I went on a tour of inspection. Hanging by a string to the ladder was a small slate and a slate pencil. This was for the diver to write messages to the attendant. Walking around the perimeter, I found two small portholes about nine inches in diameter.

These were divided into smaller holes filled with thick glass, and looked very much like a fly's eye. They were about seven feet up from the floor of The Pot, and by getting a precarious hold on the heads of a couple of bolts, I was able to lift myself high enough to look through one of them, and by placing my head in a certain position and nearly going cross-eyed, I was just able to see the time by the clock on the wall outside.

I had been down about twenty minutes when I felt the first twitching of the lips. I exercised my lips around the mouthpiece, and the twitching went off. Soon afterwards, the attendant told me the thirty minutes were up, and that I had completed the course. The pressure would be taken off the tank, and we would rise to ten feet. Here we had to remain for ten minutes, for it must be remembered that the attendant too was breathing under pressure, and as he was breathing ordinary air, he was liable to get 'the bends' if our ascent was not delayed. With great thankfulness, I heard the hissing of the air and very welcome it was too, because this time it was on its way out.

Then it happened. I suppose the release valve had been open for about ten seconds, and the gauge outside registered about forty feet, when I suddenly felt a violent twitching of my lips. I tried to wriggle them around the mouthpiece again, my mouth was blown out like a balloon, and I was blurting out oxygen through my lips so much that it was hard even to keep the mouthpiece on my mouth. The twitching of my lips increased, and I felt a terrific tingling sensation at the side of my mouth, as if someone were touching it with a live wire. This increased, until it became a definite pain, and my lips became so distorted that it felt as if my mouth were stretched to somewhere near my right ear. I tried to climb the ladder, but by this time my whole body was convulsing, and I was only just able to get my head above water. I tried to shout to the attendant to grab me before I fell back. Although my lips formed the words, no sound came. It was a horrible feeling. I could feel myself falling back into the water, and the attendant's face seemed to dissolve into a black void. In his place, mounted on that black back-cloth, I could see my grandmother. Now this was a queer thing, because I have never seen my grandparents at all. They were dead before I was born. The only thing I knew of this particular lady was from a photograph hanging on the wall at home, and it was this likeness I could see. There was no mistaking that face, with its dark, glittering eyes, the high cheek-bones, the long, hooked nose, and the swarthy gypsy-like complexion. I sang out to her to grab me. But she too faded away – blackness closed in on me – I was out.

It was an hour later when I came to – in the factory sick bay, where I had been carried on a stretcher. So I must have been in a pretty rough state. I had a shocking headache, and felt as though I'd had a monumental night on the beer and was just waking up the morning after. It was quite a cheap hangover, but I think I'd rather have paid for it in the normal way. I was given a couple of aspirins by the factory nurse, a kindly old soul who treated me with a sort of kindly-sarcastic-scolding-proud-and-loving attitude of a mother whose son has hurt his knee by falling out of a tree while stealing apples. After resting for about an hour, I went back to the camp, had some tea, got cleaned up, and went ashore to have a night on the beer, for which I had already had a hangover.

A flaking-out session, seen from the spectator's viewpoint, is much less uncomfortable than undergoing the experience as a diver. But even from the point of view of the onlooker it's a pretty grim experience. I've never seen a man hanged, but after seeing a diver hoisted out of The Pot, unconscious, at the end of that tackle, I've a good idea what one looks like. His head is slumped forward on his chest. From his mouthpiece come awful bubbling noises. His hands hang limply at his sides from sloping shoulders. His hands, all swollen and puffy, with water dripping from them, are a ghastly greyish-purple colour. When his feet are clear of the hole, he is gently lowered on to the deck, face uppermost. The water streams off his suit in little rivers down the folds, forming a pool all round him. His headpiece is removed, revealing a face of slate-grey colour, eyes closed and saliva drooling from his sagging, purple lips. At the doctor's discretion, he is either divested of his diving gear and removed to the sick bay, or left to lie where he is until he regains consciousness.

Butch Woollcott fell victim to oxygen poisoning on two subsequent occasions. 'All except one of the sixteen of us flaked out at least once,' he recalled. 'Two or three of us did it twice, but I was the only one who did it three times. It would have been even more times too, if it hadn't been for the fact that I began to recognise the symptoms of a flaking-out session coming on earlier than before, and I was able to rush up the ladder, get my head above the surface of the water, then switch my mouthpiece cock onto "air".

Many was the time that I only just made it though, and I climbed the ladder with old Oxygen Pete hot on my heels and my shoulder already beginning to convulse. I would switch on to air and the instructor would wrap his legs around my waist to stop my falling back should I lose consciousness, and I would stand there with my head spinning, half-way between being conscious and not, wondering which way I'd be going – out or not. Luckily I went the right way each time . . . While some of the fellows were going down to seventy and ninety feet for an hour or more, I couldn't even do a half-hour at fifty. In fact it became so bad that one dive lasted only eleven minutes before I had to rush up the ladder.

Woollcott continued:

Well, this sort of thing went on for four months at Siebe Gorman's. One by one, the volunteers flaked out with oxygen poisoning. We did all kinds of experiments, many under Professor Haldane and Surgeon-Lieutenant Donald, RN. Sometimes we would dive to seventy feet for twenty minutes, up to ten feet for five minutes, down to seventy again for twenty minutes, up to the surface again for five, then down to fifty for half an hour, then surface and finish. Exact notes were taken in the log of all divers' reactions.

All the time, the morale of the volunteers remained very high, and we were all very cheerful. We still treated The Pot with very great respect, though. Jokingly we used to say that there was a demon living in it who was apt to be very hostile to any hapless diver who wasn't very quick to heed the warning of 'lips'. One comedian even composed a poem, which he chalked on the blackboard. I've forgotten it now, except for the last two lines, which went like this: 'For down at the depth of seventy feet lives a guy by the name of "Oxygen Pete".' We were paid five shillings a day extra for this work.

By this time we all had a pretty good idea what the gear we were experimenting with was to be used for. But we were told nothing definite. We'd heard rumours of an attack by Italian frogmen on the *Valiant* and *Queen Elizabeth* at Alexandria.

And there was another rumour floating around of a similar attack by our own lads on German shipping – but still nothing definite. Strangely enough, round about this time, a certain friction started to spring up between some of our party. I suppose we were all keyed up and anxious to get cracking operationally. Then the rot set in. Cases of flaking out became more and more frequent, and as the good divers flaked out, so their nerve seemed to go. Many of them had had such a good run before undergoing that terrifying experience that they had no time to regain their nerve before the experiments finished. It was terrible to see the effect on some of these grand chaps. I remember one in particular, a well-built six-footer, trying to light a cigarette. The cigarette was dancing around on his lips, and his hands were shaking like those of a man with the palsy as he tried to get the match in contact with the box to strike it. I am sure that if, like me, he had passed out earlier, he would have had time to recover.

So time went on, until 15th December 1942, when the experiments at Siebe Gorman's came to an end, and after stowing our gear and saying our farewells to our friends at the factory and the camp, we returned to Blockhouse. Here, one by one, we had our last interview with Lieutenant Commander Shelford. I guess we must have looked different men from those carefree, eager, green volunteers whom he had last seen in that same little office four months before. But there was one happy man among them – and that one was me. I was told the glad news that I had been recommended to carry on diving, and that I would, if I wished it, be sent to join the next operational class in training for 'Human Torpedoes'. He didn't have to ask me twice – I said 'Yes.' I learned that there were only ten survivors, and that I had been the only one picked to carry on. I was a very proud and happy man. Proud, when I thought of the hundred volunteers that day at Pompey Barracks, proud of the men I had worked with, and of the fact that I had been one of them. I have a medal now, but it does not belong only to me – it belongs to the other guinea pigs at Siebe Gorman's and the other chaps I met later in the operational class who didn't get the same chance that I did. I was happy that I had got what I went after. I felt that now, at last, I was really going places.

By the end of the experiments in the Siebe Gorman 'pot' an aide-memoire of the practical findings was issued to the men:

1. The amount of oxygen required by a man breathing underwater is usually expressed in litres of oxygen per minute, and depends on various factors. The amount of effort used in physical action is a main factor, but the size of the man, the water temperature, his fitness, and his nervous state all have a bearing on the amount of oxygen consumed. A trained underwater swimmer consumes approximately two litres of oxygen per minute.

2. Carbon-dioxide poisoning, if carried sufficiently far, produces unconsciousness and subsequent death. It is important, therefore, for the diver to be able to recognise early symptoms of carbon-dioxide poisoning, and to take appropriate action.

3. These symptoms find different expressions in different bodies. Usually it commences with a noticeable shortness of breath and a rapidly increasing cycle of respiration. This is followed by giddiness, lack of will power to move or act, and blackout. In some cases the diver encounters symptoms of intoxication prior to blackout.

4. In training divers, it is important to induce symptoms of carbon-dioxide poisoning on dry land, under medical supervision, in order that the diver may recognise his own particular symptoms. This is usually done by a blackout parade, where the diver is slowly poisoned until approaching the stage of insensibility, when he is removed from the breathing set and revived.

5. Breathing pure oxygen underwater is only normally safe between the surface and thirty-foot depth. Below this depth, oxygen poisoning may occur, owing to alteration in the metabolism of the body. Divers in shallow diving gear can normally descend to fifty feet for short periods, and ninety to a hundred feet if crack divers. They must, however, be alert to the symptoms of oxygen poisoning, and proceed at once to shallow depths should these manifest themselves. Such symptoms are usually heralded by a twitching of the lip, eyebrow or extremities of the body, impaired lip control, hallucinations, and feelings of apprehension and vertigo.

Bill Fell described men like Butch Woollcott as 'incredibly brave'. It is an understatement. Because of the work carried out by him and a handful of volunteers at Siebe Gorman's it was determined conclusively that oxygen poisoning occurred if a diver breathed oxygen at depths greater than 30 feet (14 pounds per square inch pressure). This became the maximum safe depth for oxygen-only diving and allowed Chariot operations to proceed with confidence. Without the deliberate, calculated commitment of men like Woollcott during these perilous investigations, many lives would have inevitably been lost on operations and training to a danger too little understood.

FIVE

Trial and Error

Horsea Lake was suitable for beginners only, and the men quickly tired of its monotonous features. Within weeks, Fell began looking about for a suitable location from which to conduct the next stage of training: this time with real Chariots rather than merely a life-size mock-up, and in the sea rather than an artificial lake. Fell's requirements were 'security from inquisitive eyes, a safe anchorage, reasonable accessibility to stores and a safe diving area'. He had a location in mind, from his days prowling the Scottish Islands in HMS *Prince Charles* with his commandos. With permission granted from the Admiralty and the allocation of an old submarine support ship – HMS *Titania*, known to all as 'Tites'* – as his headquarters and the accommodation ship for his crews, his eyes fell on the Outer Hebrides, where he knew there was a plethora of inlets and isolated sea lochs where he and his men could train far from prying eyes, and in realistic sea conditions.

After some deliberation, Fell chose Loch Erisort (codenamed Port ZD), lying about 7 miles south of Stornoway on the island of Lewis, which *Titania* reached on 12 June 1942. Sladen had remained behind in HMS *Dolphin* to continue recruitment, and to see into service the first of the prototype Chariots, nicknamed the 'Real One' by the men. Unfortunately time – and the weather – proved

---

* Woollcott described *Titania* as a 'run-down old tramp steamer' when he first saw her on Loch Corrie in February 1943.

Erisort to be a bad choice, chiefly because the region was exposed to appalling conditions that limited the training the men could do on their dummy Chariots. Life was primitive at Erisort, too. They had to build a jetty and huts ashore, and facilities were dependent on *Titania*. Wintry gales soon set in and seemed to dominate the entire climate to the extent that Fell could not 'remember more than half a dozen days with winds under thirty knots during the whole time we stayed in Erisort'.

A change of location was needed, and Fell settled this time on the remote western coast of Scotland. There, on the western side of Loch Linnhe – which runs north like a dagger from Oban towards Fort William – he found the calm and sheltered waters of Loch a'Choire (Loch of the Wind), or Loch Corrie (codenamed Port HHX). It was ideally suited to his purposes. Protected from the gales that had assailed them at Erisort, Loch a'Choire had a gently sloping bottom, which allowed for shallow-water training at one end and deeper at the other. Importantly, the water was calm and clear, and was a perfect anchorage for HMS *Titania*. Oban was 10 miles away by cutter and supplies could be transported south from Fort William, 25 miles due north by truck.

By July the entire show had moved to its new location. A few weeks later the first four real Chariots had successfully completed their initial tests on Horsea and were on their way, boxed up in crates, to Glasgow by rail. The excitement when they arrived, driven by truck over the single-track road from Fort William, and had been assembled was considerable. Fell described the assembled Mark 1 Chariots, each of which looked like a green, oversized torpedo. The men called them 'Jeeps', for a reason lost in the mists of time:

The forward end of the machine was the detachable head, containing 600 lb. of very high explosive and a clock for setting it off at any specified time up to eight hours after it was detached from the main body of the Chariot. This head was so balanced that it had just neutral buoyancy in salt water, tending neither to float nor sink. Next to the head came a small watertight compartment connected to the pumping and flooding system of the craft, so that it could be filled or emptied, or the water transferred from it to a similar tank right aft. These were the trimming tanks and were operated by a small electric pump and valve box with a single lever, which, when pushed forward, pumped water from aft to forrard, and when pushed aft reversed the flow of water. When the lever pointed inwards, water was admitted from the sea, and when outwards the tanks were pumped out. The next and largest compartment contained a thirty-two-volt heavy-duty battery, which drove a motor and gave the machine a speed of four knots for four hours or three knots for six hours. [The latter gave a range of 18 miles.] It also supplied power to the pump. In the next compartment, farther aft, was the motor geared to the propeller shaft. The driver sat astride the machine about a third of its length aft from the head. He sat behind a breast-high screen inside which was mounted his instrument panel carrying a depth gauge, a compass and a clock. His pump control switch and main motor switch were at the base of the screen, and between his legs was the joystick which operated the rudder and hydroplanes. His back rested against the main ballast tank, which also formed the screen for the second diver who straddled the machine immediately behind it. The main ballast tank could be flooded directly from the sea, or emptied by air pressure from a small air reservoir. The second diver rested his back on a locker which stretched aft nearly to the tail of the machine, and in which were kept two spare breathing sets for the divers, and the magnetic clamps for attaching the warhead to the enemy target after it had been detached from the Chariot.

Butch Woollcott considered that driving one of these green contraptions was very simple, at least during daytime and in circumstances where neutral buoyancy could be maintained, observing that 'divers bestrode and controlled a species of mechanical fish'. The No. 1 controlled the rudder with a joystick, which moved left and right for turning, and forward and back for diving or ascending. The electric motor was controlled by a throttle, which gave it a maximum speed of about 3½ knots. Two levers pumped water into, and air out of, the two ballast tanks: one in the front of the vessel and the other in the rear. The skill in driving this underwater motorcycle lay in manipulating the controls to give it neutral buoyancy; allowing it to have just the right amount of air and water in the ballast tanks for it to sit perfectly still at any required depth.

It did not take long for the men under Fell to master these new 'mechanical fish' in the calm waters of the loch. However, the entire experience of operating these new vessels was new, and a range of challenges, most of which were unexpected, had to be faced, and overcome. 'We were working against time,' he recalled, as the imperative was to master this new weapon and prepare crews for battle as quickly as possible – within the constraints of the science available, and before winter made operations in northern waters impossible. Prolonged exposure to daily testing and training produced a range of mechanical issues and problems, such as explosions of hydrogen in the battery compartment, which let water into the Chariot, sending it straight to the bottom. Exhaustion among the crews was also a consideration for 'Tiny' Fell. The mental stamina required to operate in the dark and cold underwater environment was extreme. Charles Andrew, who was eventually taken off Chariot training, admitted freely that by August 1942, soon after the Mark 1 prototypes had arrived in Scotland, he began 'to suffer from what I thought was indigestion: though now I believe it was nervous tension brought on by the mental suppression of mild claustrophobia. I shall certainly always remember the feeling of near panic, instantly and automatically suppressed, which I felt when I first donned the Sladen suit.'

But the major problem remained dealing with the effects on the crews of prolonged exposure to oxygen poisoning. Fell did not have the luxury of waiting for Professor Haldane and the team at Tolworth to advise on a safe diving depth for rebreathers, so he was forced to continue training while the oxygen experiments went on in parallel. In these circumstances it was to be expected that Oxygen Pete would haunt the sea lochs of Scotland. It was especially to be found when, for no apparent reason, a Chariot would unexpectedly lose its neutral buoyancy and slip rapidly towards the seabed, carrying with it its startled crew.

This was a frightening – and worrying – turn of events, whose cause took several months to discover. The problem was that the salt waters of the sea lochs, which produced a particular buoyancy, were fed at various points by fresh water – with an entirely different buoyancy – entering from the surrounding catchment area. A Chariot trimmed to a neutral buoyancy in salt water would unknowingly enter an extensive patch of fresh water and rapidly sink to the depths, endangering both vessel and crew, and inviting a visit from Oxygen Pete. Men unable to regain control of their craft, or who were reluctant to abandon it to the depths, could be overwhelmed by oxygen poisoning in a few moments, pass out and be killed before they had a chance to react.

Woollcott's first-ever ride on a 'jeep' was very nearly his last, as he encountered what later transpired to be a patch of fresh water in the seawater loch:

When it was my turn for my first dive, I was sent out as Number One with Leading-Seaman 'Shiner' Wright as my Number Two . . . Escorting us was one of our small motor skiffs manned by Lieutenant Commander Shaw, who was our training officer. I cruised around on the surface for a while under orders from Shaw, then I was directed to make a short run underwater. I trimmed the machine down by flooding the main ballast tank and pumping water into my two trimming tanks, until only our heads showed above water. This, according to the instructions we had received, was the perfect trim to have for a perfect dive. However, when I started the machine on its way and gently pushed the joystick forward, so that the hydroplanes were in diving position, all that happened was that my head went just below the surface. Shiner's head and shoulders came out of the water, with the screw threshing the surface behind him. I stopped her, and pumped more water into the trimming tanks to make sure the screw would have plenty of water to bite on, and we sank down till the water was just lapping our goggles.

Off we went again – this time she dived perfectly. As I eased the stick forward, the nose of the jeep took on a gentle downward slope. Down we went, into those icy depths. (It was March [1943] and the water was only forty-two degrees Fahrenheit [5.5° Celsius].) The pale-green colour of the water became darker and darker as we descended. It was a marvellous sensation, and I was enjoying it immensely. When the depth gauge on the machine showed thirty feet, I decided to flatten out and carry on at that depth for a few minutes before surfacing again. I gently pulled the joystick back, and waited for the jeep to flatten out – but the jeep had other ideas. It still carried on downwards. I pulled the stick back and back until I could pull it no farther, but still the nose pointed towards the bottom, and we carried on in that direction at what seemed an alarming speed. The water got darker still, and we could see less and less – what had been light-green, friendly sort of stuff near the surface, had become a black, engulfing mass.

We were going downwards so quickly that it was impossible to keep clearing the ears and the pain in mine was terrific. I guess Shiner's were hurting too, because suddenly I received four sharp digs in the back from his forefinger, indicating that he wanted to surface. 'Yes, Shiner,' I thought, 'I want to surface too, but the machine just won't.'

As she wouldn't lift on the hydroplanes, there was only one thing for it, and that was to blow main ballast. I did this, and she gradually started to flatten out. The needle on the depth gauge showed seventy feet before this happened. When she did start towards the surface, she went with a will, and rapidly left the dark depths behind her, and with main ballast blown, her planes at 'hard to rise', and her motor going full ahead, we hit the surface with the force of a water spout and leaped about two feet in the air like a porpoise, and landed with a loud splash. When we got back to *Titania* and removed our headgear, it was found that both Shiner and I were bleeding from the ears. Happily, we suffered no lasting ill effects.

A second problem was associated with the two members of a crew becoming separated from each other and from the Chariot. This was a particular problem at night. Eventually a system was developed of connecting the men to each other by a line, a simple expedient that saved many lives. They also carried calcium flares, to alert surface crews in the event of distress. Butch Woollcott recalled one desperate occasion during training when the calcium flare saved his life. He was No. 1 on a Chariot with Midshipman Dicky Kendall, who was later to take part in the X-craft attack on the *Tirpitz* (on Donald Cameron's *X6*). His head was just above the surface, taking a compass bearing on their target, when something strange occurred to their vessel: the machine began, inexplicably, to tip backwards.

I turned in my seat to see what was happening behind me. Dick Kendall was normally only a tiny little fellow, but now he looked even shorter and I was looking right over the top of his head. So I started pumping water from the after trimming tank into the forward one, but it made no difference. In fact by now the whole machine had started to sink. So I started pumping water out of both trimming tanks, but still the chariot continued on its stem-first dive. So I blew main ballast, but that was no good either. Her downward plunge continued. There was only one thing left to do.

I turned again and shouted, 'Bail out!' We slid out of our seats and the machine carried on downwards and finally disappeared into the blackness below, leaving a trail of white phosphorescent sparks behind it . . .

The normal procedure then, was to open the by-pass valve on our breathing sets for a second or two and inflate the bag and let its buoyancy bring us to the surface and act as a lifebelt. Then the calcium flare, which was enclosed in a canvas sheath hung under our breathing bags, could be broken and trusting that the look-outs on the ship and the instructors in the skiffs were keeping a sharp watch, we could be picked up in a matter of minutes. The flare itself was attached to our harness by a short length of line, so that it could not float too far away from us.

However, as was often the case where I was concerned, things didn't work out quite as expected. For that night it so happened that I was given a brand-new breathing apparatus to wear and the by-pass valve was still rather stiff to open. And whereas when I first started out on the run I had been able to turn the little knurled wheel that controlled it, by the time I'd been immersed in the cold water of a Scottish loch for going on five hours, my hands were beginning to become rather stiff. Not stiff enough to prevent my using the controls of the chariot, but certainly too stiff to be able to get a good grip on a tight little brass wheel. So instead of blowing myself to the surface, I started to follow the machine to the bottom. After a few seconds, the increased pressure, due to my going deeper, almost flattened my bag, which made breathing somewhat difficult.

However, luck was on my side, for another precautionary measure the chariot crews took was to have about six feet of thin line roping us together from our shoulder harnesses. Thus, when Kendall inflated his bag and started heading towards the surface, he hadn't gone far when he was brought to a sudden halt, as my weight took hold. Luckily though, his bag had enough buoyancy to take the weight of both of us and he slowly gained momentum again and hauled me up with him. When we reached the surface the lessening of the outside pressure allowed my bag to resume its proper shape and my breathing was back to normal. Kendall broke his flare and within a couple of minutes the tiny beacon had brought a skiff alongside us and we were hauled inboard and taken back to the ship.

The task of the No. 1 was to drive the Chariot and navigate, both by day and at night. Diving removes some of the sensory inputs taken for granted by people on the surface, and necessitates reliance on clock and compass for navigation. This is not easy at depth, or at night – where darkness and misting can obscure the instruments from sight – and calls for great care and alertness. Virtually all crewmen lost their sense of direction under water, and were trained to rely completely on their compasses. It was found that, where possible, the Chariot should conduct its passage across a stretch of water with the heads of the crew above the surface of the sea – which also reduced dependence on the scarce oxygen – submerging only where it was absolutely necessary, such as in heavy seas, in waters where the enemy were keeping a close watch for intruders, and for the final approach to a target. When submerged, the crews would travel for no more than ten minutes before surfacing slowly and carefully to check position and direction.

Once they had reached their targets, the crews were bound to be confronted by layers of anti-submarine and anti-torpedo nets. The way through these was to either cut a hole with compressed-air shears, or simply surface and dive over the net on the surface like a porpoise – subsequently called 'porpoising': the approach adopted by the Decima Flottiglia at Alexandria. The No. 2 was responsible for cutting through the protective nets. Anti-torpedo nets were heavy objects comprising thousands of 12-inch steel rings and hanging perhaps 50 feet down from their surface buoys. They were easily avoided by the Chariot crews, who could simply ride over, or under, them. Anti-submarine nets were a different matter. Made of rectangular mesh, these were much lighter, and would drop to about 100 feet. It was possible for Chariot crews to lift them off the floor of the seabed and pull their Chariot through, although of course 100 feet was a dangerous depth for men breathing pure oxygen. Compressed-air cutters made quick work of these impediments, however. Butch Woollcott recalled that 'actually we only needed to make one cut in the wire to allow the chariot to pass through the net, but very often we'd make eight cuts and the chariot would come back to the ship with No. 2 holding aloft in triumph a complete rectangle of net as a trophy'.

It was difficult for the two crewmen to communicate with each other underwater, and a primitive form of grunts, taps and hand signals – built up between them and common to each partnership – had to suffice. 'With a rubber mouthpiece gripped between the front teeth it wasn't all that easy to speak in the old clear-cut Oxford English,' recalled Woollcott. 'However, after a team had been together for a while, a sort of spiritual partnership was formed and each began to know what the other was thinking and thus knew what was required of him in an emergency.'

The cold was always a problem. Woollcott recalled:

We still had to pile on as many sweaters as we had back in March and they managed to keep our bodies from freezing solid, but there wasn't much we could do about our hands. A pair of gloves thick enough to keep out the cold would have hampered the movement of the fingers so much that No. 1 would have had great difficulty in manipulating the controls of the machine and it would have been impossible for No. 2 to release the warhead and tie it to the magnets. So we went bare-handed most of the time. I sometimes used to wear a pair of woollen gloves, but they didn't keep much of the cold out. However, they did at least protect my hands while working under the ship and kept the barnacles at bay. Those little shells were as sharp as scalpels and used to make quite deep cuts.

A close sense of camaraderie and teamwork was built up between each pair of crews, regardless of their rank. Working at night presented an especial difficulty. Fell described it as 'sheer slavery'. Lieutenant Charles Andrew observed that dealing with nets at night meant that 'much of the fun went out of it and we were left with the real job of facing a constant challenge without any illusions concerning the possibility of quick disaster'. Woollcott agreed. Training at night was arduous, and raised insurmountable mental as well as physical barriers to some crewmen who might in fact have excelled at day work:

> At night, the water was just a void of inky blackness. It was like starting to dive all over again. It affected some of them in the same way as in that distant time when they had been asked to go to the bottom of a tank for the first time, and many of them were just as scared. As, one by one, they overcame their fears yet, once more, they found that this weird element they were probing had still one more surprise in store for them. It was as black at two feet as it was at seventy feet, but once under the surface they encountered the strange phenomenon of phosphorescence. Myriads of tiny specks of light which showed the outline of a hand – or the hooded figure astride a jeep was silhouetted in pale brilliance to the man riding behind him.

Once the task of manoeuvring the Chariot under water, and of cutting through the anti-submarine and anti-torpedo nets had been mastered, training focused mainly on the best way of approaching, and attacking, an enemy ship. As this was new to all, it was again a matter of trial and error. 'We started by just approaching the ship on the surface, then diving right under it and coming up on the other side,' recalled Woollcott. 'Next we went under and cruised around a bit, to get a general layout of the ship's bottom and pick out the best places to fix a warhead.' As soon as they could they were sent against real ships in practice runs, this time with small, hand-held limpet mines, which were fastened beneath the ship's hull by means of magnets. The hull must be clean of barnacles and suchlike for them to attach themselves properly. A method was developed of approaching the ship on the surface, after which the crew would walk the Chariot under the hull by placing the magnets on the vessel and pulling themselves along until a suitable place to leave them had been found. Approaching a darkened ship at night, however, was always dangerous, even at 2 or 3 knots. On one occasion a No. 1 was killed when he misjudged his approach to a vessel at night and his head collided with the bilge keel. He died instantly.

There is no doubt that training was rushed, and operating procedures had to be made up as they went along, but the inventiveness of the crews and the mechanics on *Titania*, servicing what were to all intents and purposes prototype Chariots, solved or overcame every challenge that faced them. Exercises which had started out lasting little more than an hour now extended to four or five, as the crews grew in confidence and experience. The men were extremely fit, and seemed to relish every challenge, even though they knew that they risked their lives each time they took their Chariots under the surface. Nineteen-year-old Midshipman Bob Aitken was sent to HMS *Dolphin* to train as a Charioteer because he was colour-blind, and the Navy was struggling to find him a place elsewhere.

As far as we all were concerned it was a marvellous summer on the west coast of Scotland. We were kept active, our days were roughly divided into three periods of eight hours each – training, keeping fit and sleeping. What better part of the world to do those three things? Also if you give a teenager what is essentially an underwater motorbike that's great fun. Between the training exercises we could chase crabs and other fish. Life was taken light-heartedly.

Fell viewed the work as strenuous, but intensely interesting. Because of the remarkable speed with which a working Chariot had been designed, and the first set of crews trained, he perhaps felt a sense of disbelief when, in late September 1942, he was able to tell the Flag Officer Submarines – from 9 November 1942 Captain (Acting Rear Admiral) Claud Barry, replacing Horton (who the previous December had been the luckless Commander of HMS *Queen Elizabeth* when it was attacked by the Decima Flottiglia) – that he thought that 'four Chariot crews were sufficiently trained to carry out an operation'.

SIX

Shetland Bus

Extraordinarily, Fell and Sladen's endeavours enabled the first British operation to be attempted only six months after 'Cassidy' had been towed for the first time around Horsea Lake. Leif Andreas Larsen was a Norwegian patriot enlisted in the service of the Royal Navy who commanded a crew of fishermen turned smugglers, which operated as part of a secret and immensely dangerous ferry service between occupied Norway and the Shetland Isles. The clandestine unit (known by mid-1942 as the Norwegian Naval Independent Unit), commanded by MI6's Major Leslie Mitchell with his deputy Sub Lieutenant David Howarth, RNVR, became known colloquially as 'The Shetland Bus'. It was set up as a joint MI6 and SOE operation to run agents to and from Norway.

Because by far the biggest problem for Britain in northern waters was the presence of the giant *Tirpitz*, a very potent threat to Britain skulking in the Norwegian fjords, it was a constant source of conversation, comment and concern in Whitehall. Germany's last remaining battleship, the *Tirpitz* was holed up 70 miles inside a sub-fjord of the mighty Trondheimsfjord. Her presence there – from January 1941 – threatened the Arctic Convoys, which ran through the icy Barents Sea to Murmansk, carrying military material from Britain and the United States in support of the Soviet Union. Nor was the prospect of her damaging the vital lifeline of convoys between North America and Britain one that Winston Churchill wished to contemplate.

After the destruction of the *Bismarck* on 27 May 1941, sinking *Tirpitz* became a priority for Britain, as her continued existence meant that a significant part of the Royal Navy had to be tied up waiting to respond to any offensive moves she might make. Britain was not to know that Hitler was terrified of losing the *Tirpitz* as well as the *Bismarck*, and that in any case limited fuel availability meant that she could not sally far, or for long, from her Norwegian hiding place. Hitler was desperate to protect his last remaining capital ship, although he also knew that placing a powerful squadron in northern Norway would serve to threaten British convoy movements, and provide a latent threat against any offensive moves the Allies made against Norway. Hitler was convinced that Norway was the door through which an eventual Allied counter-offensive against Nazi-held Europe would come.

Almost as soon as *Tirpitz* arrived in Trondheimsfjord, the RAF launched three successive heavy bomber attacks on her (in January, March and April 1942), but without success. Attacking her was not easy. She was protected in a deep anchorage surrounded by serial anti-submarine nets, steep cliffs and high mountains, as well as by multiple anti-aircraft positions and fighter protection. Her destruction required an alternative approach to the big ships, submarines or heavy bombers that would mount a traditional attack: one that entailed unconventional thinking.

The original idea for using a Q ship to attack the *Tirpitz* – carrying torpedoes strapped to the underside of its hull, and fired remotely from the cabin, all the while disguised as a harmless fishing boat – had come from David Howarth. Leif Larsen recalled how he and Howarth had discussed the possibility:

> In the spring of the year I had thought of a scheme for carrying two aircraft torpedoes underneath a fishing boat, with a release and firing mechanism which could not be detected even if the boat should be searched. I explained the plan to Larsen, and asked him if he thought he could take a boat fitted out in this

way through all the German controls into Trondheim, and let off the torpedoes at the *Tirpitz* or any other valuable target he might happen to see. If he had done so it was very doubtful whether he could have escaped. I proposed that the torpedoes should be set so that when they were released they ran on a course at right angles to that of his boat, so that all he would have to do would be to steam past his target and fire them when it was exactly abeam; and we hoped that in the excitement which would follow two underwater explosions inside the fleet anchorage nobody would take any notice of an innocent fishing boat steaming in the wrong direction. No plan was too crazy for Larsen, and he was delighted at the prospect of trying it. So Mitchell forwarded the plans of the mechanism, with the scheme for getting it into Trondheim, to the Admiralty, where it disappeared into the administrative maze and was never heard of again.

A steady stream of information about the *Tirpitz* provided by some very brave resistance workers in Norway arrived in London. Howarth and Larsen had joked in the past about using the fishing smacks of the Shetland flotilla against the *Tirpitz*, but these had been playful conversations. Not for a minute did Larsen think that he would ever find himself charged with leading a mission in *Arthur*, his 55-foot wooden fishing boat, against the most modern battleship afloat.

During the summer of 1942, Howarth and Mitchell were visited in the Shetlands by Geoffrey Sladen, who told them that the Admiralty had suggested using the fishing boats of the Shetland Bus flotilla to carry two Chariots close enough to the *Tirpitz* to allow the British to undertake an attack that mirrored the Italian triumph at Alexandria. Would it be possible? Sladen asked. Sladen was, of course, along with Fell, desperately keen to arrange a first operation for their new contraption, and it seemed that their search for a suitable task had reminded a staff officer in London of

Howarth's scheme. After a day of discussions Howarth decided that a plan was feasible:

> The two Chariots needed a crew of six men – two to drive each machine, and two 'dressers' to put them into their diving suits. The fishing boat would need four Norwegians to navigate it across the North Sea and through the controls up the fjord. The two Chariots could only be smuggled through the controls by towing them under water; but on the other hand they could not be towed across the sea. We therefore proposed they should be carried on deck to a convenient hide-out among the maze of islands and creeks off Smolen . . . There they should be hoisted overboard and towed up the sixty odd miles of the inner lead to the control point at the mouth of Trondheimsfjord, and the fifty miles of fjord which led to the anchorage. At the same time the ship's armament and radio equipment and certain other gear would be jettisoned. The ship and the Norwegian crew would have to be equipped to the last detail as Norwegian, and a hiding-place which was absolutely proof against detection must be provided for the six Chariot men and a large quantity of diving gear and stores.

Then, in August 1942, returning to Scalloway (their bolt-hole in the Shetlands) after a visit to London, Mitchell called Larsen into his office. He had a proposition for him. Would he be willing to undertake a dangerous mission against the *Tirpitz*, hidden deep in a sub-fjord within the Trondheimsfjord? Already briefed by Sladen on the concept of the Chariot, Larsen was excited beyond belief by the lure of attacking the monster that embodied the arrogance of his country's subjugation. However his biographer, Frithjof Saelen, recorded Mitchell's quiet warning to Larsen to think about the consequences before he answered: 'This thing is probably a lot more dangerous than even you anticipate.'

'You'll be taking on overwhelming odds; only the element of surprise will be on your side. The *Tirpitz* is a capital ship with some of the heaviest and most technically advanced armament in the world. She is a prize which the Germans guard very, very closely – they are only too well aware of how much the Admiralty would like to put her out of action. So you can judge the responsibility you would be carrying. Now, would you like to think it over for a few hours?'

Larsen looked him straight in the eyes. This was the chance he had been praying for.

'No,' he said. 'I'll do it.'

The following day Larsen found himself the guest of Lieutenant Colonel 'Belge' Wilson, head of SOE's Norwegian Section at 88 Chiltern Court, just above the entrance to the Baker Street underground station. Even though he considered the plan to be 'a somewhat hazardous enterprise', he was instructed to choose one of the fishing smacks used for the North Sea crossing, and to pick a crew. Six submarine crewmen would accompany them, together with two of the new submersible vessels, which were even then training 'somewhere in Scotland'. Larsen's chosen men were old friends: Palmer Bjørnoy as engineer, Johannes Kalve as deck hand and Roald Strand as radio operator, although none were given any notion of the feat they were soon to embark on. Larsen selected the *Arthur* for the mission. He had stolen this vessel while escaping from Norway after a mine-laying operation the previous October. The mysterious submersibles, each weighing two tons, were to be carried on her deck for the sea crossing, and then lifted into the sea and towed submerged for the remainder of the journey through the German checkpoints into the Trondheimsfjord and thence to their target.

SOE had placed a small team in Trondheim in February 1942, centred on two Norwegian patriots, Odd Sørli and Arthur Pevik, which had the codename 'Lark'. Two months later, a further four men joined them following training in Britain. Although the purpose of this team was to prepare for an eventual invasion of Norway, for much of the remainder of the year Lark focused on providing intelligence on the *Tirpitz*, which had arrived off Trondheim in January 1942. When Operation *Title* was first discussed in June 1942 the Lark team was asked to identify a local fishing boat that could tow the Chariots, but when this plan was dropped in favour of the *Arthur*, Lark was asked to provide copies of the shipping-control documents that would grant the *Arthur* access – by means of forged documentation – to the security zone inside which the *Tirpitz* lay. Likewise, Lark was asked to arrange a means of escape to Sweden for both the Charioteers and the crew of Larsen's fishing boat.

The *Arthur* required substantial work to make her ready. A secret compartment had to be built to hide the six submersible crew members if and when the vessel was stopped by German guard boats, and a secure means needed to be found of bolting the two Chariots to the boat. For this, a hole was bored directly through the oak keel and the bolt fastened through it. In early October, the crew still not suspecting the real nature of their forthcoming mission, the *Arthur* slipped her moorings and set sail for Loch A'Chairn Bhain – Loch Cairnbawn – a narrow deep-water loch on the Sutherland coast leading off Eddrachillis Bay, to meet up with the *Titania* and to take the Chariots and their crews on board.

Loch Cairnbawn is several miles long, with a narrow, deep channel at its eastern end, opening onto two further long, deep waterways reached through the Kylesku narrows (now bridged): Lochs Glen Dhu and Glen Coul. The area was and remains remote and sparsely populated. Its code name was HHZ. Reaching Loch Cairnbawn that evening, they tonk-tonk-tonked (the Norwegian smacks ran on two-stroke diesel engines, which gave them this distinctive sound) into the anchorage, passing the forbidding grey mass of the 35,000-ton Nelson Class battleship HMS *Rodney* on her right-hand side. The *Rodney* had been brought into Loch

Cairnbawn from Scapa Flow at 2.30 p.m. on 23 September, to allow the Chariots to practise on a vessel akin to the size of the *Tirpitz*. The visit of HMS *Rodney* was so successful that Fell was able to persuade the Admiralty the following month to send up to HHZ the brand-new 45,000-ton King George V class battleship HMS *Howe*, on virtually its first voyage out of Govan on the Clyde, for three nights for the purpose of training Fell's Chariot crews. As with HMS *Rodney*, these practice runs were tremendously success- ful – the battleship was sunk many times over – although tragedy struck on the last night, when Oxygen Pete overcame the popular South African Sub Lieutenant Jack Grogan. Hauled to the surface by his No. 2, Grogan died in his arms. It was the Charioteers' second fatality, and a salutary reminder to all of the dangers involved, even in training. With a draft of 28 feet, HMS *Howe* was right on the safe limit for oxygen diving, and every Chariot crew- man took risks in exceeding this depth so as to place their warheads under its vast steel bulk.

Larsen brought his tiny boat alongside the diving support vessel HMS *Alecto*, one of the small flotilla of vessels supporting the Chariots, where he was introduced to Fell.* Larsen felt an instant affinity with the New Zealander, as Frithjof Saelen describes:

Fell stood on the deck in overalls, his face and hands dirty and oily, and his untidy hair blowing in the wind: a man after Larsen's own heart. He took an active part in the work being carried out on his special pets, and as chief of the experiments was every- where, keeping a watchful eye on the smallest details. Every man thinks most of his own children and Fell was no exception; he considered the submarines to be technical marvels, but they had not yet been tried in operation. Now it was a question of getting

---

* HMS *Alecto* was a submarine escort vessel built in 1913 as a millionaire's yacht. She was coal-fired, long and low and narrow, with a single, tall raked funnel and a bowsprit – an unusual-looking vessel.

as near to mechanical perfection as possible so that nothing could possibly go wrong when they headed for their goal, the chief ship of the German fleet . . . Fell was a forthright, practical man who went straight to the point and sidestepped any refinements of rank.

That afternoon Larsen saw a Chariot for the first time:

The first thing Larsen saw was two heads, or something which resembled two heads, travelling through the water. They submerged temporarily, then came in sight again, this time much higher on the water. If they had been in Loch Ness they could have been taken for the monster. Two men sat astride the submarine. They manoeuvred in to the side of the *Alecto* and the craft was hoisted on board.

In the three short weeks that followed, the *Arthur* now practised towing the Chariots, and undertaking mock night-time attacks on HMS *Rodney*, which had come into Loch Broom for the purpose. The *Tirpitz*, protected by anti-submarine nets, was lying hidden in the Fetenfjord, off Aasenfjord – a branch of the mighty Trondheimsfjord, an inlet of the Norwegian Sea and at 81 miles long, Norway's third-longest fjord. The plan was for the *Arthur* to proceed to the head of the fjord at midnight and drop off the Chariots, which would carry on for the final journey over the anti-submarine nets and hopefully under the hull of the target.

The practice runs against HMS *Rodney* during mid-October were designed as far as possible to mimic the real attack, with visibility at a minimum in the cold, dark waters of the Norwegian fjord. They were very successful. On the first night, both Chariots attached their warheads without being discovered, despite a permanent watch of seventeen of *Howe*'s seamen stationed around the deck, peering into the darkness. On one night, a Chariot was spotted as it unexpectedly surfaced close to the ship, but all involved soon came to the conclusion that the Chariots had a much greater than even chance of severely maiming the *Tirpitz* if they could get close enough to deploy against her.

Morale was high. The training allowed the crew of the *Arthur* to get to know the Charioteers, and to form bonds that would be important in the testing days ahead. Sub Lieutenant 'Jock' Percy Brewster, RNVR, commanded one Chariot, and Able Seaman Bob Evans the other. Able Seaman Billy Tebb and Sergeant Don 'Shorty' Craig of the Royal Engineers, the only soldier among this complement of sailors, were their respective No. 2s. Able Seaman 'Slim' Brown and the Brazilian-born Malcolm Causer were to accompany them as reserves.

With the exercises over, HMS *Rodney* steamed out of Loch Cairnbawn and Fell's *Titania* carried the two Chariots to the Shetlands. The *Arthur* made her own way with the Charioteers to her home base at Lunna Voe, to undertake final preparations for an attack that had been given the name Operation *Title*. Butch Woollcott remembered Lunna Voe as 'a pretty grim, forbidding sort of place; just open heather-covered moors surrounded with a few low hills and not a tree in sight. The only sign of human handiwork was a stone jetty and a small shed; while on a hill overlooking the inlet was a large, bleak-looking house.'

These preparations included the production of detailed forgeries of the German documents required for all vessels using Norwegian waters, which needed to pass close scrutiny before the *Arthur* would be allowed to enter the Trondheimsfjord. The primary control station was at Agdenes on the south side of the heavily guarded entrance to the fjord, although patrol boats and guard ships would be operating all the way inside. The ship and each man of its crew would require identity cards, a fishing permit, a certified crew list, registration papers, and a certificate stamped and signed by each of the German harbourmasters at all the ports she had called at in the last three months, together with a special permit for the defence zone of Trondheim. Major Mitchell's responsibility was to provide forged papers for the boat and its crew to a level of quality that would withstand close inspection. Authenticity for these cleverly forged documents was attained by means of the simple expedient of David Howarth walking around with them in his dirty trouser pocket for a time. 'When they were finished I do not think Scotland Yard could have detected the forgery,' he recalled. 'Certainly they were masterpieces wasted on the examination officer in Trondheimsfjord.'

The cover story was that the *Arthur* was trading peat bought in Smøla. Once the vessel had entered the Trondheimsfjord and released the Chariots they would go ashore beyond Saltoy, where Norwegians from the resistance movement would meet them and help them make their way to safety in neutral Sweden – there the Norwegian Consul, Nielsen, would arrange for their arrival and repatriation. The original plan was that, following the attack, the Charioteers would rendezvous with the secret agent and his men on a road to the south of the fjord, where they would be transported the 120 miles to the Swedish border by car, if all went well, or on foot, across secret paths into Sweden, if they were being pursued. The crew of the *Arthur* would join them after first scuttling the boat.

Throughout their planning, however, the men remained ignorant of a dangerous new feature of the type of warfare they were engaged in. Quite naturally they believed that, as they were fighting in British uniform, they would be protected by the terms of the Geneva Convention. What they did not know was that a brutal new dimension had been brought to the practice of warfare by a German leader enraged by the success of British commando raids across the western flanks of the Nazi empire. On 18 October that year Hitler had issued his *Kommandobefehl* (commando order), instructing that henceforth any and all captured British 'commandos' were to be executed without mercy following interrogation. If the Charioteers were to find themselves in the hands of the Gestapo or *Sicherheitsdienst* (SD) they would be shot as saboteurs. If any of the Norwegians had been caught, they would be executed as spies, in all likelihood after a period of torture and deprivation in the Grini concentration camp outside Oslo.

David Howarth recalled the last few days of preparation at Lunna Voe, the Charioteers practising repeated use of the compass in night-time exercises:

I remember one night when we slipped a Chariot from *Arthur* in conditions like those they expected in Trondheimsfjord. It was a clear frosty night and the aurora was brilliant, hanging across half the sky like a curtain of which the folds were gently swaying as if a breeze stirred them, and reflecting a wan light from the cold calm sea. The dressers silently pushed and pulled the crew of the Chariot into their close-fitting diving dresses, and helped them to put on their leaden boots and oxygen gear. With their masks in place, black and shiny, the two men who a few moments before had been very human seemed like Wellsian monsters as they climbed clumsily over the rail and down into the water. In the water their agility returned. One submerged, to bring up the Chariot towing beneath our keel, and in a few moments it broke surface with a faint hiss of compressed air. They both swam along-side it, and in the light of the aurora we could see them making adjustments to its trim. Then they mounted astride it, and with a faint hum and the swish of the propeller the black shape gathered way, curved into the lines of light reflected from the north, and gradually sank from view till nothing but the moving heads of the two men could be seen, with a wake flowing from each. Then the water closed over their heads, the wakes vanished and the hardly perceptible sibilant noise of their movement was cut off. The aurora flickered and danced and the sea flowed silently as if they had never been there.

All the preparations were complete by 26 October 1942, when the *Arthur's* tonk-tonk-tonk advertised its departure from the pier at Lunna Voe. HMS *Alecto* had come up with Fell to say farewell, and a Spitfire flying a high-level reconnaissance had confirmed that their target had not moved. On the pier, 'Tiny' Fell and Major Mitchell calmly shook Larsen's hand, and watched the little vessel sail out into the wide harbour, and into the lion's mouth. Too emotional to say farewell on the pier, David Howarth had earlier said his individual goodbyes, and then retired to Flemington House, the unit's HQ on the Shetlands. 'These partings were always deliberately casual, but personally I often felt an emotion which I took care to conceal,' he later remembered.

This time I was more deeply moved than usual as I stood at the window and watched *Arthur* start on her journey. *Alecto* was not a big ship but she made *Arthur* seem very small, so that her fifty-five-foot hull looked like a toy as she chugged out of the harbour for the last time, cleaving the blue water into a sun-speckled wake. *Alecto* saluted her with a blast on her siren which echoed from the hills, and she answered in a smaller voice, but proudly. I was proud of her too: so small a ship, and ahead so great an adventure.

SEVEN

Arthur versus Tirpitz

The meteorologists had promised them a smooth passage, but it was not to be. Powered by mainsail, *Arthur*, weighed down by an additional 4 tons of Chariot (the submersibles were on wooden chocks on the deck, under tarpaulins, while the warheads were hidden under the cargo of peat), made barely 5 knots for the first 50 miles out of the Shetlands as it pitched and rolled its way across a heavy sea whipped up by a fresh and unexpected north-easter. The motion of the boat left all of the Charioteers, even the most experienced sailors, prostrate with seasickness. After twenty-four hours, however, the weather improved. The sea was for the most part calm and they made good progress. Just as night fell, they were able to sight a distant snowcapped mountain range on Norway's coast, about 60 miles south of Smolen. Taking his bearings, Larsen set course to ensure that by dawn they would be found sailing close to the coast, avoiding the German lookout post on the lighthouse at Grip.

The most dangerous moment in the whole journey lay in approaching the coast. In good visibility they would be easily spotted by one of the numerous Luftwaffe reconnaissance flights over the North Sea who were looking for exactly this type of intruder. Likewise, their false papers would only work once they were inside Norwegian coastal waters, when they could pass themselves off as a freighter carrying peat. If they were found outside Norwegian waters, heading east, they would be considered hostile intruders and sunk on sight.

Dawn arose the following morning – Wednesday 28 October – with the lighthouse at Grip far behind them on the starboard side, Palmer Bjørnoy pushing the little engine as hard as he could to put all the distance he could between them and the sea. Larsen looked around him, considering the incongruity of his tiny sailing boat, armed only with a machine-gun and a few pistols, heading to challenge the largest battleship afloat.

Their first test was to pass close by another fishing boat heading out to sea: it swept by with barely a glance. By 8 a.m., Larsen had anchored the vessel between the islands to the west of Edoy, and after a hearty breakfast of bacon and eggs, the men began to assemble the Chariots and attach them to their towing lines under the keel. In a mission that was to be dogged by bad luck, the battery-charging motor broke down after only fifteen minutes: it had been damaged during the crossing. They did not have a spare, but Jock Brewster judged that there was sufficient charge remaining in each of the two batteries to propel the Chariots to their targets.

It was during this activity that they had their first sight of the enemy, as a Luftwaffe plane flew low to have a look at them. The crew and Charioteers busied themselves with the nets, and politely waved at the German pilot as he circled above them. Apparently satisfied, he went on his way, but not far, spending an hour or so in the vicinity, apparently practising diving attacks on the sea. No sooner had he departed than another aircraft, this one a Messerschmitt 109, approached them at considerable speed and at low level. It passed overhead quickly, however, heading out to sea on patrol. These unwanted diversions over, the men were able to resume their work. The process was more difficult than they had envisaged, in part because by now the sea had got up. They were forced to move to a more sheltered location, but were unable to finish the work before dark, which was when they had planned to enter the Trondheimsfjord.

The work resumed at 5 a.m. next morning (Thursday 29 October) and within a couple of hours both Chariots were attached to their steel cables. Fell recorded that:

> after the towing wires had been shackled to the rings in the warheads, ballast tanks were filled until the Chariots had considerable negative buoyancy and hung tail-downwards under Arthur's stem. The hydroplanes of the machines were locked in the diving or down position and the judders were locked so that each Chariot tended to head away from its mate. This was done to keep the Chariots clear of each other and of Arthur's keel when she began to tow them.

When all was complete, the Charioteers climbed back on board and went below.

Then occurred their second contact with a Norwegian. Palmer Bjørnoy reported to Larsen that they were being approached by an elderly fisherman in a rowing boat. The old man clutched hold of one of the Arthur's gunwales, and proceeded to interrogate the visitors in a friendly but persistent way. 'What sort of folk are you, putting in here?' he asked. 'Engine trouble,' Larsen replied. 'Just as soon as we've fixed it we will be on our way.' But the man wasn't to be fobbed off with pleasantries. He began to engage them in a long conversation, asking about the fish they had caught, looking over the Arthur with a practised eye. He then spotted in the clear, still water the two dark shadows under the stern of the boat, and immediately expressed interest in them. Larsen and Bjørnoy had to think fast. The old man might be harmless, but it wasn't worth taking any risks. They decided to pretend that they were working with the Germans. Larsen told the man that they were devices used to explode mines, but it wasn't this information that eventually sent the man away. Larsen decided to terrify the old man into silence, warning him in what he considered to be his best barking tones that if he mentioned their encounter to anyone they would return and deal with him.

Taking with him a gift of scarce butter, the man hurried away, rowing his dinghy anxiously.

Later that afternoon, after completing a final check for anything that might give their origins away, Bjørnoy started the engine and they began to move out of the sound, heading for the southern point of Smøla before they entered the Trondheimsfjord. The afternoon passed without incident, the Charioteers keeping out of sight down below as a variety of fishing and trading vessels, not to mention German checkpoints, were passed without exciting any interest. The weather was calm and the sea smooth, but Bjørnoy began to be worried by a strange knocking sound from the engine. The boat and its engine were old, and they were trusting somewhat to luck that it would survive its final journey. Before long, however, smoke started to drift up through the engine hatch and *Arthur* began to lose power. Desperate to avoid being caught adrift far from land, or in the midst of one of the minefields known to guard the entrance to Trondheimsfjord, they turned towards the shelter of land. They had been given the name of a contact in the village of Hestvik on the island of Hitra, and it was to here that the limping vessel now made its slow and smoking way. The resistance contact was the local shopkeeper, Nils Strom.

As the *Arthur* finally made its way into Hitra, Bjørnoy realised that the misfiring and smoke were the result of a broken piston. There was no chance of finding a replacement: the best that could be done would be a running repair, if they could find someone in Hestvik to help. Luckily they managed to steam quietly into an inlet near the tiny port at 11 p.m. without exciting any interest. While Bjørnoy began to strip the engine, Larsen rowed ashore to find Nils Strom. A lad he met on the road into the town happened to be Strom's son, who agreed to accompany him to find his father. Larsen's biographer describes the encounter:

Larsen looked round the shelves in the shop. It was true the stock was meagre, seeming to consist mostly of matches and washing powder. He waited while Strom brought out five or six loaves of bread and some flour, watching him closely while he was packing them up.

'Have you any use for peat?' asked Larsen. This was the password he was to use, and the answer should have been 'No, I've got enough.'

Strom dropped what he was holding and turned round eagerly.

'Peat! Indeed I have – I'll take all you've got!'

Larsen was rather taken aback; this was not what he had expected. Could there be two village stores here, both owned by men called Strom? It seemed unlikely, and if that were the case he would have been told about it. The explanation must be that the password had not yet reached him, but it was best to be careful.

'Oh, well, I've got some, but in fact the cargo belongs to Sorlie, so I can't let you have much.'

Larsen thought he saw Strom start slightly when he named the agent, but he could not be quite sure.

The storekeeper stood looking at him for a while, then asked tentatively,

'You mean Andreas Sorlie from Orkanger?'

The man was no fool. Larsen had difficulty in suppressing a smile. It really was rather amusing, both of them standing there scowling and suspicious of each other.

'No,' he said. 'I mean Odd Sorlie from Trondheim.' This did the trick and he was able to explain how things were. He laid his cards on the table, disclosing that they were going up the fjord on a secret mission, but had developed engine trouble. That was why they had disturbed him so late in the evening.

By this time, Bjørnoy had confirmed that the piston head had cracked. Strom's suggestion was that they wake the local blacksmith, who was likely to be sympathetic, to see whether he could help. Strom was right. The blacksmith, once roused, lent Bjørnoy the tools and drills he required to screw a copper patch to the top of the crankcase, a fix sufficient to give it a few more miles of life. The work took the remainder of the night, but when started the engine hummed satisfactorily. After a few hours' sleep, the men got under way again. Strom waved them farewell as they left their hidden cove.

Their route now took them from Hestvik to Agdenes, on the right-hand (southern side) of the entrance to Trondheimsfjord, a journey that would take several hours, and involved repeated exposure to German guard ships, the fixed guns of Agdenes fort, as well as a minefield in the centre of the approaches. A patrol boat sat in the middle of the entrance, at which all approaching vessels had to stop and present their credentials. Larsen brought the *Arthur* confidently alongside the German vessel, as if it was something he did every day. He had ordered the Charioteers into their secret compartment, where they were to remain unless they heard shooting. But, as they drew alongside, the crew realised with horror that in the clear, calm water the Chariots, about 16 feet down, could be clearly seen underneath the bow of the vessel.

It was too late to do anything about it now, except brazen it out if anyone on the German vessel noticed anything amiss. Then, with mounting horror, Larsen observed a young German sailor leaning on the guard rail looking deep into the water as they approached. As he studied the man he became convinced that the German had seen something under the water that confused him. Thinking quickly, Larsen decided on a distraction technique. Shouting a loud greeting in German and saluting ostentatiously, he tried to get the enemy crew to look at him, rather than the water. But still the young sailor gazed into the deeps under the *Arthur*. Increasingly desperate, his mind raced. How could he distract him? At that moment Larsen saw the young man give a start: he had clearly seen something strange in the water. But before he could shout out, Kalve had thrown the heavy mooring rope directly at him. By luck the end of the rope struck the young man in the face, and he stepped back in surprise. His crewmates laughed at his embarrassment and, luckily for the *Arthur*, seemed to forget whatever he thought he had seen in the water, and stomped off downstairs.

In the meantime a portly and officious German officer clambered on board, took Larsen's proffered papers and entered the cabin. He sat and scanned the painstakingly prepared forgeries, reading each one and taking notes as he went. There was no small talk with this man, Larsen thought, as he watched nervously lest a fault be found, and the entire mission aborted or put at risk. In their secret compartment below the peat, the British Charioteers lay cramped together, wondering why the inspection was taking so long, caught in the suspense of the moment. Then, when examining a bill of lading,* the German turned to Larsen and asked: 'So you have come from Kristiansund, have you?' Larsen replied in the affirmative. 'Then do you know the harbourmaster there?' the German replied. 'He is my friend Ormann. We come from the same town in Germany.' Was this a trap, Larsen thought, to find out whether he had actually been to Kristiansund? He decided to take a risk, and replied: 'Why yes, of course I know Captain Ormann. An excellent fellow!' With that the German visibly relaxed, put the paperwork to one side and chatted for a while.

The German then walked onto the deck, perfunctorily checked the cargo of peat, and then reboarded the patrol vessel. With a cursory salute, the *Arthur* was dismissed. Waving back, Larsen lost no time in getting his propellers churning, and headed down towards the narrow Trondheimsfjord. They had safely entered the security zone within which lay the *Tirpitz*. With a good wind, they would be off Aasenfjord later that night: the Chariots would then be launched straight away.

As darkness fell, the tiny vessel entered the wider waters of the Trondheimsfjord and turned north, out of the narrow funnel of the

---

* A certificate showing the merchandise stowed on a vessel, and its intended recipient.

entrance. To the right lay the bright lights of Trondheim. It was at this time that the first omens of impending doom struck: a stiff easterly breeze and choppy seas that announced the arrival of a gale. As the seas got up Larsen throttled back, in part to reduce the chances of the men becoming seasick again. The Charioteers began the laborious process of getting into their Sladen suits in preparation for the attack. As they ploughed their way slowly past Trondheim on their starboard bow, two violent shudders seemed to strike the underside of the vessel. Jock Brewster recalled those final, fateful minutes:

The other two had finished their preliminary dressing when Brown and I went below to put on our gear. Almost immediately the weather worsened. Other conditions were still good. There was no moon, so our chances of being seen were small, and the lights of Trondheim, now lying to starboard, would help our navigation.

We hadn't got very far with our dressing when we began to hear a succession of sharp bumps. The chariots were being swung up against the keel. The weather was deteriorating rapidly. It was already a first-class storm. Speed had to be reduced, but it was out of the question to wait another twenty-four hours so near to a busy port. We could maintain a speed that would get us there in time to do the attack before daybreak. 'Press on regardless' was the only advice we could give ourselves. There was too the hope that the full force of the northeaster would blow itself out in the remaining hour or two before we reached the Aasenfjord anti-submarine net and started off on our own. Apparently such fierce storms often ended suddenly on that mountainous coast. Down below again, therefore, we continued dressing.

I was still below when it happened. It was just after ten o'clock when we heard a loud, grinding, tearing noise. The vessel jerked and shuddered. Something pretty substantial had fouled the propeller. We all guessed what it had been – one of the chariots.

There should still be at least one serviceable, so we made for the sheltered waters to have a look. Bob Evans was the most completely dressed, so I ordered him down to see what was what. He came up and reported nothing there at all.

We were dismayed. The chariots were gone and the attempt was off. I don't think anyone has ever been so disappointed as we were that night. We were ten miles from the pride of the German Navy; all our obstacles were behind us; and we might as well have been at the North Pole. Looking back, I don't remember one single curse. We were all too unhappy for that.

Larsen stated in his report:

I felt an easterly wind, but still did not think it would be too bad. Suddenly, about fifteen minutes later, with the wind ENE, we ran into two fairly large waves. The boat pitched, and we could feel a drag on the chariots, and a second afterwards one of them hit the propeller. It seemed as if when the boat rose on the first wave, the chariot was taut at the end of the towing wire, but when the boat went down into the trough, the towing wire slackened and suddenly became taut again. I was quite sure the chariots had disappeared, as I could feel it by the movement of the boat.

Brewster's dismay was felt by the entire vessel. They had come so far. Nothing stood between them and the jewel of the German fleet. As Larsen's biographer was to observe, it 'was almost too much to bear'. Fell remembered many years later that he still groaned 'when I think of what those young men must have felt, when the full significance of this disaster dawned upon them. There they were, within one mile of their launching point, and only four miles from the world's most powerful battleship, with victory in their grasp. I feel certain that nothing could have stopped them wreaking such destruction to *Tirpitz* that even if she stayed afloat she could never have fought again.'

But there was no time to grieve over what might have been. They were deep within enemy territory, and needed to make themselves scarce before they were discovered, and their true purpose exposed. They needed quickly to revise the original escape plan. It would not be possible to simply reverse their route, as they had no exit papers, and would be easily stopped by the patrol vessel at Agdenes. In any case, the hastily repaired engine would not last for much longer. Instead, they voted to head further north towards Tautra, sink the boat there and make their way as a group towards Sweden.

It was whilst they were anchored off Tautra later that night, the wind having ironically died down to a gentle breeze, that Bob Evans went over the side in his Sladen suit to find out exactly what had happened to the Chariots. He reported that the wire cables and hooks attaching them to the *Arthur* remained intact, but that the warheads to which they were joined had torn themselves free: the eye bolts were still connected to strips of metal that had previously encased the shell of the warheads. The men were rowed the 600 yards to shore, before the four-man crew took the *Arthur* out to sea, drilled additional holes in her hull to speed her sinking, and opened her cocks. They then rowed back to shore, as the fishing vessel began to sink slowly into the water. Their adventure had only just begun, but now they had nothing to show for all their extraordinary endeavours. For Larsen, the absolute imperative now was to get his entire party to safety in Sweden.

EIGHT

Better Luck Next Time!

It was Saturday 31 October when the *Arthur* slipped slowly beneath the waves. Although it was only 60 miles to Sweden, the journey would not be an easy one. Because of the presence of major units of the German battle fleet, the coastal area was very sensitive, and roads were heavily patrolled. Further inland, the country was populated by farms and the final stage would involve a strenuous climb over a plateau some 6,000 feet high, covered at this time of year by deep snow. They were not well clad for the cold, and nor were their boots designed for hard walking over frozen terrain. In the original plan they were to have been supplied with cold-weather clothing, food and equipment by their resistance contacts in the village of Vikhammer, a few miles east of Trondheim, and carried for some of their journey by car. Now they would have to walk all the way. Their food was limited to a few tins of bully beef and sardines and whatever they could forage. In addition, they were a large group of ten men – six of them armed with revolvers and wearing the uniform of the Royal Navy – and it would be hard to remain inconspicuous.

The first task was to put some distance between them and the fjord, after which they could decide how best to make their way to safety. A light dusting of snow covered the ground, which left conspicuous evidence of their presence and their numbers. As they climbed the steep wooded hills above the water they very soon found signs of the enemy. A German anti-aircraft gun position was identified, German voices in conversation above them giving it away, and as they walked over one crest in the deep fjord beyond them they saw what they thought was the *Kriegsmarine*'s modern pocket battleship *Admiral Scheer* sitting silently in the water. She was part of the *Tirpitz* battle group, and a sharp reminder of the purpose of their mission. They hurried on, a light, cold rain pattering above them on the roof of the forest. As Jock Brewster recounts:

> We had to leave the *Scheer* lying there peacefully and carry on eastwards. In the afternoon we saw three German sailors strolling along a footpath a short distance below us. They were obviously enjoying a spell of leave. I suppose we were, too, come to that. We were keeping well in among the more wooded parts of the landscape and the Jerries didn't see us.

It was at this point that the two parties decided to split up, aiming to raise their chance of safety by moving in two smaller groups. One party was led by Larsen (with Kalve, Evans, Tebb and Craig) and the other by Brewster, with Bjørnoy in support, together with Strand, Causer and Brown. Darkness was due, and the temperature falling. Larsen decided to take his group to the north, before turning east and then south-east, while Brewster's group would head directly east, passing through or around the hamlet of Markabygd. Larsen's party would strike out therefore to the north of the main road running east – what is now the national Route 72 – while Brewster's group would travel to the south. Hopefully they would not stumble across each other, and give each party the best possible chance of escape. Brewster recalled:

> We carried on through the rest of the afternoon and the evening, not allowing ourselves any organised breaks for food. That night we forced a fishing hut and had some much needed sleep. We were all pretty weary and I suppose we took very few precautions.

The nature of the whole business was such that it would have been impossible not to leave something to chance. We preferred to put speed before everything else, even at the cost of running some rather unwise risks during the daylight hours.

Larsen's group trudged through the woods and around farm-yards. The mood was downcast following the failure of the mission, but Larsen was determined to ensure that his group put as much distance between them and the coast as possible. They walked on through the night, ignoring the light rain, but getting soaked by having to force their way through undergrowth and brush against and through the wet foliage. As dawn broke on the morning of Sunday 1 November, the group huddled together under the cover of some trees at the edge of a wood, and spent a wet day sheltering from view before striking out again in the afternoon. For security they decided not to light a fire and boil up a brew, which depressed morale even further.

Brewster's group awoke in their fishing hut and decided to press on during the day:

We set off early the following morning and had a completely uneventful day. The weather was grand – had been ever since the storm had gone down less than an hour after we had lost the machines. Malcolm Causer was beginning to feel the cold, but he never complained. We had a certain amount of warm clothing – sweaters, etc. – but we could really have done with more . . . By nightfall we reckoned we were halfway across Norway. This meant we had covered twenty to thirty miles in the two days.

That night they could find nowhere to lodge and so decided to march on through the hours of darkness. It was exhausting, but their constant exertions staved off the cold, while a compass kept them heading due east. As the dawn arose on the morning of Tuesday 2 November they came across a barn at the rear of a small and neatly kept farmhouse, where they slept until awoken by voices a few hours later. They were able to slip away unseen.

Meanwhile, Larsen's group, determined now to raise their spirits, left their shelter on the edge of a forest in the early afternoon of 1 November. Two hours later they were able to use the position of the *Scheer* sitting in the Aasenfjord, far to the south-east, to pinpoint their location on the silk map Larsen carried. They continued, and well after darkness came across a farmhouse near the village of Ronglan, soon after carefully crossing the main road running north. They had hoped to be able to hide in the barn and sleep the night, but were instead spotted and welcomed by the farmer, his wife and family. They were offered a hot meal and a comfortable night in the barn under mountains of straw. Larsen, believing that he needed to provide these kind people with an explanation of their presence, spun a story that the Norwegians were resistance workers escorting Royal Air Force evaders to safety following the loss of their aircraft. Their story was not questioned.

They were on their way at first light next morning, Tuesday 2 November. Larsen was uneasy to be walking during the day, but considered it a risk worth taking because they could travel much faster than by night. His plan was to push on hard for a couple of hours before finding somewhere to hide up for the busiest part of the day. They walked quickly, alert to any sight or sound of farmers or local traffic, which would send them diving into a nearby ditch. It was increasingly cold, but the fast pace kept them all warm. Later that afternoon they set off again, still heading east. Larsen decided to use the road: there had been very little traffic on it during the day, so he and Kalve walked a few hundred yards ahead of the others, to allow the Britons behind time to find cover if they encountered anyone coming the other way. It was during this afternoon that Larsen saw that the three Britons were struggling: their feet were swollen and blistered and required attention.

On the same day – Tuesday 2 November – Brewster's group skirted a village – possibly Markabygd. 'There was no sign of the enemy,' Brewster recorded, 'so we decided to approach one of the outlying farms for bed and breakfast. We felt we deserved a comfortable bed and hot meal. Anyway, it was worth a try, we thought.' They were in luck.

We kept a likely looking farm under observation until nightfall. Then I sent Bjørnoy and Kalve down to see what they could find out. We had our rucksacks at the ready and our route planned in case we had to do a quick bunk. But fortunately there was no need. Kalve came to find us and led us down. We had a wonderful meal of soup, eggs, and potatoes, and then we were taken up to the loft. The hay was divinely comfortable and we slept soundly with someone else to do the worrying for us. Our hosts – father, mother, and two grown-up sons – were just grand. 'Entertaining' us would have meant facing a firing squad if a German patrol had chanced to find us there. But they didn't seem to be worried.

Even better, the two sons of the family escorted the men the following day – Wednesday 3 November – until the middle of the day. They set out early, rising at 3 a.m. and receiving a packed lunch of sandwiches and ersatz coffee to take with them. 'The boys were still with us at midday,' recalled Brewster, 'when we stopped for a meal in a little hut on the side of one of the hills dominating the valley.'

Soon after we restarted we got to the top of this range, and they showed us a jagged line of mountain peaks which marked the Norwegian–Swedish border. This done they turned, gave us a brief good-bye, and set off back down into the valley. They left themselves precious little time to get back to the farm before dark. I have no idea who these people were, but the physical and mental help they were to us enabled us to carry on with our trek, feeling on top of the world.

Meanwhile, Larsen's group were making progress eastward. As dusk fell they were able to find shelter in one of the last farms up the valley, for they had been steadily climbing all afternoon. As with Brewster's party, they were received with unquestioning solicitude. Larsen's biographer observed that 'the people were good Norwegians who did not count the risk when it was a question of helping others, and the men were asked inside. A room was given over to them and they had a good rest there. The people on the farm could not do enough for them, gave them food and drink and heated water for them to bathe their feet.' But Larsen was keen to press on, and their rest extended to a mere four hours, before the men were on their way again.

By this stage they were entering steep, hilly country thickly laid with snow, and offering limited shelter. It was hard going, and a particular struggle for the men already suffering from blisters and sore feet. Heavy snowdrifts further impeded their journey. Later that night, exhausted and frozen, they forced their way into a shepherd's lodge (near Storfossen) and with the help of a supply of firewood were able to keep themselves warm during the night. By coincidence, Brewster's party likewise found an empty shooting lodge, where they managed to build a fire and make flapjacks from some old flour and rancid butter they found in a food box:

On that seventh morning we tidied up the place and went on up, getting a bit excited and saying sweet things about the snow, very deep now. By early afternoon we reached the last barrier, a range of mountains 6,000 feet high. We carried on and reached Sweden early on the eighth morning, after a trying night. There was glare on the snow, and we were suffering not only from frostbite, but from snow blindness, and kept falling over rock faces and into snowdrifts. With the help of Benzedrine we eventually came to a small Swedish village, and gave ourselves up, pretty dishevelled, unshaven for ten days, hungry, but otherwise fairly all right.

Things took a harder turn for Larsen's party. The last two days of their march entailed a strenuous walk across the wide snow-covered plateau that marks the easternmost edge of Norway. Not only were the snowdrifts high, but the temperatures dipped very low, especially after dark. It was a struggle to stay warm, but Larsen knew that if they halted without cover they would not last a night. They had to keep moving, regardless of the weather. On this ultimate stage they did not stop for twenty-four hours. It was exhausting and painful toil, each step harder than the last. They worked out a pattern where they would walk in single file, the man ahead compacting the snow beneath his sea boots, into which those following placed their feet. After a while a new man would take the lead. Snowdrifts as high as their waists slowed progress and wetted them all, so that layers of solid ice built up on their clothes. Their peaked caps were useless in the cold, and they had no gloves.

Once the high ground had been reached, they confronted the vast grey-white plateau they must cross. A fierce wind lashed at their faces. Larsen was concerned that for the now exhausted men this final physical barrier would also constitute a mental one. He kept them plodding on, as day turned to night, encouraging, helping and cajoling in equal measure. Exhaustion sapped them, but they soldiered on.

Knowing that they could not survive a night in the open, they were driven to seek shelter, but the houses they encountered in this remote part of Norway were less welcoming than before, and a number of doors stayed shut in isolated hamlets. This forced them to trudge on, or otherwise suffer the rapid onset of hypothermia and death. Their weakened state also mean that they were less cautious than they might have been, and began to rely on the road – Route 72 – heading towards the hamlet of Sandvika, on the border with Sweden, to enable them to move quickly. It was to prove their undoing. Larsen described what happened next to his biographer:

There were thick woods on either side and they found some sticks which they used to walk with. They all felt much better with solid ground under their feet instead of the deep, loose snow, and the sticks helped them along. Silently they trudged on, thinking of the rest that was awaiting them. Then suddenly a voice shouted, 'Halt!'

They had just turned a corner and two figures appeared in front of them as though by magic. The group was taken completely by surprise; they were still several miles from the frontier and had not expected to encounter any trouble. Worn out as they were after their struggle through the mountains, they had relaxed their watchfulness. Now they stood staring at two revolvers covering them, their pistols completely inaccessible in their back pockets.

One of the two men confronting them had on grey-green German uniform with top boots and shoulder belt. The other was in navy blue civilian clothes or dark uniform, and his finger twitched on the trigger of his gun.

'Where are you going?' he demanded sharply.

'Who asks?' asked Larsen calmly, standing right in front of him. The German military policeman levelled the mouth of his revolver about a yard away from his head, obviously having no compunction about using it. 'I am asking you! Drop your sticks!' His voice was shrill and quivered slightly; Larsen realised that he was just as frightened as the men from the *Arthur* . . . For a moment he gathered his body, contracted his muscles and then leapt at the two men like an uncoiled spring, smashing them over backwards with the entire weight of his body. A second or two later a report went off behind him. Billy [Tebb] had got out his pistol, and the man in blue crumpled in a heap. But the German in uniform managed to fire wildly at them as he plunged off the side of the road. The rest of the group had drawn their pistols by now and shots followed the man down the slope. He disappeared into the darkness.

The exchange of fire had wounded Evans in the thigh. A hurried decision was made. Evans, the men assumed, would be protected by his uniform were he to be captured, so they bound his wound, made him comfortable, shook his hand and hurried down to the river Inna, which ran below the road, towards Sandvika. By following this they would remain off the main road and away from trouble. As it turned out, a milkman and his cart and a truck driving fast in the direction they had just come were the only traffic.

The group crossed the border unimpeded on the early morning of Thursday 5 November. They carried on, walking on the road as it ran due south to the hamlet of Skalstugan, some 6 miles from the border, where a Swedish Army post was known to be. They reached this just before reveille was sounded and were hospitably treated, Larsen explaining that he was a resistance worker from Trondheim who had escorted a number of Royal Navy sailors to safety after their motor torpedo boat had been wrecked off the coast.

According to Fell's account, both 'parties crossed into Sweden within an hour of each other and less than two miles apart'. Brewster's party came across the plateau to the south of Larsen, crossing in a remote spot at Storsjoen, due west of the Swedish border post at Skalstugan. Larsen was quietly elated. His group had travelled nearly 30 miles non-stop across terrible terrain in twenty-four hours. Evans, no doubt, was now receiving medical care at the hands of the Wehrmacht, but at least he was alive, even though he faced a stretch as a prisoner of war. He recorded that the Germans telephoned through to Skalstugan to insist that a number of escapers who had been responsible for a murder in Verdal be returned, but their request was turned down after Larsen vehemently denied involvement.

After ten days, the nine men were moved to Stockholm and on 27 November all but three, who were still in hospital (including Bjørnoy, who had a number of toes amputated for frostbite), were flown back to Scotland. Operation *Title* had been a brave effort, but had failed through no fault of the men who had come so close to success. Leif Larsen was awarded the Conspicuous Gallantry Medal, the first time it had been awarded to a non-Briton.

Admiral Sir Henry Ruthven Moore, the Vice-Chief of the Naval Staff, sent this message to the participants:

> Although we now know that through ill-luck the very gallant efforts to carry out the operation failed to achieve their object, I should like – on behalf of Flag Officer (Submarines) and of the Naval Staff – to express to you our admiration and deep appreciation of the vital part played by SOE and particularly by the Norwegian Section. Without their cooperation and valuable assistance the operation could never have been undertaken and I should like to ask you to convey our grateful thanks to all those concerned. Better luck next time!

Unfortunately, Larsen's assumption about the safety of Bob Evans was entirely misplaced. Evans became a victim of Hitler's infamous *Kommandobefehl*. After capture he was allowed to recover from his wound in a Norwegian hospital, before being taken to Grini concentration camp, 30 miles outside Oslo. On 18 January 1943 he was taken into Trandum Forest with survivors of Operation *Freshman*, a failed attempt to destroy the Vemork heavy water plant at Rjukan in November 1942, and executed by firing squad. His body was thrown into a mass grave.

It was revealed during the questioning of Rear Admiral Gerhard Wagner, Chief of Staff (Operations) in the SKL (*Seekriegsleitung* or Naval Warfare Command), at the Nuremberg Trials on 14 May 1946, that when Evans was captured he had been interviewed directly by the Commander-in-Chief, Navy, of the Norwegian North Coast, based in Narvik. Colonel-General Nikolaus von Falkenhorst, Supreme Commander of German forces in Norway at the time and the man responsible for invoking the Commando Order against Evans, was sentenced to death in 1946. The sentence was later commuted to twenty years' imprisonment, although he was released in 1953, after serving six years in prison. While von Falkenhorst, Wagner and others continued with their lives and careers (Wagner, for example, served in the Navy of the new West Germany and became, in the early 1960s, NATO's Commander Naval Forces Baltic Approaches), Evans and other victims of judicial murder at the hand of the various branches of the Wehrmacht, and of the Gestapo, remained cold in their graves.

NINE

Devastator

Well before the instructions reached Sladen and Fell to design a British equivalent of the *Maiale* and to build up a British capability to match that of the Decima Flottiglia, Sir Max Horton had initiated the search for a miniature submarine that could go where its larger brethren could not: especially the fjords of Norway, where after 1940 the *Kriegsmarine* had developed a vexing habit of hiding its capital ships. Horton had in fact displayed a long interest in the potential for such vessels, and during the interwar years had collaborated with a man who also nursed a long-held obsession with ideas, plans, patents and prototypes of miniature submarines. Indeed, Godfrey ('Bertie') Herbert had received a patent as early as 1909 for a 10-ton manned torpedo, which he called the 'Devastator'.

Herbert had been commissioned into the Royal Navy in June 1900 and volunteered for the submarine service in January 1905. When, at the outset of the First World War, he submitted his idea to the Royal Navy, it was rejected out of hand as something that suited a struggling naval power, not the world's mightiest navy. His biographer, E. Keble Chatterton, described Herbert's idea as:

> a compromise between a submarine and a torpedo; smaller than the former but larger than the latter . . . The 'Devastator' could be described as a human torpedo; or as a small submersible vessel equipped with explosive charge, propelling plant, means for navigation on or below the surface. But, also, there was a detachable

buoyant compartment for the one-man navigator, and so arranged that it could be disconnected at the required moment. Thus, suppose the Grand Fleet were approaching the enemy's fleet. On going into action one or more 'Devastators' would be hoisted out on a derrick and dropped when the enemy's leading ship was (say) 20,000 yards distant. The 'Devastator's' one-man crew would proceed, steering by compass, and start to deliver his attack . . . [at a suitable juncture the crewman, ensuring that the torpedo was on the correct course, would] . . . detach the buoyant compartment to be left in the sea containing himself, and be picked up by a destroyer or other vessel.

The explosive charge was located forward, and of such heaviness as to penetrate even the inner hull of a battleship equipped to resist torpedoes. A periscope for the navigator was also provided, together with all the control arrangements. When he should wish to be ejected, together with his compartment, the navigator had only to release compressed air and up he would come into the sea after the same method by which torpedoes are ejected from their tubes.

Rejected by the Navy, Herbert nevertheless refused to give up on his idea: he continued to develop his plan and patented it soon after the war. Nor was Herbert the only Briton contemplating the possibilities of two- and three-man submarines. Robert Davis of Siebe Gorman produced detailed drawings of such vessels in 1914: published in the company's diving manual, they looked uncannily like those eventually built in 1942. A unique feature of Davis's design was a compartment (known as the 'Wet and Dry') which enabled a diver – wearing oxygen-rebreather equipment – to enter and exit the submarine while it was submerged, allowing it to engage in acts of underwater sabotage without affecting the control of the submarine.

During the interwar years, a submariner made redundant from the Navy following the 'Geddes' Axe' retrenchment in 1922,

Lieutenant Commander Cromwell Varley, DSC – 'a tall, thick-set, fair-haired, bespectacled officer', recalled another sailor, George Simpson, at the time himself a young recruit to submarines – engaged in his own attempts, independent of the others, to design and build a working submarine. Varley seems to have borrowed Herbert's concept, constructing a 31-ton mini-submarine in his yacht-building yard on the Hamble. But whereas Herbert had seen the Devastator as something that, in large numbers, could attack an enemy force by virtue of – as his patent described – 'propelling against an enemy ship or other target a large quantity of high explosive, and of effecting this with great economy of material and personnel', Varley wanted a vessel that could go where conventional submarines could not. Harbours and other 'safe' anchorages – whether provided by natural geography or by means of anti-submarine nets – were the targets of Varley's imaginings.

Varley's, Davis's and Herbert's ideas all found support in Horton's spirited advocacy. During the First World War, Horton had recommended Herbert's plans to the First Lord of the Admiralty himself, but was rebuffed. The idea was too dangerous, it was considered, and something that an inferior nation would turn to, not for a country whose navy still ruled the waves. Unwilling to let the matter lie, however, Horton pursued the concept in the interwar years. Indeed, in 1924 he submitted plans to the Admiralty for a range of small submarines – each in the region of between 30 and 40 tons – of varying designs, all of which would need to be towed or carried to the area of operations. Horton's rationale for this sort of weapon lay in 'the increasingly effective defensive measures against submarines endeavouring to bring off a close attack. A weapon for such a purpose (to attack the enemy battle fleet when in harbour) has been looked for without real success for many years. Equipped with cutters and a stout hull, this small submarine could choose its depth to penetrate harbour defences.'

Horton found out about Varley's activities by accident. Horton's biographer described how he found himself re-engaged with the subject of mini-submarines soon after the onset of the war:

One day in 1940, his Chief Staff Officer, Captain E. R. Gibson, RN, told Horton that he had learnt that a midget submarine was being built privately on the Hamble by Commander C. H. Varley, RN, a retired submarine officer of the 1914–18 war. 'We must go there at once' said Max. 'Order the car and tell him we are coming.' Varley was not at all pleased. This midget submarine had been his pet hobby for some years, and he hoped to be able to complete the prototype in secrecy without interference from official quarters. Horton convinced him that time was the most important factor, and arranged that Varley should have every assistance from naval sources to develop the prototype. It did not fulfil all requirements, but it worked.

Horton saw Varley's revised design, which had been developed with the help of Bertie Herbert, as ideal for the Royal Navy's purposes and managed, by means of determined advocacy, to persuade the Admiralty in 1940 to commission a prototype craft from Varley's boatyard. Clear in Horton's mind was that the target of such craft should be the German capital ships that took sanctuary in the Norwegian harbours that became available to them after their invasion in 1940.

One of Horton's three 1924 designs had been for a small submarine which carried a heavy short-range torpedo underneath its belly, a concept that Varley adapted, but in which two large mines, weighing two tons each and using amatol high explosive, were shaped to be carried attached to each side of the mini-submarine, then to be placed underneath an enemy target, rather than fired *at* it. Varley's prototype – named *X3* – was laid down in September 1941 and launched into the Hamble on Sunday 15 March 1942. At the same time a second prototype – *X4* – was commissioned from the Royal Dockyards at Portsmouth: 'X' was to be the designation of all subsequent mini-submarines in British service. The vessel was designed to be manned by a crew of three: a commanding officer, a first lieutenant and an engineer, or engine room artificer (ERA). Her first crew – Lieutenant Willie Meeke, DSC, RN (in command), Lieutenant Donald Cameron, RNR (First Lieutenant), and Chief ERA Richardson – joined the Varley yard for the last few months of X3's construction. Cameron, a 26-year-old veteran of the Merchant Marine, then serving in submarines, in HMS *Sturgeon*, had managed to sneak through the selection procedures, which stipulated that for 'hazardous service' he had to be under twenty-five, and unmarried. Within months of starting initial training on X3, Cameron broke another rule: he fell in love and married the eighteen-year-old daughter – Eve – of his Portsmouth landlady, Mrs Kilpatrick.

Cyril Warren, himself soon to become an X-craft crewman, described the 30-ton vessel they confronted:

She was approximately fifty feet long overall, but, as propeller, rudder, and hydroplanes were included in this, the internal living-space length was nearer thirty-five feet, or about half the length of a cricket-pitch. The maximum diameter of the circular pressure-hull was five feet six inches, so that, with the deck-boards cutting off the bottom six inches or so, there was barely five feet of head-room. The control-room, for'ard, contained the steering and depth-keeping controls, the periscope and various navigational items, and pieces of miscellaneous machinery. Next came the escape compart-ment, known as the 'W and D', or 'Wet and Dry'. As envisaged by Sir Robert Davis in his original design, this allowed one member of the crew to leave and re-enter the submarine in diving-gear, for the purpose of cutting nets or placing explosive charges. Farther aft came the battery compartment and engine and motor-spaces.

She was, in fact, a complete submarine in miniature. Pretty well all she lacked were torpedo-tubes, for the armament of the

X-craft was to consist of two crescent-shaped explosive charges housed externally one on either side of the pressure-hull. Known as side-cargoes, these each contained two tons of amatol explosive and a time-clock. They were to be left on the bottom, beneath the hull of the target.

Propulsion for the craft, as for any other type of submarine, came from the diesel engine on the surface and from the battery-driven main motor while submerged, giving maximum speeds of approximately 6½ and 4½ knots respectively.

Another volunteer, ERA Vernon ('Ginger') Coles, had agreed to put his name down for hazardous service in September 1942. He had joined the Royal Navy in 1938 at the age of seventeen because he was bored, and here he was again, bored rigid with conventional seafaring, even in time of war. 'I looked at this and thought "Shall I or shan't I? Shall I or shan't I?" In the end I thought, yes, I'll have a go.' He wasn't impressed when he had his first glance at *X4*, under construction in a secure part of Portsmouth Dockyard:

We were ordered to go and see Lieutenant Haslett . . . and he took us over to Portsmouth dockyard. We were taken to a shed where this object was being built – although we still had no idea what it was. An armed sentry stood outside and he was given permission to take us into an inner room where there was another sentry. They opened the inner door and that's when we saw this ghastly thing – the X-craft. We looked at one another and said, 'Good heavens, is this it?' Our stomachs turned over. That was *X4* – she was just being assembled.

'Space was at a premium' in the vessel, according to Max Shean.

The crew occupied what remained after the equipment had been located. The engine room was most crowded, as you can imagine, with a bus engine alongside a three-stage air compressor within a five foot ten inch tube, the bottom of which was occupied by tanks. Yet ERAs and stokers did work in the remaining space, even with the engine running. The motor and clutches were at the back of this lot, and needed attention occasionally.

Bob Aitken, initially recruited to Chariots, was persuaded to convert to X-craft:

We slept in the battery compartment in the bow, on boards on top of the batteries. One, sometimes two men could rest there. Normally three positions were manned in the control room. Unless he was resting the commanding officer (CO) would be on the periscope and navigating, the 1st Lieutenant at the hydroplanes keeping depth and the ERA at the helm steering. Apart from relieving the 1st Lieutenant or the ERA, the diver had little to do but help with the catering.

The first production vessels (*X5–X10*) were to prove remarkably seaworthy, behaving admirably in even the worst weather the Atlantic and Arctic could throw at them, although they were not without their problems. Leakages were frequent in the periscopes and the attached charges, which had dramatic implications for trimming the vessel: the process of establishing a level and consistent buoyancy at depth. Likewise, at shallow depths it was extraordinarily hard to prevent the vessels broaching the surface unintentionally. Even though they were designed to be towed to their target area, either by full-scale submarine or a ship, the 42-horsepower Gardner diesel engine – the same as those used on the London bus – gave them a phenomenal range of 1,100 nautical miles of surface running, and they could remain submerged on her batteries for up to thirty-six hours with a maximum range submerged of 85 miles at 2 knots.

The range was limited only by crew fatigue. When en route to a target under tow the procedure that developed was for a 'passage crew' of three to operate the craft. They would be relieved just before the final run by the 'attack crew' of four, working in pairs. The decision to restrict the passage crews to three crewmen, especially for long passages, was in retrospect a mistake, as the vessel had too small a complement to allow for an effective shift pattern and to ensure safe management. 'When there were four men in the passage crew it was two men doing two hours on watch and two hours off watch, which was sustainable,' recalled Ginger Coles, who was critical of the decision to reduce the passage crews to three. 'The two hours off watch allowed you to keep the rope dry, clean and chase all electrical earths, because they were damp these boats.' With only three crew members, a single sailor had to monitor the entire boat during one whole shift. It was far too demanding for one man. The result was that two men had to stay awake, while the third attempted fitful sleep. Another submariner, John McGregor, remembered this strain: 'Nothing is worse than to watch one dial, one gauge, for two hours. You know that a sudden depth change, say from 100 to 130 feet in ten seconds, may mean the end, and you do your best to be attentive.' Even those off duty found it difficult to sleep, as Benzedrine was taken to retain the crew's alertness, which of course kept them awake when they desperately needed rest and sleep.

During an attack, with a crew of four, two men would work a four-hour shift before resting for the next four hours. One of the men on duty controlled the boat at the helm while the other carried out maintenance, prepared the food and undertook all other necessary jobs. Even with a crew of four it was hard, exhausting work. Whilst undertaking a tow the boat needed to be carefully trimmed, as it oscillated over about 100 feet as it was pulled behind the towing submarine. Any mistake in the trimming could mean that if the towing rope broke – and the hemp or manila ones did frequently, every four days of constant use according to Ginger Coles – the downward trim would send the craft plummeting to the bottom. The maximum safe diving depth of an X-craft was 300 feet. If its descent was not interrupted by the seabed or by the rapid attention of the crew it would implode when it reached destruction depth. In trials immediately after the war this was found to be at about 500 feet.

During the approach to the target the passage crew would be swapped out for three men of the attack crew, the passage crew paddling back to the towing vessel. The author Tom Waldron, who interviewed many Charioteers after the war, and James Gleeson described the roles and dispositions of the crew within the cramped confines of the X-craft:

At the forward end the helmsman sat surrounded by various levers and wheels . . . Next came the slightly raised dome, where there was a wide field bifocal periscope, which could be used when under targets or for looking for hostile aircraft. There, also, was the attacking periscope, which could be raised telescopically nine feet. This was as slender as a wireless antenna and beautifully clear. Two inches of this periscope above the water gave the Captain an excellent view of all that was going on above him, and it was nearly invisible, even to the keenest submarine look-out. Abaft the dome sat the First Lieutenant at the hydroplane controls surrounded, like the helmsman, by switches, levers and wheels. Other space in this compartment was taken up with a multitude of things – air purifiers, periscope raising gear, pumps and their motors, wheels, levers and gauges. In addition, there was the second bunk in which the occupant was forced to lie curved round various pipes and handles. Cooking was done on a double saucepan electrically heated. In this one made coffee, heated tinned foods, boiled potatoes and eggs, and washed up when finished with. The fourth compartment was almost inaccessible. It housed the gyro compass, a high-pressure air compressor, and a score of gauges and pipes and wheels and valves, not to mention the air-conditioning plant. At action stations all four were at their respective posts; the Captain working his attack instruments, doing the chart work and conning the ship by occasional glimpses through his periscope; the First Lieutenant at the main motor and hydroplanes control; the third hand . . . was dressed for shallow-water diving, with his oxygen breathing bag on and all ready, except for his face piece. He was also helmsman. The Engine Room Artificer was a Jack-of-all-trades – helping the Captain, the First Lieutenant and relieving the third hand when he left the craft to cut a way through nets or fix a mine to the target's bottom; and, of course, he was in general charge of all machinery.

The W&D compartment was complicated to use within the cramped confines of the vessel. It was particularly difficult for tall men. The diver had to get into his Sladen suit before squeezing into the compartment, adopting a foetal position and then pumping in water, equalising the pressure and exiting through the external hatch. It was a lonely, claustrophobic and unpleasant experience. No one liked using the W&D. John Lorimer explained: 'We had to climb into this compartment, shut both hatches fore and aft and, to equalise the pressure, we had to open valves to let it flood. We'd dress in our diving suits in the WD to do our chores. The one thing I really hated was sitting on the loo in this little WD, as it was flooding. I had a sense of claustrophobia.'

Horton's idea in 1940 of designing a craft able to sneak in and out of Norwegian fjords proved to be remarkably prescient. By the time that the threat of the *Tirpitz* emerged in 1942, the first X-craft were in production, and the first crews being recruited and trained. The first three recruits, who joined the X-craft service in May 1942 (to support the introduction into service of *X3* and *X4*) after a process identical to that undertaken for their Chariot colleagues, were followed by an additional nine in July and a final sixteen in August. Midshipman John Lorimer, RNVR, recalled his first view of an X-craft. He wasn't impressed. He and Sub Lieutenant David Locke, also of the RNVR, were shown over *X3* by Donald Cameron:

I remember thinking how incredibly small everything looked and wondering how such a frail craft was expected to cross the North Sea. The next day I went out for my first trip. It was just a surface run . . . During the next three weeks we went over to the Hamble occasionally, but *X3* spent most of her time in the big shed where she was built, while various Admiralty experts arrived, trying to sell their various instruments, most of which would not even get inside the craft.

X3 spent the summer of 1942 working up off Southampton while the new crews completed their training across the United Kingdom. At the end of August the men and *X3* were reunited at the new base established for X-craft at Port Bannatyne on the Isle of Bute, a short journey from the mainland across the Clyde Estuary. Loch Striven in Argyllshire lay due north. Bannatyne became known as HMS *Varbel I*, and Loch Striven as HMS *Varbel II*, for reasons to be explained. *X3* made the long journey to Faslane on the Gare Loch in secret on a railway flatbed, from which she was lifted into the water at night, before sailing down the Clyde to Port Bannatyne.

'Working up' started at once. John Lorimer, who became the No. 1 to Donald Cameron, was under way on Loch Striven on the afternoon of 4 November with two trainees – Len Gay and 'Taffy' Laites – when the craft suddenly sank in 120 feet of water. A valve designed to close off the diesel exhaust pipe had failed to do so when the X-craft began to submerge, slowly flooding the vessel. An attempt to close it manually failed when a spanner was dropped. Amazingly the three men on board all survived, as Lorimer explains:

> One of the bad things about *X3* was the location of the batteries – right aft. We sank, stern-first, at an angle of about 70 degrees, and the water in the bilges entered the batteries and created chlorine, which is lethal. We decided we had to equalise the pressure

inside and outside in order to escape. There's only one way to do that and that was to flood the craft. One of the people I was training became a bit excited, and the more excited he became the more he breathed oxygen. We had four Davis escape sets, and he finished his set and I managed to get the other set onto him. Then the other trainee managed to get the hatch open and I pushed the first man through, but it was a close-run thing.

Within twelve hours, a boom defence vessel came along and lifted *X3*, but I wasn't the most popular man because she was the prototype, and I'd been forced to sink her. She was taken to Faslane and put on a low-loader train – *X3* was crated up by shipwrights in an enormous long wooden box – and I was detailed to escort her down to Portsmouth for repair.

By this time, however, the Portsmouth Naval Dockyards had completed *X4*, which was also transported by rail to Faslane for the short hop across to Port Bannatyne, where it was given to Lieutenant Godfrey Place, RN, to command. Place was a regular officer who had joined the Royal Navy at fourteen. He had been the first lieutenant on the submarine HMS *Unbeaten* and had won a DSC for his sinking of the Italian submarine *Guglielmotti* on 17 March 1942. *Unbeaten* was in dry dock when he was asked by Commander David Ingram, RN, the commander of 'HMS *Varbel*' at Port Bannatyne from September 1942: 'How would you like to join us and sink the *Tirpitz*?' 'I just said, "Yes"', Place would later remember. 'He didn't give very much explanation of what was required to be done but I inferred that it was a small submarine venture.'

The six operational craft ordered from the Vickers-Armstrong shipyards in Barrow in Furness in May 1942 arrived between the end of 1942 and January 1943: *X5*, *X6*, *X7*, *X8*, *X9* and *X10*. Their respective commanding officers were Willie Meeke; Don Cameron; Godfrey Place; Australian Brian 'Digger' McFarlane; Terry Martin and Australian Ken Hudspeth. Together they, with all of Fell's Chariots as well as *X3* and *X4*, made up the 12th Submarine Flotilla, commanded by Captain Willie Banks, RN. Fell reported to him, as did Commander D. C. Ingram, DSC, RN, responsible for training, and Captain P. Q. Roberts, RN, commander of the X-craft depot ship HMS *Bonaventure* and Commander T. I. S. 'Tissy' Bell, RN, who was placed in command of *Varbel II*.*

One of the third batch of recruits to the X-craft programme was a 24-year-old Australian naval reservist from Perth, Maxwell ('Max') Shean. Shean, who had been studying engineering at the University of Western Australia at the outset of war, undertook initial training in the Royal Australian Navy before sailing to Britain in 1941 and joining the corvette HMS *Bluebell*. He was carrying out convoy escort duties between Gibraltar and West Africa and fighting off attacks by U-boats (he experienced five attacks in total) when he saw a notice, during a refit in the Tyne in July 1942, for volunteers for 'special and hazardous service'. The specific requirements for the volunteers were that they had to be 'below age twenty-four, unmarried, good swimmers and of strong and enduring physique'. His friend and commanding officer Lieutenant Geoffrey Walker wanted to apply, so Shean decided to join him. As it turned out, Shean was accepted following an interview with Captain Reggie Darke at HMS *Dolphin*, while Walker was instructed to remain with his corvette.†

On 14 September 1942 Shean left the Tyne for HMS *Dolphin* at Portsmouth to join a group of twelve volunteers to begin initial training in diving and submarine work as part of the newly formed 12th Submarine Flotilla. Within ten days, the group had shrunk to nine, as their first exposure to the compression tank and DSEA apparatus revealed that it was not everyone's cup of tea. At this stage they were told, in conditions of great secrecy, the purpose of their recruitment. The flotilla's training officer who revealed this

---

* Commander David Ingram replaced Bell in mid-1943.
† Walker was killed when the *Bluebell* was sunk by a torpedo from *U771* off Murmansk on 25 January 1945.

information to them was Lieutenant Arthur 'Baldy' Hezlet, DSC, RN, an enormously experienced submariner who was to remain associated with Chariots and X-craft in various forms for the remainder of the war. At the outset of the war he had been serving on the submarine HMS *H43*, before being promoted to first lieutenant on HMS *Trident*. After active service in Norway he passed the famous 'Perisher' command course and took over HMS *H44* in December 1940. Then, while in command of HMS *Unique* (based in Malta), he sank the 11,000-ton Italian troopship *Esperia*, for which he was awarded the DSC, before returning to command HMS *Trident* on convoy-protection duties to Russia. To Shean's amazement and trepidation – he admitted that his knees trembled at the news – Hezlet told them calmly that their job was to learn how to operate a new type of midget submarine in order to attack high-value enemy targets in their secure harbours, which were as good as invulnerable to conventional attack. The first and immediate target was the ship that Winston Churchill had called 'the Beast': the *Tirpitz*, still hiding deep – and well protected – within its Norwegian fjord. It all sounded 'like a one-way excursion', thought Shean.

Introductory diving training completed, the nine remaining recruits travelled north by train to Glasgow and then the Isle of Bute. The training base and shore establishment at Port Bannatyne was the requisitioned Kyles of Bute Hydropathic Hotel, which had been renamed – informally – HMS *Varbel*, a play on a mix of Cromwell Varley's name and that of Commander 'Tissy' Bell, Varley's collaborator in the design and build of both *X3* and *X4*, and the X-craft programme's first training officer. Bell was, recalled Shean, 'an energetic, single-minded man who urged us to train and strain until we were as fit as tigers'. He was also a little bit crazy. Tiny Fell acknowledged him to be a man of 'fantastic energy, but was incapable of suffering fools gladly. He was constantly falling foul of higher authority and the very young.' Fell described *Varbel II*, for the six short months in which Bell was in charge, as 'generally in a state bordering on turmoil'.

On arrival at Glasgow Shean and his group caught a train to Wemyss, after which a ferry took them across the Clyde estuary to Rothesay Bay. A two-mile journey by truck took them to the magnificent hotel which, now under its new military users, was a shadow of its former self.

Lectures by 'Baldy' Hezlet in any of a number of the rooms in the rambling vastness of the Hydro Hotel were interspersed with an increasing number of practical diving exercises in the beautiful Loch Striven (whose land base was Ardtarig House, at the north end of the loch) with both helmet (i.e. compressed-air) and DSEA rebreathers, all while wearing the Sladen suit. The aim was to increase to the maximum possible each man's familiarity with the underwater environment, new to most of the recruits. Shean recalled that 'descending the shot-rope [from the accompanying boat], pausing from time to time to move the jaw in an effort to get air to flow somewhere within the head, and to equalise pressure on the ear drums, was quite pleasant as one realised, with agreeable surprise, that one was still breathing'.

In Loch Striven had been constructed a series of anti-submarine nets, and parts of a submerged mocked-up X-craft, which enabled trainees to practise on a W&D compartment without overtaxing the only two real vessels available, *X3* and *X4*, in which training time was at a premium. While men practised on the inert device off *Varbel II* the others would team up and take *X3* and *X4* out for repeated practice runs. Shean recalled:

All day, crews would be diving, surfacing, making periscope sightings, carrying out all the evolutions of which we had to be capable, returning late afternoon to moor alongside the mother ship to recharge batteries and high-pressure air. We would make the best of our all too brief periods at the controls, forward in the control room with the steering wheel and main ballast vent and blow valves, and aft with engine, motor, trim pump and hydro-plane controls.

124

Whenever an X-craft was exercising or training, two vessels were always available at immediate notice in case of the need for rescue and salvage. One was HMS *Alecto* or HMS *Tedworth*, ships with special diving equipment. The other was one of the boom crews.

John Lorimer's memories illustrate the intensity of the training, and that it was all undertaken voluntarily. 'If you are going to do anything dangerous, the best way to accomplish it is to train, train, train, so that in the excitement of the situation you do the thing automatically. I cannot over-emphasise the drilling they put us through, the importance of it, the fact that none of us minded . . . We lived like pirates, called one another by our Christian names, but the discipline was complete.'

Following the failure of Operation *Title*, every plan and thought, wrote Tiny Fell, was now focused on one thing: the destruction of the *Tirpitz*, lying invulnerable, or so the Germans thought, under the steep cliffs of the Kåfjord in the furthest reaches of Norway – to where it had been removed after its long stay in Trondheimsfjord, protected by 'defences of every sort'.

TEN

Chariots in the Mediterranean

While the X-craft and their crews began to train intensively for this new form of underwater warfare, the Chariot crews under 'Tiny' Fell and his team continued to prepare for their own unique method of fighting. With the onset of winter precluding any further Chariot operations in northern waters for 1942, Max Horton ordered a group of T-class submarines to move to besieged Malta to reinforce the 10th Submarine Flotilla based at Marsamxett. From here, in addition to undertaking conventional protective and offensive patrols, they could operate in support of the Chariots' activities. It was a time of momentous events in North Africa, and a major role existed for the Navy: to protect British convoys making their way to Malta; to attack Axis shipping attempting to support the withdrawal of Rommel's Afrika Korps from El Alamein following Montgomery's victory in October; and to prevent disruption to the Anglo-American 'Torch' landings in November. These vessels included the newly commissioned T-class submarine HMS *P311* (it was due to be called *Tutankhamen*, but was lost to enemy action before it was formally named), HMS *Thunderbolt*, HMS *Trooper* and HMS *Unruffled*.

HMS *P311*, under the command of Lieutenant Commander Richard Cayley, RN – an 'effervescent roly-poly figure' according to Simpson – had two containers built onto her foredeck to enable her to carry her two Chariots. Her journey to ship them to Malta – along with *Thunderbolt*, *Trooper* and *Unruffled* – began on 12

126

November, and ended successfully with her arrival on 30 November. By Christmas 1942 seven Chariots and their crews were in Malta, with Geoffrey Sladen sent out to prepare them for war.

A relatively small number of operations were conducted over the following year. They took the form of offensive actions directly into the heart of the enemy's harbours and, in a new and novel use of the crews, of beach reconnaissance prior to amphibious assault of a coastline. Horton expected great things of his Chariots in the Mediterranean. 'If the Chariots can be carried to the immediate vicinity . . . of an enemy harbour,' he wrote in the paper explaining the move, 'there are no defences they cannot penetrate. They have even cut their way through barbed wire.' High hopes had been built up for Chariot operations in the Mediterranean, given that this was the birthplace of the human torpedo, but for a number of reasons these expectations were never to be fully realised.

The commander of the 10th was Commander George 'Shrimp' Simpson. He first encountered a Chariot in Lazaretto harbour, in September 1942, and was impressed with what he saw:

> The captain of this vessel assured me that he could leave Lazaretto after dark with himself and his mate, in frogmen's suits, sitting on saddles astride it and enter the Grand Harbour and knock on the bottom of a hulk inside the harbour without detection in sixty minutes. Admiral [Ralph] Leatham was willing to bet this could not be done but it was achieved with a few minutes to spare.

The first mission prepared by Simpson was a dual operation against the ports of Palermo in Sicily and La Maddalena in Sardinia. Three Chariots were to be launched from HMS *Trooper* and two from HMS *Thunderbolt* against Palermo, while two Chariots were to be launched from Cayley's *P311* against two *Regia Marina* cruisers in La Maddalena. Operation *Principal* was to strike a simultaneous blow against Italian shipping that was supposedly safe in its harbours, and so to avenge the attacks on the *Queen Elizabeth* and *Valiant*. The hope was that in addition to striking a hard physical blow against the enemy the psychological impact of this type of attack would cause the *Regia Marina* to become much more defensive, even timid. At this point in the war, the greatest threat to Allied operations in the Mediterranean was not Italian capital ships – which according to Simpson were reportedly short of fuel and confined to their ports – but their troop transports and vessels, which were supplying and supporting military operations in North Africa.

The attack on La Maddalena harbour on the north-eastern tip of Sardinia was planned for the night of New Year's Day, 1943. HMS *P311* left Marsamxett on Malta on 28 December. During the afternoon of the 30th, as it was approaching the general line between Marittimo and Skerki, it submerged: Italian motor torpedo boats were sweeping the area, probably in preparation for a convoy setting out. Both *Trooper* and *Thunderbolt* stayed back, south of Pantelleria, on Simpson's orders, awaiting news of the successful penetration by *P311*. Cayley duly reported his position at 6 p.m. on 30 December (the signal was sent at 1.30 a.m. next morning), indicating that he had managed to infiltrate through the dangerous Sicilian strait. The winds were reported to be strong at the Chariots' point of disembarkation but it was decided not to postpone the operation, as a delay would have a detrimental effect on the morale of the Charioteers. But nothing was heard from Cayley or his crew again, and the submarine has never been found. Simpson's supposition was that she was destroyed by an anti-ship mine. All ten Charioteers on board, together with her crew, perished. 'So passed,' he observed, 'a gallant leader and his brave company.'

This left five Chariots (Numbers 15, 16, 19, 22 and 23) on HMS *Thunderbolt* and *Trooper* for the attack on Palermo harbour. This proved only to be a partial success, however. When the Chariots left the submarine, it was in the teeth of a Force 5 gale, the worst weather the men had ever seen. One feature of operations in the Mediterranean during winter, for which the crews trained in

North West Scotland were unprepared, was the stormy weather and heavy seas. Chariot No. 16, operated by Sub Lieutenant Rodney Dove and Leading Seaman Jimmy Freel, was hit by a massive wave on launching that swept away the limpet mines they were going to deploy against secondary targets. They were able nevertheless to enter the harbour and place their main warhead on the 8,500-ton troopship *Viminale*, disabling it. The two men then made their way to shore, in an exhausted state, and became prisoners of war.

The other two Chariots launched from HMS *Trooper* that night failed to reach the harbour. Sub Lieutenant H. L. H. Stevens, RNVR, and Leading Seaman Carter on Chariot No. 23 (whose target was the MV *Ankara*, a cargo ship used for transporting German Panzers to North Africa) struggled against huge waves to find the entrance to Palermo harbour, and were forced to head back out to sea, where they were lucky enough to be recovered by HMS *Unruffled*. On the third Chariot (No. 19) the No. 1, Lieutenant H. F. Cook, RNVR, was so violently and repeatedly sick – a condition probably brought on inside the bowels of HMS *Trooper* as it pitched and yawed through tremendous seas – that Able Seaman Worthy was forced to drive him to the rocky shore before attempting to carry on against their target – the liner *Galiano* – alone. But he simply could not handle the Chariot by himself in the rough seas, and returned to the rocks where he had dropped off Cook. He could not find him. His No. 1 was never seen again, presumed drowned.

The two crews from HMS *Thunderbolt* likewise found the conditions appalling, and succeeded in getting away from their mother ship only with the greatest difficulty. While inside HMS *Thunderbolt* during the approach run, the men could feel the strength of the seas, giving them a good indication of just how difficult the situation would be 'on top'. Chariot No. 15 (Able Seaman W. Simpson and Petty Officer Milne) struggled from the outset, the state of the sea making their Chariot difficult to manage. Then disaster struck.

A battery exploded, sending their machine plummeting to the depths. Simpson was unable to extricate himself and return to the surface, and Milne only managed to do so – from a depth of 95 feet – with great difficulty. He was lucky to make it to the shore.

The only one of the crews that set off – Lieutenant Greenland and Signalman Alex Ferrier (Chariot No. 22) – did find their way into the harbour. As they approached the land after leaving *Thunderbolt*, struggling to manage their pitching vessel, they were relieved to see the welcoming Palermo lighthouse blinking in the distance, the light being reflected off the low clouds. Once inside the harbour, the sea conditions improved dramatically: the men glided in towards their target at a depth of about 10 feet under a surface that was like a millpond, an amazing contrast with what they'd just experienced. The anti-submarine net at the entrance was easily broached by diving underneath it, although the anti-torpedo net around their target, the uncompleted cruiser *Ulpio Traiano*, proved to be the greatest problem they faced inside the harbour, as Greenland explained:

> We had one helluva job with the net which seemed too big and was lying on the bottom in folds. Don't ask me just what happened next. All I remember is that we got under it and were blowing towards the top . . . As we neared the surface, I did my Mongol-horseman-act, sliding round and underneath the Chariot whilst hanging on with one hand, which amazed Ferrier. I had neglected to inform him of my intention.

They managed to attach their warhead to the hull of the unfinished vessel, and set the timer for two hours, before attaching their four limpet mines to three other targets. Now entirely beat, they made their way to a set of stone steps in the dockyard, scuttled the Chariot and made off into the town. They hadn't left the dockyard before a shattering explosion at 8 a.m. sank the *Ulpio Traiano*. For reasons they did not understand, none of the limpet mines exploded. They were arrested the following day as they tried to escape from the town, and became prisoners of war.

Operation *Principal* was criticised at the time for its limited results and high casualties. One T-class submarine was lost, as were all the Chariots and six of the seven crews that had been deployed. It seemed poor recompense for the enormous effort undertaken in terms of transporting submarines, which had to be diverted from other offensive operations, and of the sacrifice of the men who had been asked to carry out their operation in the face of enormous and probably unmanageable seas. The primary reason for failure was the atrocious conditions, which dramatically increased the difficulty the men, on their unprotected Chariots, had to face. That two crews even managed to slip into Palermo harbour and attack their targets demonstrated their remarkable degree of professionalism, courage and commitment. Of the fourteen Charioteers (excluding the 'dressers' killed when HMS *P311* was sunk), eight died on Operation *Principal* and four were captured, an unsustainable casualty rate of 86 per cent.

A week after the end of *Principal*, a further call was made on the Malta-based Charioteers: this time to the south, in Axis-held Libya. In early 1943, the Germans and their Italian allies were being pushed back across North Africa following the 8th Army's victory at El Alamein in October the previous year, and the successful Operation *Torch* landings a month later. In their retreat westward, the Germans were preparing to deny the port of Tripoli to the Allies by sinking blockships across the narrow harbour entrance. Vice-Admiral Sir Henry Harwood, Commander-in-Chief Levant, urgently asked the 10th Submarine Flotilla whether they could destroy the blockships before they were placed in position, and as a result Operation *Welcome* was launched. 'There were few suggestions I had ever liked less,' recorded Simpson. 'The approaches to Tripoli were strewn with mines, it was approaching full moon and [anti-submarine] patrols would be a certainty, but the great importance was clear to all.' The enormous losses on Operation *Principal* weighed heavily on everyone's minds. Nevertheless, on 17 January HMS *Thunderbolt* sailed from Malta with two crews. Lieutenant Geoffrey Larkin, RNVR and Petty Officer Conrad Berey on Chariot No. 12, and Chief ERA Stanley Buxton and Sub Lieutenant H. L. H. Stevens on No. 13.

The Chariots were successfully launched about 8 miles off the Libyan coast in beautifully calm weather on the night of 18 January, the RAF helpfully bombing the town to both provide a distraction to the approaching saboteurs and help them identify the location of the harbour entrance. A German E-boat was sighted emerging from the harbour and stopping about two miles away, but the British submarine, which had surfaced ready to disembark the Chariots, managed to launch the two craft – a process that took twenty minutes, after which *Thunderbolt* quietly submerged and the two crews were on their way.

As they came closer to the target and prepared to dive, Larkin and Berey found to their dismay that they could not submerge: their hydroplanes had been damaged, possibly in the act of leaving the submarine. There was now no way that they could enter the harbour securely, or get underneath their target to lay their charges. Frustratingly, the entire mission, for them at least, had been in vain. They had no choice but to scuttle their craft and attempt to escape to meet up with the advancing British 8th Army.

Meanwhile, Sub Lieutenant Stevens and Chief ERA Buxton made their way towards the harbour mole. They had not yet submerged when, only a few hundred yards ahead of them, two large explosions signalled that the Germans had beaten them, sinking two vessels in the entrance. They had arrived too late. Nevertheless, they made their way into the harbour and chose another target, which proved to be another blockship waiting to be dragged and sunk across the entrance the following day. After placing their limpet mines, they managed to make their way to the rocky mole, which, after some initial difficulty, they managed to climb after scuttling their craft and dropping their suits and equipment into the water. Attempting to escape from Tripoli, however, they walked into an Italian Army camp and were taken prisoner. When the Italians surrendered later that year, Stevens and Buxton escaped from their POW camp in Italy in the confusion and made their way to Rome, where they managed to find sanctuary in the Vatican until the Allies entered the Eternal City in June 1944.

Meanwhile, in Libya, Larkin and Berey managed successfully to evade permanent capture, after a series of escapades. Heading west, towards the advancing Allied armies, they avoided German and Italian sentries for five days until one morning their luck ran out: they chose to sleep in a park that also became home to a German motorised unit. Captured, they were well treated, but after several days of indifferent guarding they managed to steal away from their captors. Their greatest difficulty now was finding food, but they were hospitably entertained by an Italian farmer, whose greatest concern was that the advancing troops were not the dreaded Australians. Within a few days, to everyone's satisfaction, the first troops of the 8th Army to arrive turned out to be British. 'What are you two doing here?' Larkin and Berey were asked. 'Waiting for you chaps' came Larkin's laconic reply.

In the post-operational analysis of *Principal* by the Admiralty the loss of *P311* was not considered to demonstrate any fundamental flaw in the Chariot concept. Indeed, the Admiralty believed strongly that, although the tactic might well have been compromised, strong opportunities remained to continue to use this particular approach against enemy ships in their harbours. In the words of Rear Admiral Claud Barry in a secret memorandum to three of the naval commanders-in-chief (Mediterranean, Home Fleet and Levant) on 23 February 1943, enemy 'defence against this weapon has proved difficult, and given suitable targets it is considered that future successes are to be expected'. 'Four chariot operations have so far taken place, one in Home Waters and three in the Mediterranean,' he wrote.

> In three of these the chariots have penetrated the enemy harbours and at Palermo an enemy cruiser was sunk and probable other damage done. It seems that the attack against Maddalena did not materialise as the carrier submarine was probably sunk on passage. In Home Waters the chariots penetrated a particularly difficult enemy base. The chariots have therefore proved their ability to enter enemy defended harbours. The loss of 20 men in these operations was unfortunate, but must always be accepted in operations of this nature.

Twenty-four crews were currently in training. Three Chariots were en route for the Mediterranean to replace those recently lost, and a further twenty-four were in production, ready for use by May 1943. 'This programme is only tentative and is capable of expansion if required,' Barry concluded, inviting the C-in-Cs to consider operations in their own commands that would benefit from this type of attack.

The Charioteers undertook two further sets of activity across the Mediterranean in 1943 and early 1944. The first was to reconnoitre beaches in Sicily in advance of the invasion of the toe of Italy in July 1943, known as Operation *Husky*, and the second proved to be a remarkable joint Anglo-Italian operation against the German-held base at La Spezia, the home port of the Decima Flottiglia. Operation *Torch* – the Allied landings in North Africa, both on the Atlantic and Mediterranean coasts, in November 1943 – demonstrated the importance of understanding the terrain likely to be encountered by landing craft, and any underwater obstacles that might exist. This was a science that reached new levels of sophistication for the Normandy Landings in June 1944 (and in which X-craft played a distinguished role), and which began with the Malta-based Chariots of the 10th Submarine Flotilla in 1943.

Petty Officer Charles Kirby recalled reconnoitring Gela Beach on Sicily – location of the American amphibious assault – from HMS *Unrivalled* in May that year:

> We were lying about a mile off shore. The submarine half submerged to enable the Chariots to float off . . . we did two good runs on Gela Beach . . . On one occasion I went within a few yards of the water's edge and saw some sentries on the beach; this was far enough for me to go inshore so as to see that it was possible for amphibious troops to land. On our return an Italian destroyer was spotted a mile or so away, which was enough to get us under-water as quickly as possible.

Three U-class submarines – *Unrivalled*, *Unseen* and *Unison* – were involved in these beach-reconnaissance missions with a Chariot carried on the casing. On approaching the beach (always at night), the submarine would trim to the point at which the Chariot could simply be driven off. The mother submarine would then sink to the bottom and the Chariot would head in to the beach to conduct the reconnaissance.

The invasion of Sicily in July precipitated the fall of Mussolini and eventually the end of Italian resistance to the Allies. In the months that followed, the last Chariot operation in the Mediterranean was undertaken, and this one had a twist. Since the collapse of Italian resistance, part of the Decima Mas – led by Commander Valerio Borghese – had elected to remain under German command while the remainder decided to throw in their lot with the Allies. The latter, named *Mariassalto* and commanded by Capitano di Fregatta Ernesto Forza, included a number of men, such as Luigi de la Penne, who had been released from British POW camps in Egypt. Forza suggested a joint assault against the German-held port of La Spezia, which it was believed the Germans were preparing to block in the face of the slow but steady Allied advance north. This was agreed, and in April 1944 Operation *QWZ* was authorised. Led by Commander Patrick Heathfield of the Royal Navy, it comprised the Italian destroyer *Grecale*, an Italian motor torpedo boat (MS74), two British Chariots and an Italian assault swimmer ('Gamma') team – under the command of de la Penne – who would enter the harbour in inflatable speedboats they had nicknamed *Tacchina* ('Turkeys'). The Chariot tasked with sinking the 10,000-ton Trento-class heavy cruiser *Bolzano* was crewed by Sub Lieutenant Malcolm Causer and Able Seaman Harry Smith; that tasked with sinking the heavy cruiser *Gorizia* was crewed by Petty Officer Conrad Berey and Stoker Ken Lawrence.

On 21 June, following a journey from Bastia on Corsica, the *Grecale* and MS74 arrived at the dropping position at 5.30 p.m., after which the British crews transferred to MS74 and the two *Tacchina* made their way towards the harbour at speed. A few hundred yards off the mole, close to midnight, the Chariots were launched, by means of an ingenious mechanism that allowed them to slide down rollers on the boat's stern. It was certainly 'the best means of transportation that I have ever come across', considered Berey. At the same time, de la Penne dropped off his frogmen. After making their way carefully into the harbour, busy even in the small hours of the night, evading three anti-torpedo nets and a half-sunken vessel, they came to the dark mass ahead of the *Bolzano*. 'In a few moments,' Causer recalled, 'we came scraping along the underside of the huge hull.'

We switched off the motor, clamped on with the magnets and immediately began to pull ourselves and the Chariot along the ship's hull, moving the magnets one at a time. We continued this progress underneath the ship until I reckoned we were halfway along and, as far as I could assess, under the boiler rooms. Once settled in this position, I proceeded to stick magnets on the ship's bottom without myself getting off the Chariot. The loose ends of the lanyards hanging from the magnets I secured to the torpedo warhead. As soon as several of these were safely made fast I got off my saddle. That was a mistake in the circumstances as I was holding one heavy magnet in my hand. The weight of this was such that I immediately started on my way to the bottom, so quickly let the offending item slip out of my fingers and rose up again on my slightly positive buoyancy. Smith by this time was also off his seat and was up alongside the warhead, making sure it was properly secured. These things could not be too well checked. As it was almost 4.30 a.m. when we decided the charge was well and truly fast, having exchanged the thumbs-up with a fair degree of swagger about the gesture, I turned the handle of the time fuse setting until I felt two distinct clicks. Two clicks two hours, so the balloon should go up as near as dammit at 6.30 a.m. Back to our seats, therefore, a final check of everything, and then I pulled the release gear that freed the warhead from the Chariot.

Their attack was dramatically successful. At 6.30 a.m. two large explosions hurled water high in the air and the cruiser rolled onto her side. The following day, a photo reconnaissance aircraft took shots of the *Bolzano* on its side at its moorings. Unfortunately, Berey's Chariot malfunctioned, and he and Lawrence spent a considerable amount of time simply trying to control their unruly beast. It appeared that there was an air leak in the ballast tank, which made the entire device uncontrollable. Reluctantly, close to the mole that formed the breakwater to La Spezia harbour they were forced to scuttle their vessel and make for the rocks. All four men managed to escape into the arms of the Italian partisans, and the joint Anglo-Italian Chariot operation provided an unlikely end to a story that had begun with the development in La Spezia of the original *Maiali* eight years before.

ELEVEN

HMS *Varbel*

When the first production (Vickers Armstrong) X-craft – numbered *X5* to *X10* – were delivered in early 1943, it was hoped that the work-up period would take no more than two months, to enable an operation against the *Tirpitz* to take place in early March 1943. This would mean that the attack would occur before the arrival of the Arctic summer made a secret approach impossible: some darkness was needed. Commander George Davies, RN, a member of Claud Barry's Northways staff, was responsible for drawing together the detailed planning. But a March operation proved entirely unrealistic.

The six craft prepared intensively in secret with their crews in the protected waters off Port Bannatyne and the old hunting lodge at the head of Loch Striven from the moment they arrived. Not only was the X-craft itself a new form of underwater weapon, but its crews likewise were new to the vessels, many even new to submarines. Every aspect of operating these craft, transporting them to the target area and undertaking an attack needed to be repeatedly practised. As with all first-generation vessels, they experienced teething problems that took time to resolve. Likewise, the means of getting them to the target area involved considerable planning, and debate. One option was to hoist all six aboard a mother ship, like the support vessel HMS *Bonaventure*,* and travel most of the way to Norway as passengers, but of course *Bonaventure* would stand out like a sore thumb off the intensively patrolled enemy coast, and wouldn't stand a chance of getting through the German defensive screen. Another option was for each of them to be lifted onto a smaller vessel and transported the same way, although the minimum size of each individual mother ship would need to be significant, as they would have to be able to lift a 30-ton craft from the water and place it on her deck, or in her hold. Six such mother ships (for the attack was always intended to include all the available X-craft available) would also be easy to spot by the watching Germans.

The solution arrived at was to tow each X-craft to a point off the north Norwegian coast by conventional T and S Class submarine. This decision, made in February 1943, was not universally appreciated by the Submarine Service, some of whom regarded this duty to be a diversion from the important task of patrolling, but a consideration of the threat posed by the *Tirpitz* usually brought detractors around.

Each of the six X-craft had satisfactorily completed its initial seaworthiness trials by April, although a number of modifications were made to each of the six craft in a dry dock brought to Port Bannatyne for the purpose. However, it quickly became clear that the full training of the crews – in respect of the mechanics of long-distance towing, approaching an enemy ship in harbour, cutting through the anti-submarine nets and placing their two amatol charges precisely underneath the hull of the enemy vessel – would be far from complete by early March, and that an operation against the *Tirpitz* would need to be moved to the early autumn, before the bad Arctic weather set in. Rear Admiral Claud Barry accordingly postponed the operation until September.

---

* HMS *Bonaventure*, known either as *Bono* or B/V, had been commissioned into the Royal Navy from the Clan Line, who had built her to handle heavy lifts. She could lift four X-craft onto her foredeck, two onto her afterdeck, and two into her afterhold. She had specialists in all trades, a well-equipped workshop, and accommodation for crews of six X-craft.

The additional time needed to prepare fully for the considerable task of crossing a thousand miles of the North and Arctic Seas to launch a terminal blow against the *Tirpitz* in six tiny steel coffins required every minute of the remaining months available. More time was required, for instance, to master the intricacies of penetrating an anti-submarine net. This was far from easy when first attempted, and one life was lost in early trials. Sub Lieutenant David Locke, who had first been shown around *X3* by Donald Cameron, fell victim to Oxygen Pete on 31 May 1942 when trying to cut through a practice net. Accordingly, the Australians Max Shean and Henry 'Tiger' Henty-Creer were charged with experimenting with all of the options until a quick, easy and safe procedure could be found. The plan they came up with was to gently manoeuvre the bow of the boat into one of the diamond-shaped spaces of the net, at a depth no greater than 30 feet, to prevent the diver suffering from oxygen poisoning. Keeping the motor running at 'slow speed ahead' would keep the X-craft in position while the diver exited the W&D compartment and, with the newly developed compressed-air cutter, cut a diamond shape out of the net some 9 feet wide and 9 feet deep. The vessel's commander, who would be watching through the short 'night' periscope, would then gently increase speed to push the X-craft through the newly made hole, at which point the diver would rejoin through the W&D compartment. Repeated practice demonstrated that the process worked perfectly. On their first attempt, Shean managed to exit the vessel, cut through the net and re-enter the W&D compartment after *X5* had slid through the hole, in twelve minutes.

Towing the X-craft to the area of release prior to the attack likewise required extensive practice. When first carried out, this revealed a series of unexpected handling characteristics: it was incredibly hard to maintain the X-craft on an even keel and at a steady depth when being towed. The crews had not anticipated just how difficult, and potentially dangerous, the process was. Max Shean was commanding officer for the passage crew for Donald

Cameron's *X6*, on towing practice behind the T-class submarine HMS *Tuna*. Because there were too few of the new nylon ropes, designed to tow gliders, available, most of the X-craft were to be towed to Norway on ropes made of manila. Unfortunately, they had a habit of snapping after four or five days' constant use. The problem was that the ropes were placed under constant strain, one moment slack and the next as taut as a piano wire. If the tow broke while the vessel was in the downward leg of an oscillation, it could mean disaster for the X-craft – especially if the craft was trimmed so that it travelled slightly bow down, by means of flooding the forward ballast tanks – as it would follow the same slant down. Unless rapid and decisive action was taken, the X-craft could quickly breach its 300-foot depth limit, which in deep water would inevitably mean the destruction of the vessel if it went much lower.

It proved very hard to learn how to manage the oscillations in an X-craft being towed, as Shean describes:

The manila tow rope was about two inches thick, six hundred feet long, and had a telephone wire which usually broke, laid up within each strand. We also had a radio transceiver, and if these forms of communication failed, Submarine Underwater Explosive signals (Suzies) would be used, one to attract attention, two to dive, and three to surface . . .

Instructions were passed to us to dive and to surface each hour if the telephone failed, and to report by radio. Down we went, and up went the speed. This was easy to tell by the attendant noises. There was always something to rattle outside the hull. The hydroplane operator was having difficulty keeping a uniform depth of fifty feet. Presently she broke surface, took a bow down angle, and plummeted down, twenty feet, thirty, forty, fifty. Hydroplanes were, by this time, set amidships. Sixty, seventy, eighty, ninety, one hundred feet. There she steadied for a second while her bow came up. Ninety feet, eighty, and so on while the planes were reset to dive to try to slow her rate of rise. Regardless of this, she splashed through the surface again, and porpoised once more for the depths at a steep angle . . .

We had reached one hundred and twenty feet by this time. I ordered the operator to let me have a try and put the planes to dive, holding her at that depth. Slowly I reduced the angle on the planes. Her bow started to rise, pulled up by the tow rope. Very gradually, by anticipating her movements, these were brought under control, but it was an uneasy state of equilibrium, just on the balance. At fifty feet, she needed bow down angle to keep down at that depth. Some water was pumped into the compensating tank, and some from aft to forward. Eventually, she sat level at fifty feet, with planes amidships. So far, so good, but if the tow should part, we would no longer be pulled upwards, and with extra trim weight, and some of that forward, she would go deep.

This was explained to the crew. 'If the noise suddenly stops, immediately pump out, pump aft, put planes to rise, and run the motor half speed ahead. If that does not restore control, shut main vents, and blow.' The tow rope, being six hundred feet long, and our designed depth three hundred feet, even if the tow did not break it would be possible to reach a dangerous depth.

By the time he had handed over to Cameron and Lorimer they had travelled a very uncomfortable 250 miles. It was the closest he had come to exhaustion so far in his naval career. What on earth would a 1,200-mile* tow – to Norway – be like?

There were many accidents on X-craft during this work-up period. Charlie Reed recalled one occasion:

In my training period in X-craft, I remember we had just completed our net cutting run and skipper Lieutenant Ernie Page suggested lying on the bottom in Loch Striven and having a quiet cup of tea

---

* This was an average distance. The total distance travelled was between 1,000 and 1,500 miles.

142

before surfacing. We did this but on trying to surface the rudder guard hooked into an old net. Next thing we knew the boat literally stood on end. Everything loose fell aft. We tried all sorts to break free to no avail and settled on the bottom again thinking of abandoning ship when suddenly for no apparent reason the boat freed herself. Quite a heart-stopping time was had by us all.

But a few incidents had tragic consequences. A month following the accidental sinking of *X3* with Lorimer, Gay and Laites on board, *X4* was at sea off the Isle of Bute when Sub Lieutenant Morgan Thomas was swept out of the W&D compartment. His body was never found.

Collisions were rare, but had serious consequences. An X-craft being readied for service in the Far East, the vessels for which had the designation 'XE' – this one was *XE11* – was launched at Faslane on 19 February 1945. The commanding officer was the 24-year-old Lieutenant Aubrey 'Eustace' Staples, a Rhodesian serving in the South African Naval Forces, together with Sub Lieutenant Bill Morrison, Diver Midshipman Gordon Newman and ERA J. Robson. Morrison explained what happened:

At approximately 11.20 a.m. while coming up to 10 feet, there was a considerable bump up forward in the battery compartment indicating that we had collided with or hit something. The craft heeled over quite an angle before righting itself. The CO asked me to open the battery compartment hatch to ascertain any damage. As I was reporting no apparent damage, there developed a fairly loud grating noise which appeared to be running on our hull from fore to aft. Suddenly the noise of a ship's engine and propeller was obvious and almost simultaneously a major collision rent a huge gash on our pressure hull, causing a cascade of seawater about 6 inches broad shooting into our control room just aft of the main periscope on the port side behind the main control position.

The CO immediately ordered 'Full Ahead, Group Up, Hydrophones, Hard to Rise', and ordered me to open up the hatch, as we would all scramble out on breaking surface. I pulled the hatch clips to the open position but could not open the hatch against the sea pressure, and suffered great pain in my neck and shoulders trying to push open the hatch with my head with every ounce of strength I could muster. By this time the craft was flooding furiously and developed an extreme stern-down angle. All lighting and power had gone and I realised I was standing not on the deck of the W/D compartment, but on the bulkhead which sectioned off the W/D compartment from the control room, with my head in a pocket of air which was trapped in a corner of the W&D compartment with most of the area of the escape hatch.

I was aware that Swatton (the ERA replacing Robson, who had been given the day off) was halfway in the W&D escape chamber with me, where he had been ordered by the CO to be ready to scramble out while helping me to open the hatch. As I was having my last thoughts of the life and times of Bill Morrison, the craft suddenly hit bottom, rolled on to an even keel, and the air pocket spread evenly over the top of the W/D escape chamber. As I had left the clips of the hatch in the open position, the pressure of the trapped air blew open the hatch, shooting the trapped air bubble to the surface with myself and Swatton who had managed to squeeze himself wholly into the small chamber with me.

Alas, we both got jammed in the hatchway with the upward thrust of the air bubble. I managed to retract myself into the chamber, at the same time giving him a good push out of the compartment up towards the surface. My lungs were still full of air as compressed at 200 feet and I stretched my arms into the control room to feel if I could locate anyone else, but to no avail. I immediately pushed myself out of the hatch and propelled myself to the surface. I was unconscious before surfacing, and the next thing I remember was lying on my back on the deck of the ship we

A Mark 1 Chariot in a training run on Loch Striven: the Chariot was the British Navy's version of the first 'human torpedo', the Italian *Maiale*. In the Mark 2 version the diver (in the rear seat) faced backwards. © *Imperial War Museum*

An X-craft exercising on Loch Striven in Scotland. Lieutenant Jack Smart, who was to command an XE-craft in combat in the Far East, is standing on the deck. These four-man midget submarines weighed 30 tons, and carried two huge explosive charges – weighing two tons each – one attached to each side of the hull. Two operational models were produced, initially with the intention of taking on the Tirpitz: they subsequently found several other uses in Europe and the Far East. © *Imperial War Museum*

A photograph of a British 'frogman' in 1945 (the name was invented by the press in 1943) wearing the latest version of the 'Sladen Suit' and a rebreather set, which was based on the original design invented by Robert Davies as a device for assisting in an escape from a stricken submarine. All Charioteers and X-craft divers wore variations of this suit. © *Imperial War Museum*

The *Tirpitz* hidden in a Norwegian fjord. Three X-craft successfully attacked this huge battleship in September 1943, it having luckily survived an attempted attack by Chariots the previous year. The *Tirpitz* was at this stage of the war the German fleet's most powerful ship, and although she saw little action, her mere presence tied down significant British resources and was a constant worry to Winston Churchill, who called her 'the Beast'. In the photograph below she lies in the remote Kåfjord in the far north of Norway, where the Germans believed she was immune from attack by the Royal Navy. They were mistaken. *Bridgeman (above), Corbis (below)*

A proud Sub-Lieutenant John Britnell triumphantly raises the skull and cross-bones on X24 after its daring attack on Bergen harbour in September 1944. Unfortunately the wind wasn't strong enough to help show off the flag to its best effect, the sign of a merchant vessel on the flag denoting a successful attack. © *Trustees of the Royal Navy Submarine Museum*

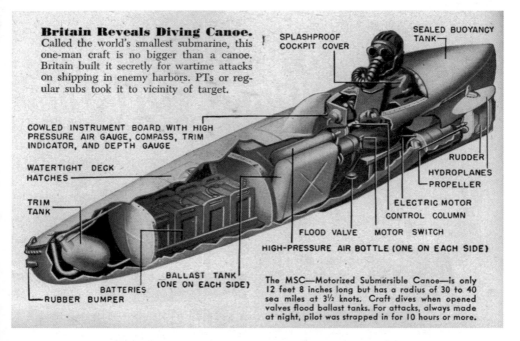

Britain Reveals Diving Canoe.
Called the world's smallest submarine, this one-man craft is no bigger than a canoe. Britain built it secretly for wartime attacks on shipping in enemy harbors. PTs or regular subs took it to vicinity of target.

SPLASHPROOF COCKPIT COVER

SEALED BUOYANCY TANK

COWLED INSTRUMENT BOARD WITH HIGH PRESSURE AIR GAUGE, COMPASS, TRIM INDICATOR, AND DEPTH GAUGE

WATERTIGHT DECK HATCHES

TRIM TANK

RUDDER

HYDROPLANES

PROPELLER

ELECTRIC MOTOR

CONTROL COLUMN

FLOOD VALVE   MOTOR SWITCH

HIGH-PRESSURE AIR BOTTLE (ONE ON EACH SIDE)

BALLAST TANK (ONE ON EACH SIDE)

BATTERIES

RUBBER BUMPER

The MSC—Motorized Submersible Canoe—is only 12 feet 8 inches long but has a radius of 30 to 40 sea miles at 3½ knots. Craft dives when opened valves flood ballast tanks. For attacks, always made at night, pilot was strapped in for 10 hours or more.

The Motorized Submersible Canoe (MSC) or 'Sleeping Beauty', as depicted in *Popular Mechanics* magazine in 1947 – although this smallest of mini-submarines ultimately saw limited use.

The Passage and Attack crews of X7 just before setting out on Operation Source in September 1943. Back row, left to right: Sub-Lieutenant Bob Aitken, Lieutenant Godfrey Place, Sub-Lieutenant Bill Whittam, Lieutenant Peter Philip. Front row, left to right: Leading Seaman Mick Magennis, Stoker John Luck, ERA W.M. Whitley. © *Imperial War Museum*

The Passage and Attack crews of X6 just before setting out to attack the *Tirpitz* in September 1943. Back row, left to right: Lieutenant A. Wilson, Lieutenant Donald Cameron, Sub-Lieutenant John Lorimer. Front row, left to right: Sub-Lieutenant Dicky Kendall, ERA Edmund Goddard, Leading Seaman L.S. McGregor; Stoker Oxley. © *Imperial War Museum*

Mick Magennis and Ian Fraser, both of whom received the Victoria Cross for their role in the attack on the Japanese cruiser *Takao* in Singapore Harbour in 1945. © *Imperial War Museum*

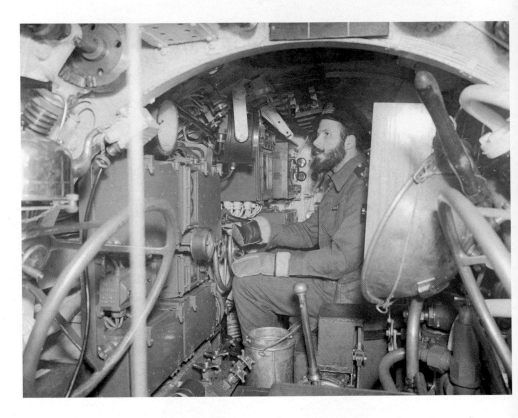

Sub-Lt K.C.J. Robinson at the controls of an X-craft, showing how cramped conditions aboard the vessels could be. © *Imperial War Museum*

had collided with, being given artificial respiration, around about noon.

Later it transpired what had happened since 11.15 a.m. was that in the course of our calibration exercises, taking approximately three hours, the tide had carried us while in static trim out of our exercise area into another area where the boom defence vessel *Norina* had been laying a buoy while lying stationary. Her task was completed at precisely the same time as we decided to come up to 10 feet to do our last calibration. This gave our first impact, and then the grating noise was the tide carrying us along her keel. Her ripping our pressure hull gave an awareness of some mishap and she stood by the area as a precaution.

Very shortly, ERA Swatton broke surface and swam around fully conscious, wondering what had happened to his 'Jimmy', who he assumed had escaped with him. His assumption was correct, as a few minutes later I broke surface lying on my back unconscious, about ten feet from him. He swam to me and as he was holding me I apparently spouted like a whale, convincing him that there was some life left in me – he held on to me! All of this was witnessed by the vessel with which we collided, and she lowered a boat which picked us up to rush us to Port Bannatyne.

The craft was located and recovered a few days later by helmet divers operating from the vessel we had collided with. The craft was in an area marked on charts as varying between 30 and 35 fathoms. The divers that took part in the salvage confirmed their depth indicators showed the depth between 210 and 215 feet.

When the three bodies were recovered they each had a DSEA set around their necks and bodies, but they were not connected or switched on, as they were either killed by being drowned or overcome by pressure before being able to switch on the oxygen supply.

During the work-up training the X-craft and their crews now regularly travelled to, and operated from, Loch Cairnbawn, which had become the forward operating base for HMS *Bonaventure*, HMS *Titania* and Chariot operations. Repeated towing, approach and anti-submarine net operations were the order of the day for both operational (i.e. attack) and passage crews. Given that there were effectively two crews for every X-craft, the vessels were used intensively, although time was also required for servicing, repairs and modifications.

One area of additional preparation recalled by Max Shean was the need for crews to be aware of, and avoid, unwanted attention from the air. During one exercise, in which six Swordfish of the Fleet Air Arm searched for all six operational X-craft in the area of the Minches, south-west of HHZ, Shean managed to bag himself a seat in one of the aircraft. Acting as observer for his pilot, flying from Stornoway on the Isle of Harris, he was shocked to see just how vulnerable the X-craft were to eagle-eyed pilots who knew what they were looking for:

We flew at two thousand feet, and at eighty knots. If we were higher, the craft would appear too small to be seen, especially in the choppy waters, and, if too low, the field of cover would be reduced. After being in the air for half an hour, I saw a tiny white arrowhead, with another one immediately behind it, pointing south. I slapped the fuselage with my hand, as the pilot had done earlier, to attract attention. He looked at me and I pointed to the white arrows. He nodded, and next moment the Swordfish's tail went up, and all I could see was sky. At the bottom of his nearly vertical dive, the pilot pulled up again and there, almost within handshaking distance, was a skipper scrambling down the hatch of an X-craft. As we climbed back to our patrol altitude, I watched the craft as she slowly submerged. If she were our enemy, we should have made a kill.

X-craft took about sixty seconds to submerge from full buoyancy and, in such a sea, it would not be safe to proceed at reduced buoyancy. It took less than a minute for the Swordfish to dive from two thousand feet, so it was imperative for an X-craft to keep a good lookout for enemy aircraft at all times. The noise of his own diesel probably prevented the skipper from hearing us coming. We spotted one more craft before our endurance limit was reached, and we returned to Stornoway.

As the days began to get shorter, the final preparations were made. The window available to Northways for launching an operation against the *Tirpitz* (and the accompanying battleship *Scharnhorst*) – now called Operation *Source* – was dictated by the end of the summer period with its long days, and the onset of autumn and the potential for rough weather. The period between 20 and 25 September had been agreed, as it promised a good balance of darkness and moonlight to help the craft navigate their way unseen into the fjord system. Planning now focused on preparing the X-craft, towing submarines and crews ready for the departure from HHZ. A 'slipping' date (D-Day) of 20 September was eventually determined, dependent on the actual time it took to travel to Söröy Island, off the Kåfjord where the *Tirpitz* lay hidden. Along with their support ship, HMS *Titania*, the towing submarines – *Thrasher*, *Truculent*, *Syrtis*, *Sea Nymph*, *Stubborn* and *Sceptre* – duly crept into HHZ at two-hourly intervals on 6 September. Two 'spare' vessels, HMSs *Satyr* and *Seadog*, would be positioned at Scapa Flow in case they were required. The men were desperate for action, after such a long period of preparation. Ginger Coles remembered how:

As the date for the operation came closer, things became quite exciting. The adrenalin started flowing; everybody was keen to go. The boats were ready, the crews were ready and it was quite something to get together and talk about the same things ... all the crews were at the same peak. Everybody was excited.

We were given a survival pack, which included money and maps, compasses, and little packs of hacksaw blades and files, which had to be hid in different parts of the body in case we got ashore. We also were taught a secret code to use if we were taken prisoner so we could send messages back to this country in the POW mail, although we were strictly ordered not to use Red Cross mail for this purpose. Whether anyone used it or not, I don't know. We were also taught methods of breaking out of prison camps by Commander Newton, Royal Navy, who'd already escaped from a prison camp in Italy.

The men had known that the operation was imminent when, from 1 September, HHZ was locked down. Letters could be written, but not sent. Secrecy had always been a hallmark of Chariot and X-craft training. 'While we were training we couldn't tell any of our friends or family what we were doing or where we were doing it,' recalled Bob Aitken. 'So we just had to talk about walking, sailing or other recreational activities, without mentioning which part of the country or the world we were in.' But now the screw was tightened. All leave was cancelled. Visits in and out of HHZ were strictly controlled. The men were encouraged to prepare their wills, leaving them with their personal documentation in the hands of the paymaster.

On 5 September, each of the X-craft was winched onto HMS *Bonaventure* to receive their explosive side charges, and that night the six X-craft captains received the first intimation of their target. The pre-war adventurer Lieutenant Commander Patrick Dalzel-Job – now an intelligence officer and commando, the original inspiration for Ian Fleming's James Bond – was responsible for providing the intelligence briefing before the attack. He had sailed his schooner in the waters of the Altafjord in 1938 and 1939, and knew it well. Looking at these men, about to embark on a mission of paramount import to the naval security of the British Isles, entombed in tiny steel coffins that might indeed become their graves, Dalzel-Job was overcome with emotion. 'I think it fair to say that there has very seldom been gathered together in one place so splendid a group of courageous and dedicated young men, as were then on board HMS *Bonaventure* and HMS *Titania* in Loch Cairnbawn . . . They had come from all over the British Isles and British Commonwealth – especially from Australia and South Africa . . .'

The men had, of course, guessed long before that the *Tirpitz* was the primary object of their preparations, but none spoke of it. Wartime secrecy was such that even loose talk about what they were doing might prejudice the entire operation, and cost countless lives. To a man, and a woman, the crews working on the X-craft kept their mouths shut. Newlywed Eve Cameron could only surmise what her husband was up to – he never told her. The importance of success was clear to all. John Lorimer mused that if they were successful 'the British Home fleet could give its [full] protection to the U-boat haunted Atlantic convoys and the lives of thousands of merchant seamen might be saved'. Norwegian resistance workers audaciously made close-up notes and drawings of the *Tirpitz* in her lair, by pretending to be fishermen. The crews were briefed on what to do if captured, how to deal with life as a prisoner of war, and issued with escape equipment – including compasses and silk maps – to enable them to make their way, independently or in groups, to Sweden, as well as contact information for Norwegian resistance workers, which they had to memorise. Suddenly everything, Shean considered, was getting serious.

TWELVE

The 1,200-Mile Tow

Worryingly, the first Spitfire reconnaissance undertaken from the Soviet Vaenga airfield, near Murmansk on 7 September – flown by Flight Lieutenant Donald Furniss – showed that the *Tirpitz* was no longer in the Altafjord,* although when the flights were retaken on 10 September she was back in her berth. The heavy cruiser *Lützow* was confirmed in Langefjord after another flight four days later. The photographs were flown from Russia by RAF Catalina seaplane. The *Kriegsmarine*'s Norwegian Squadron had in fact been at sea in an operation to bombard Spitsbergen. As it transpired it was the first and only time *Tirpitz*'s guns would be used for this purpose.

Back at HHZ the final preparations were being undertaken, with the X-craft crews – both for passage and attack – getting to know their towing submarines. Max Shean was at this stage a supernumerary, and could only look on with frustration as his colleagues prepared for war, while he would be left behind. After all this time in training, it was difficult to watch one's friends prepare to depart on such a significant operation, even though all expected it to be hazardous. Crew selection had been confirmed in July, and Shean had been irritated to find that the noisy exhibitionist and fellow Australian Henry 'Tiger' (so called because of his vivid red hair) Henty-Creer had been appointed over him to take

* During the war the British referred to the Altafjord as 'Alten Fjord'. All references in this book have been changed to Altafjord.

command of *X5*, replacing Willie Meek, who had returned to conventional submarines. All other commands remained the same. Donald Cameron continued in charge of *X6*, the newly married Godfrey Place *X7*, while the two Australians – Lieutenant Brian 'Digger' McFarlane (RAN) and Lieutenant Ken Hudspeth (RANVR) – commanded *X8* and *X10* respectively. The historian Léonce Peillard described Hudspeth as 'a young schoolmaster from Tasmania . . . a modest, intelligent, responsible man'.

Dalzel-Job observed that the three commanding officers allocated for the attack on the *Tirpitz* 'made an interesting contrast: Don Cameron, RNR, tall, steady, and quietly humorous; Godfrey Place, RN, dark and rather pale-faced, with a lively and slightly sardonic sense of fun; and Henry Henty-Creer, RNVR, slim, with reddish hair, and looking little more than a boy'. He was impressed with Henty-Creer's studious preparation for the mission, something that belied his exuberant, devil-may-care exterior:

It seemed to me that Henty-Creer was in some ways rather different from the other X-craft officers. Even among the arduous and often dirty work of final training, he was always neat and tidy in appearance; and he was equally careful in studying the Intelligence material, photographs and charts which I had assembled for briefing the midget submarine officers. Henty-Creer would spend any spare time he had in the last few days – and there was little enough of it – in checking and re-checking the information we had, and in discussing such details as the appearance of inlets and islands from different directions, the positions of German defences, and the places where X-craft could lie on the bottom in the fjords if need arose. Just before leaving HMS *Bonaventure*, he asked rather diffidently if he could have the original chart and coast photographs, which I had annotated in colour for the briefing. I told him that I would be delighted for him to take them – I knew he would put them to the best possible use and no one else would need them when the submarines had gone.

Command of *X9* remained with Terry Martin. Three of the six X-craft commands for the attack on the *Tirpitz*, therefore, were given to Australian officers. Then, on 10 September, the evening before the operation was to begin, the diver in the attack crew of *X9* pulled out, as did another crew member. It had always been a feature of X-craft training that only volunteers would be taken on live operations, and there was no hard feeling if a crewman decided to withdraw, for any reason. Shean and Ginger Coles were therefore appointed to fill the empty places, Shean as diver and Coles as ERA. They were both delighted, and took their place in the attack crew on board HMS *Syrtis* commanded by Lieutenant Martin Jupp, RN, along with Lieutenant Terry Martin and the first lieutenant, Sub Lieutenant Joe Brooks*. For the passage, three crewmen were responsible for *X9*, under the command of Sub Lieutenant Paddy Kearon. Ginger Coles was not impressed, however, to see that *X9* had a manila rope. 'We were envious of the other boats with nylon tow ropes.'

> You can imagine the surprise when there were only three nylon tow ropes available for the final operation; they went to *X5*, *X6* and *X10*, commanded by Navy captains. We knew very well that we didn't have a tow rope which would last any more than five days but we were told not to worry because the towing submarine had a spare cable. It's all very well to change a tow rope when you're on a canoe lake at Portsmouth, but when you're out in the middle of the North Sea getting close to the Arctic Circle it's quite a problem – you've only got 18 inches free board above the water line.

On the morning of Saturday 11 September, each of the towing submarines was in HHZ completing its victualling on either side

---

* Martin Jupp was killed on 28 March 1944 when the *Syrtis* was lost in the Bodo area of northern Norway, probably to an enemy sea mine.

of HMS *Alecto*, the submarine support vessel: three to each side. Winter had come early in the Highlands, and snowcapped peaks looked down on the preparations, although the weather remained calm and the day clear. The six X-craft sat alongside their own 'mother hen', HMS *Bonaventure*. Apart from the last-minute bustle that characterises the start of all operations, the men were calmly confident as they prepared for the hook-ups between each of the towing submarines and their X-craft: they had rehearsed this endlessly the previous week. The first two pairs to leave – HMS *Truculent* towing *X6* and HMS *Syrtis* towing *X9* – were to depart at 4 p.m.

Admiral Sir Claud Barry had flown up to Loch Cairnbawn the previous night to say farewell to his X-men. The experiment begun by his predecessor Max Horton was about to bear fruit. By Shean's account it was a helpful visit, inspiring the men 'with his enthusiastic support'. Barry recalled afterwards that 'any doubts I might have entertained about its outcome could not possibly have survived the infectious confidence of these young men who were just leaving us. They were like boys on the last day of school, their spirits ran so high'. Barry had dined with the twelve X-craft commanders on Tiny Fell's HMS *Titania* the previous night. Cameron wrote an account of the evening to his wife: 'Excellent dinner, sitting on Claud's left between him and Willie Banks. Usual shop. Very optimistic, perhaps a trifle over-optimistic.' Coles, who often recorded the different treatment of officers and men, recalled that there was no such send-off for the men of the crews: instead, they enjoyed a barrel of beer in 'a little cowshed on the beach'.

The plan was for each pair of submarines to travel independently to Norway from a starting point to the west of the Shetland Islands, with every boat following a carefully choreographed course. Each pair – towing submarine and X-craft – would leave the Shetlands at two-hour intervals, and run on parallel tracks some 10 miles apart until they converged at a point off Söröy

Island.* There the X-craft would be slipped from their tows, and make their way directly to the target area. For most of the 1,200-mile journey, the towing submarine would be submerged during the day and would run surfaced – with the X-craft submerged at a depth of about 20 feet – at night, but for the final 200-mile stretch (about two days' travel time) it would also dive during the day, to reduce the chance of detection by German combat air patrols. At a point 150 miles off Altafjord, each pair would then switch course for Söröy Island. Once there, the X-craft would slip from their towing submarines – this was D-Day, planned for 20 September – and travel at night on the surface across the minefield. Once clear of this, and at dawn, they would dive, making their way independently via Stjernsund to Altafjord, where they would wait on the bottom for H-Hour. Every effort was made to try to conduct a coordinated attack on the *Tirpitz* – always the primary target – between 8 a.m. and 9 a.m. on 22 September. In the meantime, each of the six towing submarines would remain on patrol until 27 September, when they would rendezvous with the returning X-craft following the successful attack.

On a bright, sunny afternoon, the first two pairs connected their 600-foot-long tow ropes and began to make their way out of Loch Cairnbawn. The calm of the sea and the blue of the sky made Shean compare the scene to a regatta. At 6 p.m., HMS *Thrasher* and *X5*, together with HMS *Sea Nymph* and *X8*, and HMS *Stubborn* with *X7*, made their way successively out of the port. HMS *Sceptre*, towing *X10*, departed the following morning. When HMS *Truculent* left with *X6* that afternoon Cameron watched *Bonaventure* salute them as they passed. Rather pensively he wrote to Eve: 'I look at the familiar hills and islands and wonder when I shall see them again.' Cameron had managed to get one of the few nylon ropes for the tow. The two other nylon ropes were deployed to HMS *Thrasher* (*X5*) and HMS *Sceptre* (*X10*). *X7*, *X8* and *X9* all

---

* Some of the official reports suggest that the separation distance was 20 miles.

had to put up with manila ropes which were so heavy that balsa floats were attached to them to reduce their tendency to sink.

The first four days of the 1,200-mile journey went largely as planned. The routine was that during the day each X-craft would remain submerged, rising to vent the vessel with fresh air briefly (about 15 minutes was sufficient) at the set times of 6 a.m., 12 noon and 6 p.m. each day. This was known as 'guffing'. After dark, the X-craft would also surface for a period of an hour or two to recharge their batteries. It was only once the six pairs of submarines were under way that Claud Barry made the final target selection, based on the results of the Spitfires' aerial reconnaissance on 10 September – showing the *Lützow* in the Langefjord, the *Scharnhorst* in the first part of the Kåfjord, and the *Tirpitz*, behind its twin layers of anti-submarine netting, in the far end of the Kåfjord – and passed on their orders to the respective submarines three days after they had left HHZ. A range of options had been prepared in advance, depending on the exact location of the various ships within the *Kriegsmarine*'s Norwegian Squadron. No. 4 Plan was adopted, which entailed three simultaneous attacks:

Attack 1: *X5*, *X6* and *X7* were to attack the *Tirpitz* in the far end of Kåfjord

Attack 2: *X9* and *X10* would attack the *Scharnhorst*, in the entrance to Kåfjord

Attack 3: *X8* was to attack the *Lützow* in Langefjord, a tributary of Altafjord.

'We were all in top spirits when the target direction was received,' recalled Cameron. 'It was high time to get cracking.' Towing worked reasonably well when both craft were submerged. However, with the towing submarine surfaced, in rough weather, life on the X-craft was turbulent, uncomfortable and dangerous. In these conditions the X-craft would find itself in a jerking flurry – reflecting the variations in the towing submarine's speed, as it surged through heavy water – with the tiny vessel pulled first one way and then the other, corkscrewing at the same time. What with the unpredictable movement, the men inside were constantly battling seasickness, and the endless drip of condensation threatened repeated short-circuits of the electrical equipment. Despite their agonising discomfort they had to be constantly on the alert, watching the Clynometer* and depth gauge at all times to ensure that any sudden drop in depth could be immediately countered.

Even experienced crews struggled with the harsh conditions. The South African Peter Philip – described by the historian Léonce Peillard as 'short and sturdy, with a beaky nose . . . [who] stood out as a man of great enthusiasm, stamina and precision' – succumbed like many others. He was the passage captain on *X7*. His logbook records that when they surfaced at 10 p.m. on Sunday 12 September he was 'very sick, very sick indeed, and ought to be bloody well ashamed of himself . . . 10.05 p.m. – C.O. clearing up his own mess in apology'. His log records the extreme difficulty experienced during the passage by crews who had to operate in claustrophobic, darkened conditions while being bounced to and fro by the swell which 'at thirty feet [was] sufficient to knock cups off shelves'. The ERA on *X7* was West Belfast-born Leading Seaman Mick Magennis:

From the start we ran into trouble. We were zooming up and down first breaking the surface, then plunging dangerously . . . Mac Phillips [*sic*], our South African Captain, flooded in more ballast. The weight gave us greater stability. We were kept up by the pull of the tow . . . But when the tow broke we had a terrific scare. I was operating the planes, stoker John Luck was sat at the steering and periscope controls, Lieutenant Phillips was dozing on our one bunk above the batteries. We took it in turns to change round. Lieutenant Phillips ordered to blow all tanks. The depth

---

* Sometimes called the 'inclinometer', this was a spirit level that showed the angle of the boat.

gauge still rose 110 feet, 120 feet, 130 feet. I was in a cold sweat as it approached 150 feet and slowly we started to surface. The third time we broke the line we dived well below the limit of 160 feet. It was a hair-raising, horrifying experience. At an angle of sixty degrees with the tail down, there is nothing worse than a sub that goes into a back slide. I was standing alongside the periscope to work the blows. John Luck dropped back into the engine room. He had to fall into it because of the crazy angle we had taken up. The engine clutch was jamming. We could get no drive from the propellers. John was working on the clutch itself. The propellers started to turn and slowly we surfaced. Lieutenant Phillips had to get on deck to fix the new tow. Rough seas made it dangerous to open the hatch. On the tiny lurching deck he had only the upright induction tube to cling to. He was out there for a whole perishing hour. Another damper was a collision with the tow submarine. It was yawing frighteningly. One crash and it would have sent the midget to the bottom. So it went on for eight weary days.

At 11 a.m. on 15 September Philip recorded the conditions as:

worse than I have ever known them, even on the surface. We are rolling as well as pitching, and every few minutes our bows are hauled over to port with a corkscrew motion. We heel over, and rise, then go down in a power dive. Perfectly bloody. I expect the tow to part at any moment. Also I have a vague suspicion that one, if not both of our side charges have gone, or are at least flooded. Heigh-ho. P.S. The telephone appears to have packed up, too.

Philip's fear about the ability of the manila tow ropes to withstand this type of stress was well founded. The strain of these conditions made breakages inevitable, and on the fifth day of the tow the first two breaks occurred. Both *X7* and *X8* suffered broken tows, and although *X7*'s was rapidly identified by both crews, and reattached, the plight for *X8* was much more serious. HMS *Sea Nymph* realised that she had entirely lost contact with her X-craft at 6 a.m. on Wednesday 15 September, and it was only by retracing her course that the two vessels were reunited, after thirty-six hours. Tragically, the fact that the tow between HMS *Syrtis* and *X9* had broken was not spotted until the towing submarine stopped to allow *X9* to vent at 9 a.m. on Thursday 16 September, 240 miles from the slipping position. The last contact with *X9* had been earlier that morning, after diving following battery recharging at 1.20 a.m. – seven hours and forty minutes before. The X-craft could be wandering anywhere across a vast expanse of sea.

Jupp immediately ordered the rope to be hauled aboard, as a precursor to turning the submarine around and retracing its course. At this stage there was no suggestion that *X9* would not be found: her crew would even now be searching for *Syrtis*. The freezing temperatures in these sub-Arctic waters made recovering the rope a difficult job, and just as the final length was being hauled in it caught fast, held somewhere under the submarine, probably under the port propeller. A diver was required to recover it. The *X9* attack crew diver was Max Shean, who takes up the story:

My diving suits were aboard *X9*. All that *Syrtis* had were the standard DSEA escape sets which provided breathing only; no protection from the cold water, neither had they any weights to compensate for their positive buoyancy.

I dressed in a pair of overalls and the DSEA set with some steel weights from the engine room, and went aft along the casing, where a rope had been rigged for support. Lieutenant Jupp urged me to be quick. If we were surprised by enemy aircraft he would have to dive immediately. I climbed, with a lifeline attached, onto the after hydroplanes, switched to oxygen, and launched myself into the North Atlantic Ocean. It was cold. When my face went under, it took my breath away. I was floating. The weights were not only too light, but loose as well. They were long pieces of metal which swung about with my every movement. It was impossible to get down.

The water was absolutely clear. In the few moments that I could remain submerged, I noted the shafts of sunlight descending into the depths. It made me feel giddy. I tried to see the propellers, but, as *Syrtis* pitched in the heavy swell, the hydroplanes smacked the surface with an almighty, splash, which forced me to the surface again. I was cold all over, and more frightened than I have ever been. This was not Loch Striven diving. It was beyond my ability to get down to the propellers. In a proper suit, correctly weighted, insulated from the cold, I could have swum down, but, floating as I was, and being pumped to the surface with every swell, it was more than I could do. But there was no giving up. The rope had to be cleared, otherwise we were limited to the use of the starboard propeller only.

I swam along the surface to get clear of the hydroplanes, and looked down. There were the infinite light beams converging toward the great deep, and there was the port propeller with the rope around it, not tight but in a big loop. That was fortunate so long as the propeller was not rotated. I looked up to the First Lieutenant on deck and removed my mouthpiece: 'Do not turn the port propeller. Let out some slack on the tow, and carry it as far aft as you can.' This they did. I saw, to my enormous relief, that the bight of rope was now lying aft of the propeller.

'Right. Heave in now.'

The rope straightened above the propeller and slid across the top of the big shaft as the casing party heaved it aboard. Eventually the end came up, frayed from the break and having been towed for some time afterwards.

The casing party hauled me back to the hydroplanes and up on deck. The crew were complimentary as we hurried forward and up into the conning tower. *Syrtis* was already under way on diesels, and heading back along the way she had come.

'Well done, Shean,' from Jupp, and down I went to change.

The rush of engine air down the conning tower, as I stiffly clambered down the ladder, was hardly felt. I was numb.

Despite hours of searching, HMS *Syrtis* was unable to find any sign of *X9*. She had vanished from the ocean. The submarine saw a slick of engine oil at one stage, but that might not even have come from the X-craft. Finally Jupp decided that he could not locate her: *X9* could, of course, be even then making her way to safety, but for the attack crew – now without an X-craft – the operation was off. Jupp turned *Syrtis* northwards to a point at which he was allowed to transmit and signalled the news to Northways House. The hope was that *X9* would either find its way back to Shetland under its own steam, or would wash up on the Norwegian coast. It was not to be, however, as no trace of *X9* was ever found. If the craft had been trimmed to prevent excessive oscillation there is a good chance that if the rope broke on the downward leg she would have continued to the depths and, without instant correction, to her grave.

While the exhausted passage crew of *X8* had been rescued, problems with the vessel continued. The attack crew, who had swapped places on the boat, noticed at once that it was impossible to achieve a steady trim on the vessel, and that the X-craft had a lopsided tilt to the right. The CO – Brian McFarlane – concluded that the starboard charge was leaking, and that if he was unable to compensate for the problem the X-craft would slowly sink. The only choice was to jettison his starboard charge. That would right the vessel, resolve the trim, and leave him with a single two-ton charge of explosive to lay under the hull of the *Lützow*. Setting it to 'safe', meaning that it would not detonate, McFarlane duly released the errant charge. Immediately, *X8* righted herself, and began to follow HMS *Sea Nymph* on a comfortable trim. Fifteen minutes later, however, at 7.50 p.m., the charge – now perhaps 1,000 yards distant towards the seabed – exploded.

The effect of the blast was catastrophic. On *X8* it threw the men hard against the hull of their cramped vessel and a list began, this time to the left. *Sea Nymph* also received a battering, but remained serviceable. McFarlane realised to his chagrin that the remaining charge had now been damaged, and that he had no choice but to jettison it, effectively ending the mission. This time ignoring the 'safe' setting on the charge's timer, they set it to explode in two hours' time, and dropped it at 4.55 p.m. HMS *Sea Nymph* increased speed to put as much distance between them and the resulting explosion. When the device detonated at 6.40 p.m. they were perhaps three and a half miles away, but the explosion was extraordinary. The towing submarine was knocked about, with a number of lights going out. Far away the men on *X7* heard the explosions. Philip noted that they were 'very loud, bloody loud. Depth Charge? Bomb? Torpedo? Anyway, it shook us considerably.' Two hours later, there was 'another bloody great bang. Sounds like someone's getting hell, and it might even be us.'

The damage inflicted on *X8* by the second explosion proved fatal. Her W&D compartment flooded, her seams buckled and she was gradually settling in the water. Lieutenant John Oakley, DSC, commanding officer of the *Sea Nymph*, made the hard but inevitable decision. At 3.50 a.m., in the strange half-light of the sub-Arctic night, shouting across to Digger McFarlane, he ordered: 'Scuttle the boat. The show's over.' After a long journey, *X8* sank to the depths, some 150 miles west of North Cape. With McFarlane's crew back on board their towing submarine, both *X8* and *X9* had been lost, together with the three crew of *X9* – Sub Lieutenant Paddy Kearon, Ordinary Seaman A. H. Harte and Stoker G. H. Hollett. The loss of their friends was deeply felt, according to Shean, as well as the ending of their chance of striking against the enemy:

I thought of Paddy. He was a cheerful Irishman, short, slightly on the heavy side of average, fair, with a broad countenance and a smile to go with it. He had a third officer WRNS acquaintance at HMS *Ambrose*, the submarine base for Allied boats, at Dundee, where my Mary was now a Wren herself. On his last leave, Paddy had gone to Dundee to see 'Touche' as he called her, and carried a letter from me to Mary . . . Leading Torpedo Operator 'Darkie' Harte was a quiet, industrious Londoner. Stoker 'Ginger' Hollett was a ball of fire, always cheerful, always doing something in the boat of his own initiative; a very good submariner.

By the evening of 18 September, the remaining three submarines and their X-craft reached their slipping-off zones, and made final preparations for D-Day, although HMS *Stubborn*, with *X7* back on tow, did not arrive in her designated position until just before the time came to slip off and launch the final attack. The work of the *X7* passage crew, led by the South African Peter Philip, was a minor miracle. Having overcome childhood polio, Philip, who in peacetime was known to thousands of children as 'Uncle Peter' on Capetown Radio's *Children's Hour*, repeatedly replaced the broken rope to keep *X6* in the fight. Philip's log recorded his last day before handing over to the attack crew:

06.30. Been at sea now for 6½ days, 156 hours. I've got so used to the routine by now that it doesn't bother me much. But oh for the fleshpots and a pint, a bath, a shave, a haircut, a good long sleep.
13.20. Magennis began preparing a culinary masterpiece, lamb's tongues, tomato soup, baked beans, tinned peas (entrée), followed by tinned blackberries and ditto milk.
18.45. Four SUEs! For this we are truly grateful. CO and Stoker Luck dressed in watch-keeping suits, and ship's crew went to cleaning stations.
20.10. Surfaced. Change-over.

Midget-less, *Sea Nymph* and *Syrtis* placed themselves in a position to assist with any recovery, should it be required. On HMS *Truculent* Donald Cameron recorded in his diary that the entire ship's crew had mustered in the control room to hear their commanding officer, Lieutenant Robbie Alexander – described by Peillard as 'a burly, cheerful, red-faced man with an infectious laugh' – read a moving service from the Book of Common Prayer. Glancing at his confident-looking comrades – John Lorimer, Edmund Goddard and Dicky Kendall (who had spent an adventurous time with Butch Woollcott training on Chariots) – he asked himself the age-old question of men before battle:

Is it a pose, or do they really feel that way? If so, I envy them. I have that just-before-the-battle mother feeling. Wonder how they will bear up under fire for the first time, and how I will behave though not under fire for the first time. At least responsible for my share of the operation, I hope. Exercises were fun at Port Bannatyne and Loch Cairnbawn, where if things went wrong, up you popped and came alongside *Bonaventure* for a gin. Feel somehow that gin would be last thing the Germans would think of in a similar case. If I were a true Brit, the job would be the thing, but I can't help thinking what the feelings of my next of kin will be if I make a hash of the thing.

The truth was that all the men were afraid. John Lorimer recalled 'almost losing my nerve' as he crossed over to *X6* that night. 'How small we felt sitting in the dinghy,' Dicky Kendall recalled. 'Suddenly we came upon the craft and slid into her like ferrets down a rabbit-hole.' Ten miles apart, each of the surfaced towing submarines and their X-craft were close to the enemy shore, and dangerously open to discovery. At 3 a.m. on the morning of D-Day – Monday 20 September – Martin Jupp on HMS *Syrtis* saw the unmistakeable silhouette of an enemy U-boat at a distance of 1,500 yards, and crash-dived. Frustratingly – for reasons of operational security – he had been forbidden to fire on any enemy target – unless it were the *Tirpitz* herself – and this juicy target was allowed to traverse unhindered. Fortunately, none of the six British submarines was detected by the enemy.

Later that morning, a further piece of excitement occurred as a German anti-ship mine, most likely ripped free from the minefield off Söröy Island, floated gently past HMS *Stubborn* as she towed *X7*, and caught herself in the bow of the X-craft. The detonation of a mine of this size would have instantly destroyed both vessels. 'Everybody's nerves were taut as piano wire,' wrote Peter Philip, who had thought that once off *X7* he was safe, 'expecting any minute to see mine, side-charges, *X7* and possibly *Stubborn* as well, go up in a sheet of flame'. HMS *Stubborn* was brought to a halt and, in the trailing *X7*, the newly transferred attack crew heard an unusual sound above them. Lieutenant Godfrey Place lifted his head out of the hatch to see the reason. 'I went up on deck and saw a green and black German mine caught in our tow wire and bumping against the bow,' he recalled. 'One of the mine's horns had already broken so I quickly pushed it off with my foot while I freed its mooring wire from our tow. I breathed a sigh of relief as I watched the mine floating astern.' The relieved crew on HMS *Stubborn* let out a cheer when the mine floated away. Place waved back and recorded nonchalantly in his report: 'That's the first time I've shoved a mine clear by its horns!'

Despite the enormous difficulties encountered and overcome in the extraordinary journey to the Arctic Circle, the fact that four X-craft lay off the Söröy minefield ready for D-Day with the loss of only three men was something of a miracle. There were many at Northways who feared that the considerable challenge of getting to Söröy in the first place – especially with only three nylon tow ropes between them – was too much to ask of these untried vessels and their raw if enthusiastic crews. Claud Barry later offered his congratulations to the passage crews: the ten-day tow – undertaken for the most part under extreme sea conditions – demanded intense levels of professionalism, commitment and courage.

Between 6.30 p.m. and 8 p.m. that evening, *X5* (Henry Henty-Creer), *X6* (Don Cameron), *X7* (Godfrey Place) and *X10* (Ken

Hudspeth) all said farewell to their towing submarines and began to make their way on the surface across the minefield towards the entrance to Söröy Sound. Their mother ships sank quietly beneath the waves to await the successful return of their charges.

THIRTEEN

Kåfjord

At 6.45 p.m., as *X6* (which Donald Cameron had nicknamed *Piscis minimus maximorum adpetens*, or, loosely, 'the smallest fish with the biggest appetite' – *Piker* for short, all crews giving their craft unofficial names) began to make her way across the minefield on her own, heading for Stjernsund, Cameron wrote to Eve:

Free at last and left to my own resources. Monarch of all I survey, a little tin god in a little tin fish. Crawl back to my conning position, but not before fair amount of cold Atlantic has found its way through my wristbands and into my boots. Not wearing watch-keeping suit, find it too cumbersome for quick action . . . Look astern to where Robbie now indistinct smudge turning to northward and his patrol area. Feel very much alone, darling, and cross my fingers . . . No time to worry about things now if we are to make the grade on time, so return to business in hand.

Check up with John [Lorimer] on our position, and settle down to keeping a look-out. Below, the boys are getting used to patrol routine again, with the great exception that we are now in hostile waters, not off rugged but comparatively friendly coasts of Scotland – which adds a certain amount of excitement. Quite excited myself at prospect before us, and only hope everything will be O.K. Flooded charge worrying us not a little.

An hour passes very quickly as we drone along climbing steadily up crests and sliding into troughs of swell. Wind has fallen

166

away to a light breeze hardly rippling surface, and *Piker*'s casing dry for first time for weeks. Tired of speaking down induction trunk and trying to make myself heard above din of engine; decided to con [trol] and keep my look-out standing in W and D. Much warmer there and easier for me if we had to crash-dive. Gather my appearance there caused momentary stir, as men inside thought they'd missed an order and we were about to dive – my fault for not informing them of my intentions. Everything going very well ... Reckoned our speed about 4 knots – [Pitometer] log not to be relied on.*

At 9.25 p.m. Cameron's log continued:

Altered course to negotiate minefield as ordered. A declared German one, forming barrier across entrance to Stjernsund, but our intelligence on the matter very scant. Mines were there, we knew, but not the type, etc . . . Having no idea of the swept channels we hoped for the best ... we had very little to fear really, with our shallow draught and by keeping outside the 100-fathom line. Night wonderfully still, and moon by now well on its way above horizon. We were treated to a wonderful display of Northern lights. High land to eastward now in sight, with moon glistening on snow-drifts; also entrance to Stjernsund. Close inshore to the N.E. picked up lights of a small craft. She was three to four miles off, but kept her under observation till out of sight. Some of the Inner Lead lights were burning, though sectors to seaward were obscured. Beginning to feel cold and hungry, so had John to relieve me. With engine running temperature inside almost as low as outside, but I warmed my feet on the gyro motor and swallowed hot cocoa. A pleasant change to sit on a comfortable seat. In the middle of checking up our position when first alarm went. John came tumbling down to say a vessel's

---

* Pitometer logs measure speed relative to the water.

lights were in sight to Northwards. Panic stations. Stopped engine and prepared to dive. Climbed up on top to investigate. Sure enough, a light low down on horizon but quite a distance off. Watched for a while through glasses until it suddenly dawned on me that it was a star. Relief, and carried on towards Stjernsund. Had told John to keep a look-out for Godfrey or Henty, but he had seen neither when I relieved him at midnight.

His next entry was at midnight:

The sky was now lightening to the eastward, the short Arctic night coming to an end.

A fresh off-shore breeze had sprung up, raising a choppy sea.

The high land ahead now showed up as a jagged black wall with the entrance to Stjernsund a narrow grey chasm. To the north Söröy loomed darkly, and to the southwards the mountains round Oksfjord. Trimmed down at this juncture, taking all possible precaution against being spotted by enemy observation posts on Söröy and at entrance to Oksfjord. Latter, in addition to gun batteries, had torpedo tubes covering entrance to Stjernsund and the fleet anchorage at Altafjord. Still no sign of Godfrey or Henty-Creer, but expect they will turn up at the rendezvous tomorrow. Dawn came very quickly, and at 02.15 still three miles west of Stjernsund, decided to dive and end my misery. Was so stiff with cold I found great difficulty in bending to open the hatch, and my hands were quite numb.

X6 dived, spending the rest of the day creeping through the sound at a depth of 60 feet. Unfortunately, the periscope kept misting up, making it unusable after a few minutes. The crew were forced repeatedly to dismantle, clean and reassemble the infernal device, just for a quick glimpse of the world above. At 4 p.m. Cameron recorded:

Periscope depth. Fixed position 6 miles north of Tommerholmen Island. Visibility deteriorating with dusk. Still no sign of surface craft.

6 p.m. Periscope depth. Tommerholmen just visible ahead as a dark blob. Too dangerous to remain at periscope depth. 80 feet, and prepared for the night's activities. Decided to nurse the periscope during night and wrap it up with electric heater.

6.30 p.m. Estimated position 1 mile north of Tommerholmen. Came to low buoyancy and took all round sweep through night periscope. All clear. Decided to open hatch and investigate. Air of great tension in the craft. Opened up and crawled on to casing. Beautiful evening, atmosphere clear and everything still. Leading lights at Alten, Bosskop and Lieffshavn burning brightly. As yet no sign of surface traffic, so motored close inshore to a small brushwood cover to start charging.

First shock of evening while twenty yards off beach: sudden blaze of light among the trees. Came from open door of a small hut, local inhabitants a trifle careless with blackout. Sound of voices, then the light disappeared and I heard the door shutting. Swallowed very hard and found my knees trembling. Carried on charging. Next alarm as small coasting vessel came round point keeping close inshore. Broke charge and dived out of it.

Surfaced half an hour later to be sent down again almost at once by craft proceeding in opposite direction. Movement seems to start with the night in Norwegian shipping circles. Thank God they burn navigation lights. Surfaced after she had passed and motored down to the lee of Tommelholm. Hoped I wouldn't be molested there. As this was the rendezvous position, kept my eyes open for Godfrey and Henty. Some difficulty maintaining position between Tommerholmen and Brattholmen owing to current. This meant interrupting charging, but as surface traffic kept well clear to both sides of me, considered it was worth it.

Also on *X6*, Dicky Kendall's log described events that afternoon, Tuesday 21 September:

At 16.30, as it became dark, we surfaced only ten miles from our target and moved slowly up and down between the islands charging our batteries. This was the familiar pattern, Don or John half out of the hatch on watch, 'Nigger' [Goddard] looking after the engine and motors, and myself at the wheel. 'Let's have some food, John,' I said. He switched on the electric kettle and brought back some eggs to boil and some cocoa, cheese and sardines. 'Lucky the craft smells,' I thought, 'the cheese must be getting a bit ancient.' Suddenly the hatch crashed down – 'Cut engines, dive, dive, dive! A torpedo boat!' said Don. Her searchlight went right across us. Ten feet down we could hear her coming nearer – straight towards us – 20 feet. Nearly on us – had they seen us? Thud, thud, thud, of the twin propellers – 40 feet. We waited for the crushing effect of depth-charges. None came, and gradually the noise died away. 'Periscope depth . . . up periscope. O.K.,' said Don, 'Surface.' So much for the eggs – John squeezed forward and looked at the mess on the deck and cleared it up. Just cheese and biscuits now and sardines.

Donald Cameron's log continued at 9 p.m.:

Treated to firework display from destroyer base at Lieffshavn. Star shells and searchlights. Thought at first that one of the others had been spotted, but apart from above no action was taken. Believe *Scharnhorst* responsible.

Sat on casing and watched lights go by on both sides. Boom at entrance to Kåfjord brilliantly floodlit. Saw headlights of a car twisting and turning along shore road till it finally disappeared in direction of Kaa. Wondered if it might carry German admiral and speculated on his reactions tomorrow if all went well. Moon rising above mountains and everything brushed with silver . . .

felt very homesick indeed. Elation of sitting in middle of enemy's fleet anchorage vied with feeling of a small boy very much alone and wanting to go home and be comforted. Was not conscious of fear, just of wanting someone to talk to. Cheered myself up with visions of my leave and the thought of having waited two years for this . . .

At midnight . . . John relieved me for a spell and I went below to take stock of our position. Rooted out patrol orders, made sure of my time for attacking and destroyed them by burning. Had a look at periscope in its night clothing, and released the charge connections just in case they got caught up next morning. Before doing so, tried to set both firing clocks to six-hour setting, as I reckoned I wanted that time to make myself scarce in. Clock in flooded starboard charge worked perfectly, but each time I set switch on port charge the fuse blew. Very annoying, as I was now left with a flooded charge set to six hours which would probably fail to explode, and a perfect charge with only a two-hour setting – not leaving me much time to get clear. My idea was to attack at 6.30 a.m., lay my charges, and run for it. Given two hours, I might possibly just make outer A/S boom, and if so had whole fjord in which to elude the inevitable hunt; if not, I would be penned in, in narrow confines of Kåfjord, and could look forward to a sticky time.

He managed to wedge her bow between two rocks at Tommerholmen, so as to lie out of the wind. 'How incongruous the affair was, was brought home to us on the night before the attack,' he wrote afterwards. 'There we were, in an enemy harbour, about to attack the big fellow himself – or herself – with earphones clamped to our ears, listening with one ear to a BBC programme, and to harbour craft circling about us with the other.'

At 1 a.m. on the morning of Wednesday, 22 September, he lifted *X6* off the bottom, brought her to a depth of 60 feet and steered her towards Kåfjord.

Piker with one charge flooded, one defective clock, an air leak in No. 1 Blow which meant we left a trail of bubbles wherever we went, a nasty list to starboard, very little ballast water to play with – and Kåfjord might prove much fresher than Altafjord . . . if I went in to attack and was successful, only one of my charges might explode, but the gaff would be blown and the enemy on the look-out for Godfrey and Henty.

If I waited for a day, the others could make their attacks, and I could limp around and perhaps do a little damage. *If* the others were in the fijord? – and in a fit state to operate, I would not compromise them. If the others were in the fijord? They had not turned up at the rendezvous. They might be in a worse plight than I. If I waited any longer, my periscope might be completely unserviceable and attack out of the question. What was I to do?

Shut the hatch, went below, and headed for Kåfjord and *Tirpitz*.

X10, commanded by the young Tasmanian Ken Hudspeth, and towed by HMS *Sceptre*, made the dangerous passage to Norway without difficulty, Hudspeth saying farewell to his towing submarine in the early hours of 21 September. From here on, however, *X10* suffered from a series of problems that resulted in its ultimate failure to press home its attack. During the first day the periscope refused to work, the gyrocompass failed and water appeared to have leaked into all the electrical equipment. These issues had to be dealt with, so Hudspeth took *X10* off to a remote fjord on the north coast of Sjernoy, where the entire day – 21 September – was spent sitting on the sea bottom effecting repairs. Unfortunately none of these worked, and at the end of a tiring day neither periscope nor gyroscope was operable. Hudspeth resolved that they would carry out their attack regardless, and by midnight had made their way into Altafjord. Steering for Kåfjord they discovered, on encountering a German patrol boat, and diving to evade it, that their compass was inoperable, and the periscope motor burned out, filling *X10* with acrid smoke. They now had no way of navigating in a submerged state. There was nothing else to do but to bottom the craft again, and attempt to repeat the repairs. In the early hours of the day of the attack – 22 September – Hudspeth placed *X10* on the bottom south-east of Tommerholmen, in the hope that repairs would enable his defective craft to take part in the final attack later that morning.

Over an hour after Cameron and *X6* had entered the minefield on the evening of 20 September, Godfrey Place's *X7* likewise said farewell to HMS *Stubborn* and proceeded into the minefield. Like Cameron, Place's plan was to travel on the surface until it got too light to take risks, and then submerge to periscope depth into the Stjernsund. Three and a quarter hours later, the path of *X6* happened to converge with that of Henty-Greer's *X5*, with Söröy island on their left-hand side. Place and Henty-Greer, both standing on the casing, exchanged shouts of greeting and wished each other good luck. 'We made a fairly steady passage up Stjernsund into Altafjord proper,' recalled Place, 'coming up to periscope depth every so often but otherwise had a quiet day dived deep – at about ninety feet I thought we'd be out of sight – in really very pleasant weather indeed.'

The next day went incident-free, and took them without trouble into Altafjord. Then, at 4.30 p.m. on 21 September, he saw a large battleship next to Aarøy Island which he judged – correctly as it turned out – to be the *Scharnhorst*. For a moment he thought that it might be *Tirpitz* away from her known hideaway in Kåfjord, but realised that she wasn't large enough. The *Scharnhorst* was out of her berth, Place thought, to undertake some live firing practice, but, though tempting, she wasn't his target; he left her alone.

From the point at which they slipped off, the X-craft were not expected to meet up or communicate with each other. Instead, a plan had been agreed in which specific time brackets were allocated to their attacks. If they could not achieve the successful dropping of their charges during one time bracket, they were to wait for the next. The first bracket for firing their charges was between 8 a.m. and 9 a.m. on 22 September. Thereafter, the next span was between 12 noon and 1 p.m., and every four hours thereafter.

That night *X7* reached her designated waiting point off the Brattholmen islands, spending the evening busy with the thousand and one tasks necessary to keep the vessels in good condition, including carefully repairing one of the exhaust pipes. At 1 a.m. on the morning of 22 September – exactly the same time as Cameron and *X6* set off, from a position close by – *X7* began its final journey. By 3.40 a.m. they were entering the Kåfjord, diving to avoid an oncoming German vessel, when Place found himself suddenly stuck in the grasp of an anti-submarine net in the middle of the fjord, at a depth of 30 feet. He had experienced this many times in training, but had been taken by surprise by the net's location. It must have been one recently vacated by the *Lützow*, he thought. Unlike British nets, Place found this one hard to shake off. It took about an hour to break free and head towards his target. Sub Lieutenant Bob Aitken, *X7*'s diver, later recalled:

> The bow had caught on something we couldn't see and we couldn't move. All we could do was to shuffle the boat forward and astern, making it alternatively more and less buoyant, hoping to shake off the net. With no success after about 30 minutes the CO told me to get dressed and go and see what the problem was. Getting into a diving suit in an X-craft without assistance took a long time and was quite exhausting. Before I was ready to dive the CO said, 'Take it off. I don't know how it happened, but we're now free,' and we were on our way again.

Then, at about 5.45 a.m. Place recalled that 'we had our first view of the target, the *Tirpitz*, quite plainly, very clear. And we approached, fixed ourselves, and then went deep at about two hundred yards . . . range to go under the anti-torpedo nets that were surrounding the ship.'

All our information about German anti-torpedo nets had been based on either air reconnaissance or our knowledge of our own nets. Our own nets don't go below forty or fifty feet at the most and are rather like chain mail, heavy steel rings interlocking. But in fact the Germans' nets weren't like that at all, they were very fine four-inch mesh, criss-cross material with this very thin wire, and they did go undoubtedly a great deal deeper so it did take us a considerable time to get in. In fact, having tried it all depths, I thought, 'Well, we're just simply going to have to come up to the surface and have a look properly through the night periscope.' Miraculously, at that moment when we came up to the surface, there was no intervening net and the *Tirpitz* was a matter of fifty, sixty feet away.

The time was now 7.10 a.m.

So we went down as fast as we could and collided with the ship's bow at, I think, about twenty-five feet and slid on gently underneath in the full shadow of the hull. We were by then in an ideal position for attacking and dropped the first charge, as I estimated, under 'A' turret and went towards the stern of the ship and dropped the other charge under 'X' turret. And being somewhat in doubt as to how we'd got in, I thought I'd go back to the point where we'd penetrated the nets. But it's very difficult in a very small area . . . so in fact we spent most of the next three-quarters of an hour trying to find a way out. I think we went into quite a number of positions, passing under the ship two or three times to try various bits.

Our charges were set for an hour and now it occurred to me that we needed to take somewhat drastic measures to get out. So in fact we did a sort of 'flop' operation: hitting the net, holding ourselves down, blowing the bow tank to absolutely full buoyancy, going as fast as we could, so that you came up at a terrific angle, and at the same time going full ahead on the motor, and we scraped over the top of the net and got out.

175

Like *X7* and *X10*, Cameron's *X6* had its own array of technical problems to contend with. The starboard charge was partly flooded and the vessel was releasing a trail of air bubbles on the surface; the clock of the port charge did not work; the periscope was misted up and to all intents and purposes unserviceable. At 4 a.m., just as Place was struggling with the first of his nets in *X7*, Cameron wrote:

> Periscope depth. A green film over the eyepieces except for a tiny pin-hole in the top left-hand corner. In spite of all precautions it was worse than yesterday. Gave order to steer north and away from our target, dive to sixty feet and removed eyepiece.
>
> Cleaned eyepiece as best I could and replaced. Look of dejection on everyone's face finally decided me. We had waited and trained for two years for this show, and at last moment faulty workmanship or bad joss was doing its best to deprive us of it all. There might be no other craft within miles, for all I knew we were the only starter. Felt very bloody-minded and brought her back to her original course. It might not be good policy, it might spoil and destroy the element of surprise, we might be intercepted and sunk before reaching our target, but we were going to have a very good shot at it. Faces resumed normal expression.

To compound his problems, the periscope motor – with a splutter, sparks and some acrid smoke – now ceased working. Striving to repair both the periscope and the fogged lens, they managed to achieve a jury rig efficient enough for Cameron to see the *Tirpitz*'s net buoys ahead. At 4.45 a.m. he wrote in his log:

> Approaching entrance to Kåfjord. Periscope extremely bad. Patrol vessel sighted bearing Red 60. Ferry-boat with tall white funnel bearing Green 10 and heading North. Altered course to avoid ferry-boat, this brought me very close to patrol vessel . . . Patrol

vessel appeared to be stationary, passed her distance cable. Altered course to make entrance to A/S net. Vision very poor.

Cameron suddenly saw the blurred shape of the enemy vessel entering into the anti-submarine net and, in a moment of inspiration, decided to follow in the wake of the German vessel. Surfacing, he judged that the German sailors would be looking forward, and would not spot the following X-craft. He was right, and this moment of audacity allowed *X6* successfully to enter the beast's lair.

The time was now 5.05 p.m. Diving again, Cameron and the crew struggled once more with the fogged-up periscope, dismantling and assembling it again. It worked well enough to enable them to avoid a number of small ships in the fjord. Cameron's log continued:

More draining of periscope, atmosphere a trifle tense, but crew behaving very well. Dicky doing his best both as helmsman and periscope brake. Brake had seized up to add to our troubles and needed kicking whenever I wanted to operate periscope. Trim-pump also showing signs of packing up. About to come to periscope depth again when a dark shadow and ominous scraping warned me this would be inadvisable.

Stopped motors and investigated. Could see the bank rising on my starboard hand and a few fish. Overhead was a black shape like a pontoon with wires hanging from it. Hadn't foggiest idea what this was, but it looked rather nasty. Did not appear to be caught up in anything, so decided to go ahead slowly. Scraping and scratching we drew clear, so stopped and trimmed up. Periscope very fogged, but could just make out dark blobs which I took to be the flotation of the A/T nets, and pushed towards a space in this chain.

By 7.05 a.m., *X6* was close to the *Tirpitz*, but its periscope brought only blurs and shadows. Suddenly the vessel struck rocks, and only managed to avoid porpoising thanks to energetic action by her crew to keep her submerged, but a volume of mud was disturbed, and rose to the surface. On the battleship an alert lookout recorded suspicious activity in the water, but his sighting was dismissed, Cameron later found out, as a porpoise. With only a vague idea now of where the *Tirpitz* lay, Cameron crossed the fjord, but was soon caught in anti-submarine nets at a depth of 70 feet. At 7.20 a.m., while attempting to free herself from the nets, *X6* shot to the surface. In showing herself to the lookouts on the *Tirpitz*, Cameron also had a chance to fix his own location, and steer his vessel the remaining 60 yards towards the giant battleship. The enemy, fully alert by this stage, had opened up on *X6* with all manner of small-calibre weapons and grenades. Luckily, *X6* was so close that the larger-calibre weapons onboard could not be depressed enough to hit her.

A few short minutes later, Cameron was underneath her hull, and at 7.21 a.m. gave the order for both mines to be released. This act of releasing 4 tons of explosive charge served to shoot *X6* to the surface, where she struck the underside of the *Tirpitz*'s hull. She slid to the surface on the battleship's left-hand side. Her two charges had been deposited immediately beneath the B Turret.

There was now no option but to surrender themselves, and scuttle the X-craft. The hatch was opened, equipment smashed with hammers and the Kingston valves opened, flooding her and sending her to join the charges she had just dropped, now lying on the sea bed 120 feet below. The men climbed out just as a German craft appeared alongside, allowing them to step from their sinking X-craft into captivity. Donald Cameron, water up to his waist, had had the presence of mind to collect his pipe and tobacco before stepping out of the rapidly sinking *Piker*. The German lighter had managed to attach a line to *X7*, but this had to be quickly cut as it sank beneath the waves, threatening to drag the German vessel with it. They were then transferred to the *Tirpitz*. It 'was the most magnificent ship I'd ever seen,' recalled Lorimer. 'It seemed an awful pity to blow her up, but there we are.'

Place now had to work out how to get *X7* away, first through the nets and then back through the control boom at the head of Kåfjord. Lacking a compass, however, he couldn't tell quite where he was. Within moments they were entangled in the nets, but by dint of deft manoeuvring managed to extricate the vessel. By now the entire hornets' nest in the fjord had been roused to fury, and *X7*'s progress was tracked – as she surfaced repeatedly – by eager marksmen across the *Tirpitz*, including those manning the light anti-aircraft weapons. Two destroyers also rushed to the area to drop depth charges.

X7 had dived again to a depth of 60 feet and had hit yet another net when, at 8.12 a.m., the charges went off underneath the *Tirpitz*, with 'a continuous roar that seemed to last whole minutes'. This explosion allowed them to slip through the net, but Place immediately rested on the bottom at 125 feet to assess the damage. 'The after hatch lifted and quite a volume of water came in,' he would remember later:

> there were one or two spurting leaks but nothing very dramatic round and about. Unfortunately, in the next half an hour, we were unable to maintain any sort of depth. There was so much water inside the boat that as soon as you got the bow-up angle it all washed down to the end and you came up to the surface, and as soon as you got a bow-down angle it switched down to the other end and of course you went rocketing down to the bottom again.

It was evident that *X7* could not escape submerged, as her diving gauges and compass were out of order, so Place ordered that they surface and attempt to flee at sea level. The time was now 8.14 a.m. This manoeuvre naturally drew a storm of enemy fire, too much to survive in, so he had to dive again. But *X7* remained blind, and a few minutes later, when he tried to surface again to ascertain his location, even more enemy fire now holed *X7*. He could not escape. 'We can't go on,' he ordered. 'Stand by to abandon ship.'

Surfacing, and surrounded on all sides by the clatter of falling fire striking the hull, Place took responsibility for putting his head out of the hatch and surrendering, waving a dirty white naval sweater in the process. Surprisingly, given the amount of ordnance directed at *X7* from the *Tirpitz*, he was not hit, but as he climbed out of the hatch his valiant X-craft began to sink beneath him. Within minutes he was alone in the sea, but finding himself close to a floating gunnery target, he swam to it and clambered aboard.

On board the *Tirpitz*, where they had been taken, the four men of *X6* had been brought to the wardroom for questioning when Dicky Kendall noticed a flurry of excitement around them. The Germans had spotted another X-craft in the fjord, which turned out to be *X7*:

The light armament trained to starboard. Rapid orders shouted. This crew was too damned efficient. They opened fire – crump, crump, crump; my ears hurt from the noise. There outside the torpedo net a small periscope cut through the water. The shells burst round it. 'For God's sake dive!' I stood fists clenched, urging, urging, but at this range, they couldn't miss. Another salvo – the periscope disappeared altogether, and the German sailors cheered, some turning and laughing at us. Who was it, I thought – Henty or Godfrey? You wait, you bastards, but how long? I glanced at my watch again. Still six minutes to go.

The English-speaking lieutenant came up to us. I followed the others into a small alley just by X gun turret. He motioned Don and John to follow him, Goddard and I remained. Interrogation, I supposed – they wouldn't get anything out of those two. I turned my back on the guard and took another look at my watch. Two minutes left, what would happen? I wondered what I'd do – jump for the door and get out on deck at all costs, I thought.

Then as I turned to face the guard again, crash! My knees buck-led as the explosion hurled the ship out of the water. Complete darkness in the alley as all the lights shattered. Fire-sprinklers showered foam on us, I was grabbed by the guard and pushed through the door into the bright sunlight. What a change in those few moments! The ship started to list rapidly to port. Steam gushed from broken pipes. Seamen ran in all directions. Oil flowed from the shattered hull covering the water of the fiord. Injured men were being brought up on deck. Bursts of machine-gun fire were interspersed with the loud crashes of the secondary armament firing wildly. It was impossible to take it all in. All around was confusion. Don and John were out on deck. I suddenly realized I was deadly tired, but had a wonderful feeling of relief. In exaltation I looked at the others. They were grinning too. We'd succeeded, even though we now faced the prospect of a German prison camp for the rest of the war.

'Our reception aboard the *Tirpitz* was rather frigid,' Cameron recalled. After the explosion there were 'an extremely unpleasant few minutes before the enemy regained his composure and shep-herded us back on deck again'. The damage caused by the explosion of at least eight tons of explosive on the seabed under, or slightly to the side of, the *Tirpitz* (Captain Meyer had the wit to haul the ship to the right a few metres, using his anchor chains, away from the point at which *X6* sank on the port side) was catastrophic – although the survivors were naturally disappointed that they had been unable to sink the vessel. The ship absorbed a vast shockwave from the explosions that twisted its structure, buckled and split parts of the hull, leading to extensive flooding, smashed its entire electrical system and broke thousands of bolts. Thrown physically into the air, it settled with a pronounced list to the left – three of the massive gun turrets jamming on their mountings. *Tirpitz* was most de-cidedly put out of action, and took six months of intense effort to repair to a state where it could again raise steam on the high seas.

The four survivors of *X6* were joined by Godfrey Place close to 9 a.m., soaking wet, and dressed incongruously in waterlogged long johns, a vest and a huge pair of boots borrowed from Peter Philip during the handover from the passage crew ('Five guineas from Jermyn Street,' recalled Philip, who tried unsuccessfully to recover them from Place, a man with a penchant for borrowing other men's kit). It was an amusing moment amidst all the excitement.

Then, at 8.43 a.m., a further X-craft was sighted 650 yards on the opposite side of the fjord, far enough away for the heavier anti-ship and anti-aircraft armament to get her range and send her beneath the waves in a fury of shell splashes. This must have been *X5*. Her presence – seen by John Lorimer from the quarterdeck of the *Tirpitz* – clearly demonstrated that she came close to her target. She may indeed have laid her 2-ton eggs underneath the *Tirpitz* and could have been making good her escape, but although much mystery surrounds her movements, no trace of *X5* or her gallant crew has ever been found. It seems likely that Henty-Creer managed to escape the dangerous confines of Kåfjord but foundered elsewhere, unknown and alone. It was a tragic end for a courageous crew.

The final survivor from *X7* was recovered at 11.15 a.m. The exhausted Sub Lieutenant Bob Aitken told his story to the others later that day, after first catching a few hours' sleep:

I heard you, Godfrey, saying: 'Here goes the last of the Places.' Then in a few seconds we were back at the bottom. Luckily the W and D hatch had been shut in time, I don't know how. Bill Whittam took charge at once, had the DSEA sets taken from their stowage positions, and put on. I checked them on him and ERA Bill Whitley. The craft was more or less dry, and we were all pretty calm. The pressure at 120 feet was nothing after training by Chads.* Meanwhile the vents had been opened. We had decided

---

* Chadwick, one of the Charioteer and X-craft diving instructors at HMS *Dolphin*.

to flood the craft so that we could use both hatches at once. Willie would go by the aft one, Bill by the forward one – and then me – using whichever was clear first. With the water up to our ankles, we had a first try. But with the D.S.E.A. on we found we couldn't pass each other. I was nearest the W and D, and Bill told me to go out first by that, then help him and Whitley. All this time the water was rising, but too slowly. We had lost our early confidence a bit. We were now thinking of the air getting less, of the time when we'd have water up to our mouth, eyes, over our eyes and our heads.

It was reaching our knees, and it was icy. We tried to open three other vents, but they were blocked or stuck, somehow. There was nothing to be done. We waited like this – for half an hour. The water, or ice rather, was up to our thighs. We could still only wait. It reached an electrical circuit, the fuse-wires exploded. Smoke, gas from the batteries, all the rest of it, you can imagine. From then on we were forced to start breathing our escape-oxygen. And it was utter darkness, 120 feet down, a coffin. The two others were standing near me. An hour later the water was up to our chest, its icy grip was like a vice. *X7* was near enough flooded, so I went into the W and D and tried to open the forward hatch. The pressure wasn't balanced yet, we had to go on waiting. My oxygen bottle was empty or almost empty. I groped through the water and the night to where I had left Whitley, propped up against the periscope. I wanted to ask him for help in lifting the hatch. My hand met a void, or rather the water; but my foot knocked against a body – Whitley had slipped.

I leant over and put my hand on his face, his chest, his oxygen bottle. The breathing-bag was empty, flat, completely flat, the two emergency oxylets were empty too. Poor old Whitley couldn't be still alive, and even if he was, I couldn't hope to lift him, get him out and bring him to the surface. I nearly fainted myself – and I'd emptied my bottles too so I took a few steps aft, towards Bill, with great difficulty because of the water and the complete darkness. I felt as if I had only enough oxygen left for a few seconds. I quickly opened my two emergency small bottles, but at that depth they seemed to give me no more than a breath apiece. Bill was almost certainly dead too, so here I was in a flooded submarine with two dead men at 120 feet, my last oxygen reserves gone – all I had was the breath in my lungs.

I remember scrambling back into the escape compartment for one more go at the hatch. Then things went black, and I must have fainted. But I suppose I must have somehow got the hatch open at last – and when my eyes opened, I saw a stream of oxygen bubbles all round me as I sped up to the surface. The cold air and the sun revived me. Yes, I at last saw the sky after two hours and a half down there at the bottom of the fjord. The Germans fished me out, gave me some hot coffee and a blanket, asked a few questions – and that's it. I don't want to talk about it anymore, please don't ask me anymore, ever.

Despite intense efforts by Ken Hudspeth and his crew, *X10* was unable to execute her attack. Her technical difficulties, together with the fact that her target, the *Scharnhorst*, had moved from her berth, meant that a very frustrated Hudspeth was forced to abort his mission, and return to the slipping-off point. There, late on the night of 27 September, they were met by HMS *Stubborn* and returned safely to Britain. The battered *X10* could not survive a second tow, however, and Northways instructed her captain to scuttle her in light of the imminent arrival of a gale.

By 7 October, the last of the patrolling submarines had returned without incident to Lerwick. HMS *Syrtis* berthed at Shetland, where Shean recalled that 'we had our first hot bath in weeks at the servicemen's quarters ashore'. He was despondent at the loss of his friends, and the fact that it was now known that the *Tirpitz* was still afloat. On reflection, however, he realised that the attack was 'a splendid achievement. Compare it with the sinking of the sister ship, *Bismarck*, which took a large fleet of the Royal Navy and the loss of the battle cruiser *Hood* with all but three of her crew.' He was right. Desperately unhappy to discover that their target had not sunk, the surviving crew were nevertheless consoled by the reality that Operation *Source* had neutralised Germany's greatest battleship, and the single most powerful maritime threat to Britain, for a critical period of the war. Losses were hurtful, but arguably fewer than expected: three men from the passage crew of *X9*, four from the attack crew of *X5*, and two men killed in the sinking of *X7*, from which Godfrey Place and Bob Aitken had escaped. Six men were taken prisoner.

The attack by *X6*, *X7* and possibly also *X5* was dramatically successful; in part because the *Tirpitz* was taken by surprise. Certainly no one on the German side was expecting an attack by midget submarines, and especially not ones that had travelled over a thousand miles from Britain. When interrogated after the attack, the captured crews had considerable trouble persuading their German captors that they were British sailors at all, and not Norwegian or Soviet saboteurs who had made their way from the relative closeness of the Kola Peninsula. Indeed, Rear Admiral Claud Barry recorded in his dispatch that the 'Senior British Naval Officer, North Russia has stated in a monthly report of proceedings that there was an enemy air raid on Polyarnoe on the 24th September, apparently directed against the submarine base. This may have been in connection with Operation "Source", and it is considered not unlikely that the enemy thought the X-craft were operated from Kola Inlet.' British offensive ingenuity had been decisively demonstrated, and the *Tirpitz*'s defensive flaws exposed against a threat of this unconventional kind.

On 23 September, Winston Churchill received a copy of a German message that reported: 'A midget submarine was destroyed inside the *Tirpitz*'s net barrage at 07.30. 4 Englishmen were taken prisoner.' More was to come. The following day a second signal reported:

Heavy explosion 60 metres to port of Tirpitz at 10.12. (Submarine destroyed by time bombs.) 500 cubic metres of water in ship. A second submarine was destroyed by time bomb; at 10.35 Commanding Officer was taken prisoner. A third submarine was fired on when 600 metres distant on the starboard beam, several hits being observed.

She had not been sunk, but as the prime minister noted, 'There was an agreeable new fact before us. The *Tirpitz* had been disabled by the audacious and heroic attack of our midget submarines ... Thus we had an easement, probably of some months, in the Arctic waters.' Rear Admiral Claud Barry, in his dispatch, afforded full recognition to the three commanding officers – Henty-Creer, Cameron and Place – 'who pressed home their attack and who failed to return':

> In the full knowledge of the hazards they were to encounter, these gallant crews penetrated into a heavily defended fleet anchorage. There, with cool courage and determination and in spite of all the modern devices that ingenuity could devise for their detection and destruction, they pressed home their attack to the full and some must have penetrated to inside the A/T net defences surrounding the TIRPITZ. It is clear that courage and enterprise of the very highest order in the close presence of the enemy were shown by these very gallant gentlemen, whose daring attack will surely go down to history as one of the most courageous acts of all time.

Tirpitz was not to sink until destroyed – with the loss over 1,000 of her crew – by Lancaster bombers on 12 November 1944, but her vulnerability had first been demonstrated by the X-craft and their remarkable crews in Operation *Source*. A few days after his return to Britain, Mick Magennis was enjoying a pint of beer with his brother Bill in Chatham when he heard the well-known voice of the BBC presenter Alvar Lidell reading the news:

For the first time the Admiralty have revealed the existence of midget submarines. They announce they have carried out an attack on the main units of the German navy in their well protected anchorage at Kåfjord in Altafjord. They have travelled 1,000 miles from their base, penetrated minefields, dodged nets, gun defences, and listening posts, and negotiated intricate fjords. Within a range of 200 yards, and inside the final screen of protecting nets, they delivered their attack and damaged the *Tirpitz*, which reared out of the water unable to escape. The submarine commanders scuttled their craft and were taken prisoner.

Of course, he and the other passage crews, together with the men of *X10*, had returned to Britain with no knowledge of whether the attack had been successful, and were on tenterhooks to find out the result. On hearing confirmation that the attack had been in part successful, and that his comrades – or at least some of them – were safe, although in enemy captivity, Mick couldn't help but let out a joyous yell, raising eyebrows around him. He wasn't allowed to tell anyone in the pub that he had just come back from the attack. In any case, no one would have believed him.

FOURTEEN

New Ideas

The desperate days of defeat between 1940 and 1942 produced many ingenious and even improbable ideas for taking the war to enemy capital ships skulking in their harbours. These concepts came from a variety of sources: some based on a foundation of professional knowledge and experience, others spurred simply by the need to 'do something'. Many did not see the light of day, failing the most elementary tests for practicability and remaining on the drawing board. But a good number made it through into production and operational service, although it is fair to say that several of these failed the test of longevity. Some, like the X-craft, had had a long gestation, the Admiralty simply adopting the product of many years of experiment and development by men convinced of the virtue of their idea. Others, like the Chariot, were ideas inherited from the enemy.

Some initiatives, such as the canoes of Major 'Blondie' Hasler and his Cockleshell Heroes for instance, who carried out the successful attack on Bordeaux harbour in December 1942, were a military extension of an already proven capability. The Commandos had already developed the concept of taking canoes into enemy harbours. In 1940 Roger ('Jumbo') Courtney, the well-known African big-game hunter and canoe enthusiast – he had once canoed down the Nile from Lake Victoria, a distance of 2,300 miles, carrying a sack of potatoes and an elephant spear; his only possessions other than the clothes on his back and the boots on his feet – managed to persuade Admiral Roger Keyes, the first and short-lived Director of Combined Operations, of the potential offered by canoes to target enemy shipping in harbour with magnetic mines that could be attached by hand to their hulls. He presented a paper proposing an attack from the sea using folding canoes called Folbots. This was initially dismissed out of hand on the grounds that ships were too large and complex to be boarded, let alone damaged, by one man.

But the forty-year-old Lieutenant Courtney persisted, demonstrating spectacularly to a sceptical naval staff the validity of his idea that in certain circumstances ships at anchor were uniquely vulnerable to sabotage. He proceeded to swim out undetected to the commando ship HMS *Glengyle*, which was anchored in the River Clyde, and removed the cover from one of its anti-aircraft guns to prove where he had been, before swimming back to shore. He then interrupted, still in his dripping swimming trunks, a meeting of naval officers, throwing the pom-pom cover melodramatically onto the table. On another occasion, he planted huge white chalk marks down the side of a vessel to demonstrate the ability of swimmers or canoeists to get close to ships without being seen, and to lay mines against their hulls.

The idea of using canoes – canoeing was a fast-growing pre-war water sport popular on both fresh and seawater – to launch pinprick raids against the enemy was one that came to a number of inventive minds at the beginning of the war. On 15 July 1940, Engineer Lieutenant G. M. D. Wright, RN, of HMS *Triumph*, for example, wrote to the commander of the 2nd Submarine Flotilla on HMS *Forth* (a submarine support ship) suggesting the use of the well-known civilian single and two-man Folbot collapsible canoes against the enemy. In addition to carrying a load of up to 400 pounds, Wright argued, a canoe could, in suitable conditions, be 'sent from a submarine into a harbour where enemy ships were suspected of lying [to bring about] considerable damage'. Wright listed the virtues of canoes:

1. complete silence
2. no silhouette
3. easy manoeuvrability
4. a man in training could maintain 4 knots for over an hour
5. seaworthy qualities in a small breaking or large unbreaking sea
6. when collapsed would take up no room in a submarine.

Courtney's point, and Wright's arguments, were made. Max Horton asked on 2 August 1940 for permission to supply a one-man Folbot for trials. These were satisfactorily carried out at the Special Service ('Commando') training centre at Lochailort; and Keyes authorised Second Lieutenant Courtney to raise a troop of eleven men as part of No. 8 Commando. Thirty Folbots were ordered from their manufacturer in London's East End.

During 1941, from Malta and Alexandria, Courtney did much to develop the art of raiding from the sea with a group of men in the Special Boat Sections of the Army Commandos. Launched from submarines in the Mediterranean, small detachments of men would paddle into the shore, attacking airfields, bridges, roads and trains and carrying out reconnaissance of the enemy coast. In Europe, the first attack against an enemy ship was carried out by Courtney's deputy, Captain Gerald Montanaro of the Royal Engineers, the commander of 101 Troop of the Special Boat Section based in Dover harbour. On the night of 11 April 1942, Montanaro, together with Private F. A. Preece of the King's Shropshire Light Infantry, launched their Folbot from a motor torpedo boat in the dark, three miles from Boulogne harbour. Their target was a heavily laden German freighter, perhaps of 4,000 tons, carrying a cargo, as it turned out, of copper ore. The canoe carried eight of the newly designed limpet mines, activated by acetone fuses. The two crewmen wore kapok-lined survival 'Octopus' suits of the type that had just begun to be issued to fighter pilots, which were designed to keep a man afloat and warm enough to survive for twenty-four hours at sea. Under cover of darkness and with blackened faces the two men made their way through the heavily defended harbour, brightly lit by searchlights, to place eight limpet mines (all on four-hour fuses) on the hull of the vessel. Some drunken Germans at one point threw a beer bottle into the water, wetting the men with the splash.

Their collapsible canoe was scarcely up to the task, however, and was damaged during the approach to the target when it struck a submerged concrete ledge. They found that they had to scrape the barnacles off the freighter's hull before the magnets on the limpets would stick, at least one refusing to hold and dropping into the sea. They then slipped away into the night, the Folbot wallowing dangerously with four inches of water inside it, making the task of paddling exhausting and the vessel ungainly and difficult to control. The two men only just managed to find their way back to the waiting motor launch and drag themselves back on to it before the Folbot sank beneath them. The launch then powered its way home to Dover. Aerial photographs the following day showed that their target had sunk. Later intelligence suggested the Germans had executed a number of innocent Frenchmen, believing that the sinking was the result of sabotage by the Resistance. But this, and spectacular operations like that of Hasler's Cockleshell Heroes at the end of the year, could not hope to carry enough explosive to disable a modern battleship, nor indeed to penetrate heavily defended harbours. Freighters – weighing in the region of 4,000 tons – were one thing: the *Tirpitz* and its like, at over 40,000 tons, were a different proposition altogether.*

All ideas, whatever their origin, were derived from the desperate urgency Britain had in these early, bleak years of the war to counter a threat that appeared overwhelming, almost insurmountable. But if canoes against the *Tirpitz* were too small, and conventional submarines too large and their weapon delivery

---

* See the author's *Operation Suicide: The Remarkable Story of the Cockleshell Raid* (London: Quercus, 2012).

systems easily defended against, what were the alternatives? In an unusual move, Rear Admiral John Godfrey, the head of Naval Intelligence, decided to ask his staff for ideas. On 1 March 1942 he wrote a letter that asked all 'members of staff (male or female)' to rack their brains to think of ways of bring the *Tirpitz* to heel, 'however fantastic or unattainable they might seem at first sight'. A copy addressee was Sir Frank Nelson, head of the Special Operations Executive, who passed the letter to his own staff. Lieutenant Colonel John Dolphin, inventor, engineer, entrepreneur and member of the Territorial Army, who was then commanding SOE's Station IX – at the requisitioned luxury hotel The Frythe, near Welwyn, responsible for the development of ingenious gadgets for SOE – responded almost immediately. Dolphin had been examining the possibility of a pedal-powered one-man submarine, capable of placing explosive charges directly underneath an enemy ship, and explained in a response to Godfrey on 3 March the principles behind the concept:

> The submarine would tow a special delayed-action explosive charge of, say, 600 pounds of suitable explosive using the magnetic principle to make this charge adhere to the bottom of the ship. Such a submarine should be able to dive below the booms which protect the *Tirpitz* and the charge should be sufficient to sink her. It might be necessary to fasten the submarine beneath an ordinary Norwegian fishing boat, which would proceed up the fjord until near the *Tirpitz*, when the submarine would be released and would proceed independently on its task.

More details were submitted next day. The weapon was designed to be disposed of once its primary function had been achieved. After placing the explosives on the hull of the enemy vessel, the 'pilot' – dressed in a specially designed diving suit equipped with an oxygen rebreather – would scuttle his vessel and escape across Norway with the help of the resistance.

However, the plan that Dolphin submitted demonstrated to those who examined it that it had been prepared in haste, and by people with no technical expertise in building submersible vessels. Dolphin believed, for example, that to construct and test the vessel would take no more than six weeks, which would mean that an attack on the *Tirpitz* could be launched by mid-April. It was a hopelessly optimistic claim. Nevertheless, and as a measure of just how frantic the Admiralty were for a solution, *any* solution, they approved the plan – desperate days called for desperate measures after all – and three days later the sum of £3,000 had been allocated for Project *Frodesley*.* So was born what became known as the Welman (all equipment developed at Welwyn received the prefix 'Wel'). SOE were to continue to develop the concept, while the Admiralty – through Max Horton at Northways – maintained a watching brief to see if anything could be learned.

The files in the National Archives describe a process of trial and error as a prototype was quickly assembled, and in which Dolphin's early and optimistic timeline was quickly shattered. In fact the Welman became, over time, a very different submersible beast to that originally envisaged. The original concept, that an SOE agent with a modicum of training could pilot the craft, was quickly dropped when the realities of managing underwater vessels were grasped. It was soon realised that pedal power was good only for the boating lake: it simply could not provide the strength required to propel a one-ton craft, even in quiet seas, and a battery-powered engine was required. Equally, the idea of the pilot's head and shoulders sitting outside the craft was also junked and an oxygenated, enclosed cabin incorporated in the design. By 10 April, an initial report talked of slow progress: Dolphin's optimistic assertion of an attack on *Tirpitz* as early as mid-April was shown to be quite wrong-headed. A further report a month later offered the hope that 'the submarine will be ready for depth and trimming tests in

---

* Worth nearly £600,000 in 2015 values.

about six weeks' time. If these prove satisfactory, fitting out will be completed during August.' Frederick Boyce and Douglas Everett's evaluation of equipment design and manufacture at Station IX observes that the device 'was the largest project to be undertaken by SOE's research and development team. It also happens to be the best documented and yet the least understandable.' Nevertheless, by dint of Dolphin's persistence, a prototype was available by the end of June 1942, although it took a further seventeen months before the first Welman operation was allowed to proceed.

In retrospect, the project should have been scrapped at this point. The trawl net for new ideas had been cast in March, at about the time that the Admiralty was instructing 'Tiny' Fell to design an equivalent to the Italian *Maiale* – an already proven concept – and when Cromwell Varley's X-craft prototype had been requisitioned by the Royal Navy and tenders placed with Vickers Armstrong for the production of operational craft. Continuing to expend scarce resources in developing an SOE-originated concept led by gifted amateurs rather than submersible design engineers now became a distraction for both SOE and the Royal Navy. The suggested modus operandi of the vessel was remarkably fanciful in one late 1942 report by SOE:

> It is ideally suited to any form of stealthy approach, whether in daylight or bright moonlight. It is therefore submitted that much alarm and despondency could be caused by a determined Welman operator who could get close enough in to pick off enemy sentries with a silenced carbine.

By the end of 1942, at a point when a live Chariot operation (*Title*) had already been launched, and Chariots dispatched for operational service to Malta, a small number of Welman prototypes were under trial at Helford in Cornwall. It was at this stage that SOE recognised the limit of its competence, and the project was handed to the Admiralty; specifically, to 'Tiny' Fell. He had after all demonstrated remarkable success in building a Chariot from virtually nothing, creating a tiny offensive fleet, training the crews, and sending the first teams on live operations. To be fair to Dolphin, the Admiralty remained interested in the idea, and allowed its development to continue. In Claud Barry's memorandum to the naval C-in-Cs for the Home Fleet, Mediterranean and Levant about the progress being made with Chariots on 23 February 1943 he advertised the Welman, the trials for which he described as 'most promising':

> This is a diminutive submarine driven by one man from inside the craft, and carries a detachable limpet head charge with 560 lbs of explosive. Craft has an average speed of 3 knots for 24 miles or 33 miles at 2.2 knots. The total weight of craft is 2½ tons. Craft is only 18 feet long, 2 ft. 6 ins. beam and 3 feet 6 inches overall height which includes a small conning tower with observation scuttles. The diving depth is 300 feet. It can be carried recessed into the casing of the submarine without a container and released from submerged. Preliminary trials of releasing from a dived submarine have been satisfactorily completed. It should be possible to carry two or even three WELMAN in (S) or (T) [submarine] classes. They should also be capable of transport in a variety of craft from M.T.B.'s upwards.

Lieutenant Commander Patrick Dalzel-Job considered them 'fascinating toys, if nothing else, and it was the greatest fun exploring under water among the rock-channels and islands of the sea-loch, with big and little fishes darting and mouthing a few inches from one's eyes. At night, the cupola windows usually moved through a blizzard of flashing phosphorescent sparks. Having no periscope, underwater vision was limited to a few feet.' But Fell was not happy with the 'baby' that was thus passed to him, observing caustically that the vessel had been 'invented by a colonel, whose ingenuity defeated the practicability of his invention'.

The basic problem with the 20-foot-long vessel was its limited range and payload, combined with the fact that its single crewman made it difficult to operate for more than short periods of time. Nor could it cut its way through an enemy anti-submarine or anti-torpedo net, and if beached was liable to capsize and flood. The requirements on the crewman were enormous. He had to operate the craft, maintain its trim in all waters and conditions, navigate, steer and, when the enemy target was reached, attach its 425-pound time-fused explosive charge magnetically to its hull, before scuttling the craft and making good his escape. One of the greatest deficiencies lay in its lack of a periscope. Each time the operator wished to find out where he was he had to surface to look out of the glass conning tower, exposing himself and his craft to detection.

As it happened, the Welman boats required constant attention due to technical issues. In both a Chariot and an X-craft there was more than one man available on board to rectify any problems that occurred when the craft was at sea: in the Welman the operator was on his own. Throughout 1943, Fell nevertheless attempted to make the vessels a success, training sailors of the Royal Norwegian Navy for an operation against German-held harbours in their occupied homeland:

I remember one cold evening when a young Norwegian was trying to trim his Wellman [*sic*] alongside *Titania*. We could see him through the windows round his little conning-tower, struggling with something inside the craft. We made signs to him to come out but, before he could do so, the Wellman sank in 180 feet of water, and only a small line of bubbles rose to the surface to mark the spot. We knew the Wellman must be flooding and that the driver must drown in a very short space of time, long before helmet divers could be dressed and boats manned to attempt a rescue. Minutes dragged by and then big bubbles came up, followed a moment later by the Norwegian. He was unconscious and bleeding from ears and nose and mouth, but he had done a 'free escape' from 180 feet, that is come up without any form of breathing apparatus. This was by far the greatest depth from which anyone had ever escaped.

Dalzel-Job described some hair-raising moments when trying to master these craft, following a course of instruction that was limited 'to nothing more than being told the purpose of the few controls; the rest was trial and error'.

On my first run, I descended to 140 feet below the surface of the loch; it was quite dark down there, and there were some odd creaking noises in the boat, so I came up rather hurriedly. Only afterwards was I told that Welmans had not been tested below one hundred feet! There were other hazards. On one night exercise, I carried out what seemed to me to be an unusually effective practice attack on a big supply ship anchored near the entrance of the loch. I judged the distance and course quite accurately, and my Welman bumped into the ship's hull at the right depth without too much shock. I slid under the round of the bilge by judicious use of motor and buoyancy-tanks, and the releasing of the dummy charge went smoothly. Then I flooded the buoyancy-tanks, to drop clear of the ship, and set course and speed to get well away before coming to the surface to check my position. After two minutes on a steady course, when I should have been a cable's length from the ship, I blew tanks very carefully, so as to avoid any tell-tale bubbles.

Nothing happened; the needle of the depth-gauge did not move, and there was no thinning of the black darkness overhead. I blew tanks again, until bubbles began to rumble. Still nothing happened, so I opened the air-valves wide, careless of the disturbance it would make on the surface. Obstinately, the Welman refused to rise, and now I had very little compressed air in the cylinder, which meant that continued blowing of tanks would soon leave me with no means at all for coming up to the surface. I closed the valves, and stopped to think.

Without expecting to see anything in the water at that depth, I felt for my electric torch, and shone the beam through the cupola window in front of me. A few inches from my eyes, the light fell on the barnacled bottom and rudder of the ship under which I had set my dummy charge.

I realized with some surprise that I had not moved at all during my supposed two hundred-yard withdrawal, so that there I still was, close to the great blades of the ship's propeller. It was not a good place to be, especially as I appeared to be jammed on some obstruction which kept the Welman from dropping clear and which also stopped me from opening the escape hatch. No one would think of looking for a missing one-man submarine in such a position, and I wondered whether the end would come with my oxygen giving out or with the big propeller starting to turn. I tried flooding the buoyancy-tanks again. Nothing at all happened, until suddenly I felt a slight lurch, and the hull of the ship above me swayed out of the torch-light. The Welman's depth-gauge needle began to move quickly; I had just enough compressed air to stop the descent and to get back to the surface clear of the ship.

'Tiny' Fell records that in July 1943 he was told by Claud Barry that 'the time for using Welman craft had passed, and that he saw little chance of being able to lay on any major operations for our craft.' The reality was that with Operation *Source* in the process of being planned, with execution due in September, the threat posed by enemy harbours in North West Europe had almost entirely receded. The situation was different in the Mediterranean and the Far East, but for the time being the focus was on achieving success against the *Tirpitz* with X-craft. A reprieve to this decision, however, came almost immediately, when the Admiralty asked Fell to plan a raid on Bergen harbour to destroy the Laksevaag floating dock, together with other shipping. With most of his operational Chariot crews already in the Mediterranean, and the X-craft focused on the upcoming raid against Kåfjord, only the Welman was available. It was agreed, therefore, to attempt an operation against Bergen in November, once the current effort associated with Operation *Source* was behind them. Thus was Operation *Barbara* born. Despite the personal courage of the four crewmen involved, all the worst characteristics of the Welman evidenced themselves during the operation, and the mission failed.

The plan was to transport four Welman craft on two motor torpedo boats of the Royal Norwegian Navy from Lunna Voe in the Shetlands, dropping them off outside Bergen harbour at night. This procedure went entirely to plan, the two MTBs slipping out of Lunna Voe on 20 November. However, the four crew involved, two Norwegian soldiers – Lieutenant C. A. Johnsen (*W45*) and Second Lieutenant B. Pedersen (*W46*) and two British sailors – Lieutenant J. Holmes, RN (*W47*) and Lieutenant B. Marris, RNVR (*W48*) – struggled to overcome the inherent difficulties of managing the craft on their own. The problem was that, while driving the craft was quite straightforward, when it came to solving problems, or tackling a spate of sudden difficulties, one pair of hands was too few. Nor could the craft communicate with another, so that once deployed, each vessel was alone.

During the early morning of 21 November the four Welmans were successfully launched from the MTBs at the entrance to Solviksund and travelled together to one of the many small islands that strew the seaward approach to Bergen, where they were to wait until nightfall before beginning the final penetration of the harbour. Holmes remained submerged for most of the way to the rendezvous off the supposedly uninhabited island of Hjelteholm, where they would wait for twenty-four hours before proceeding:

After scouting around, we found that Hjelteholm was not such a suitable place to hide the craft as we had been led to believe . . . After a while I surfaced, in time to see a U-boat outward bound. This was at 7.30 a.m. Meanwhile Lieutenants Johnsen and Pedersen had broken into the nearest and most suitable summer house where we settled down for the day ... The island was supposed to be uninhabited and unused in winter but ... [at about 2.30 p.m.] two rowing boats with two fishermen arrived and Lieutenants Johnsen and Pedersen went out and 'captured' them and brought them into the summer house. One man who had been on the island during the morning had seen my Welman, which he had assumed to be a large torpedo. He then went out and found some fishermen and they all came back to examine it ... The man who had been on the island before was taken by the fishermen to another island to catch a boat back to Bergen. This man was known to Lieutenant Johnsen who let him go because he trusted him and because, if he was detained, his absence would cause enquiries to be made.

When darkness fell that night, each Welman set off at fifteen-minute intervals, Lieutenant Pedersen leaving first at 6.45 p.m. German searchlights were seen playing on the water ahead, even before they set off. Holmes's experience supported the complaint that, being devised by SOE, the vessels fell short of the standards of naval construction.

I left at about 7 p.m. and the other two at fifteen-minute intervals thereafter. I dived in towards Byfjord but soon discovered that my boat was making a considerable amount of water. Eventually I had to use bursts of full speed to maintain my depth. Soon after I had passed Stange light I observed two searchlights on Gjerdingsnes and Klampevik which were focused across the centre of the fjord. Within a few seconds the entire area round Bergen was illuminated. I stopped, trimmed right down and waited. It soon became apparent that I could not negotiate the minefields on the surface. Since my boat was not in an efficient diving state, I decided to return to Hjelteholm where I thought I might find Lieutenants Marris and Johnsen. I carried out a direct submerged run towards Faerøy – and hit it! Thereafter by various ways I reached Hjelteholm at about midnight. During this period the searchlights were continually active . . . I then unloaded my gear, removed my oxygen bottles, pumped out my boat and carried out some minor repairs . . . At about 1.30 a.m. I returned to Byfjord. Again my boat was leaking considerably and I decided it was impossible to continue. I returned to Hjelteholm once more, removed my gear and scuttled my craft before daylight.

Lieutenant Johnsen found that he could not penetrate the enemy harbour defences at all. The Germans were on full alert:

Suddenly three searchlights came straight at me, an unnerving experience. I tried to dive underneath them but they remained switched on and several motor vessels, with searchlights on, passed over the top of me. I switched off my motor and direction indicator (D.I.) and thought to fool them but they still kept on. In desperation I dived down to 60 feet, sat on the bottom and stopped my motor and D.I. When I switched off, everything was stopped and the searchlights disappeared. Every time I switched on my D.I. or oxygen the search-lights came on again. They were so powerful that I could see every stone around me on the bottom at 60 feet.

Although Johnsen escaped and eventually scuttled his Welman at Vidnes, Second Lieutenant Pedersen was caught by searchlights from a patrol boat and was forced to surrender, attempting to scuttle his boat before he was captured. Marris, who had previously had to push his vessel off some rocks, found himself lost in the maze of islands in the Bergen fjord and scuttled his Welman near Bratholm. Pedersen was never heard of again, while the three other survivors, having lost contact with each other during the operation, met at a prearranged rendezvous and were able to regroup. They were collected by an MTB on 5 February 1944 and returned to the Shetlands.

A number of half-hearted attempts were made to relaunch the operation, but to no avail. It proved to be the first and only opportunity to use the Welman in combat. Unlike the Chariot and the X-craft, which both achieved a measure of operational success, the Welman did not repay its users with any return on the investment that was spent on it. One-man vessels of this type, weight and complexity ultimately proved too demanding for single pilots.

However, there was a separate one-man vessel that showed promise, developed in parallel to the Welman. This was the brainchild of another Station IX inventor, Major Quentin Reeves, who pushed hard to evolve a canoe that could undertake the final approach to its target underwater. Reeves envisioned a canoe that could travel to an enemy harbour in the traditional way, but then become, in effect, a submarine, submerging at the final stage of penetrating the harbour, to allow the 'pilot' or 'driver' to place limpet mines on the hulls of enemy vessels. The Motorised Submersible Canoe (MSC) was deployed only on a handful of occasions, all in the Far East – once in tragic circumstances – and earns its place in the pantheon of secret submersibles designed, built and deployed by the British during the war. Made of mild steel, and nicknamed the 'Sleeping Beauty', after Reeves was found asleep in it one day, it underwent its first successful trials at the Queen Mary Reservoir, Staines, in December 1943. It was nearly 13 feet long, had a beam of 27 inches, and was battery-powered with a maximum range of about 30 nautical miles. When it submerged it was designed to dive just under the surface, with the diver using an oxygen rebreather set. Its maximum depth was 50 feet and it was armed with limpet mines.

Reeves described the first successful practice run in the Sleeping Beauty when it ventured onto the Queen Mary Reservoir:

There was about a square mile of water, with scarcely a ripple on the surface . . . We crossed the reservoir for about three hundred yards. The craft handled beautifully on the surface, making barely a ripple from the streamlined hull. At the far side, I stopped after turning the bows to face the sun, gave a 'thumbs up' signal, and opened the three-inch flooding valve.

We glided away from the surface like a large fish. Neutralising the hydroplanes, with the control stick at normal, we ceased going down and silently glided forward . . . I depressed the control stick, rose a little and flattened out. It was all absurdly easy, and I was gaining confidence every moment, and could now relax. I switched off to check trim. The tiny specks of green algae in the water ceased to stream past my goggles, and we hung in the water on a dead trim. I leaned over the side to look below. The craft remained perfectly still and didn't tip – it might have been set in solid glass. Forgetting that I myself was neutrally buoyant and, therefore, couldn't exert a force underwater, I was rather surprised at this lack of movement, and sat back to think out this strange phenomenon. I was rudely interrupted by darkness arising round me, and a sharp pain in my ears. We had sunk considerably. It was time to rise. Switching to 'Slow Ahead' and planes at 'Hard to Rise' we moved ahead and upwards, taking on a steep climbing angle. I held the angle, and we broke surface into the light of day. I remembered that the anxious men who had built her were waiting in the speedboat, so looked around; they were about a quarter-of-a-mile astern, so I gave them a reassuring wave.

Once more I dived, levelled out and switched to 'Full Speed'. The craft gave a slight shudder, shot ahead—and I was pushed hard back against the shoulder-rest and head support by the surge of water rushing against me. This was a bit unexpected, but rather fun, and the little green specks in the water were really racing past my goggles now. I kept my head well down, stared at the instrument panel, and hunched my shoulders . . . The movement through the water whipped my goggles off my eyes, and I shut them good and tight to keep the water out, but was temporarily blinded. I fumbled with the controls, and surfaced . . .

It was all perfectly easy and controllable now, so I decided to throw the craft about a bit underwater and she behaved beautifully . . . All the dread of failure, and worry that things might go wrong, banished in a few minutes, and it was a happy team which gathered round the craft when hauled up on the bank.

But as good as the idea was, its real value during wartime was entirely dependent on the quality and quantity of targets it was fit to take on: unfortunately it emerged just too late in the conflict to prove useful. The best-known occasion when MSCs were used on a live operation was Operation *Rimau*, a raid on Singapore harbour in September 1944 by commandos from the joint Australian, British and New Zealand 'Z Force'. After being detected by a Japanese patrol boat, the canoes had to be scuttled along with the junk they were carried in. Ten of the attacking force were taken prisoner by the Japanese and subsequently beheaded.

Operating in the Far East at the time and based in Ceylon (modern Sri Lanka), Butch Woollcott and his colleagues were issued with Sleeping Beauties. They loved them. Woollcott described them as a 'new toy':

It was a very handy little craft and in the hands of an experienced operator it could be made to throw itself around under water almost as well as a fish. Another great advantage it had was that being small and light it could be carried actually inside a submarine, as the fore hatch was quite large enough to allow it to pass through.

On one occasion only was a Sleeping Beauty deployed in anger and successfully returned to its mother ship. This was operated by ERA W. S. Honeyfield from the S-class submarine HMS *Statesman*, commanded by Lieutenant Robert (Bob) Bulkeley off the coast of Malaya in April 1945. Bulkeley considered the MSC 'quite a brilliant idea' and regretted that it did not see more extensive action:

When the target became visible, a compass bearing would be taken and the craft run in submerged until the ship was reached. On approach, the first step was to pull out the plug in the bottom of the cockpit. Using the silent engine, one could then cruise along so that only the eyes and the top of the head were visible above the surface. Finally by flooding both tanks, the operator could cruise at any depth he wished and, after some practice – not of course for real – one could even loop the loop underwater.

It was a simple and intriguing device, primarily for attacking ships in harbour. When appropriate, a magnetic plate attached to the bow rope enabled the operator to anchor the 'Beauty' to the ship's bottom while he climbed out to fix the charges. The nine limpets would be placed in position and retirement effected in the same manner as the approach. In theory these limpet mines could sink two 10,000-ton ships, if correctly placed. Sadly, the opportunity never arose.

Bulkeley commanded HMS *Statesman* during a total of nine spectacularly successful patrols against Japanese coastal traffic around the Malay Archipelago in 1944 and 1945. On one of these he decided to deploy Honeyfield in the Sleeping Beauty he carried on board. Bulkeley described the action:

At 8.50 a.m. on Wednesday 11th April 1945, *Statesman* surfaced in position to attack by gunfire a convoy of five small motor lighters, estimated at seventy tons each. In the ensuing action three lighters were sunk and two beached themselves, out of range of our gun. Shortly afterwards *Statesman* was attacked by an aircraft and had to clear the area. On returning to the position in the afternoon, it was observed that the lighters had disappeared and it was thought that they had probably taken refuge up a river close by.

It seemed to me that this was an excellent opportunity to try out the Sleeping Beauty to destroy the two lighters which had got away. The driver, E.R.A. Honeyfield, was accordingly instructed that after launching he was to proceed on course until reaching the mouth of a river near where three lighters were sunk and where he might expect to find two more, to which he was to attach his limpets. If the lighters were not at the mouth of the river, he was to proceed upstream until reaching a native village. If the lighters had not been sighted by then, or whenever he had attacked them successfully, he was to retire and proceed to seaward from the mouth of the river on the reverse course to the approach, until making rendezvous with *Statesman*. This sounds simple on paper but would require a brave, determined and resourceful man, which Honeyfield was, to accomplish successfully.

At 6.36 p.m. *Statesman* surfaced and closed the coast slowly and silently on main motors. At 7.20 p.m. the ship was stopped, the torpedo loading hatch opened, the launch party came on deck and started to get the *Sleeping Beauty* out of the hatch. [Following some delays] *Statesman* was then trimmed down until the top of the casing was only slightly above water, and we closed the coast whilst Honeyfield got dressed.

By 8.55 p.m. we were in the launching position. Just eight minutes later the S.B. had been launched and had cleared *Statesman*. We retired to seawards on main motors until, after battery charging, it was time to return inshore for the pick-up. At 11.05 p.m. I stopped engines and continued silently on motors, keeping a listening watch on Asdics . . . At 11.30 p.m. the S.B. was heard and by 11.37 p.m. it had been recovered, secured on deck and Honeyfield and the recovery party had retired below.

Unfortunately this operation did not achieve its aim. Honeyfield reported that on leaving the ship he proceeded inshore on the appointed course and eventually found himself among some breakers on the beach. He turned to seaward to get clear of these and found that his compass was still registering approximately SW, and he found it impossible to steer any course with it. Thinking that the very strong magnets on his limpets might be affecting it, he ditched these and also his knife. But none of this had any effect and he soon found himself on the beach again, this time about fifty yards away from a vessel of some sort.

I consider that this was most probably the more southerly of the two lighters which had beached themselves after my attack in the morning, that it had never got off the beach and that I had not seen it when I made my inspection in the afternoon. As Honeyfield had unfortunately, but quite reasonably, got rid of all his limpets, he was unable to do anything. So he made to seaward again and when clear of the coast came to half buoyancy, partially undressed and dug out from his inner garments his emergency jungle compass which had a dial about the size of a sixpence. Using this he navigated himself back to the rendezvous and was duly picked up. Although the operation itself did not achieve its aim, I consider that E.R.A. Honeyfield showed great courage and resourcefulness when he was completely lost off a hostile coast and managing, in spite of everything, to find his way back to the pick-up position.

It proved to be the only time a Sleeping Beauty was launched in anger against the enemy. This was a pity, but it is clear that it arrived in the Allies' inventory too late to prove useful. One can only im-agine the enthusiasm for this remarkable device that would have been shown by Major Blondie Hasler of the 'Cockleshell Heroes', had Sleeping Beauties been available for this dramatic attack. Hasler had envisaged such a machine in early 1942 (which he had named an Underwater Glider), but was not to trial a prototype Sleeping Beauty until October 1943.

FIFTEEN

Chariot Adventures

At the same time that Operation *Source* was getting under way, the remaining British-based Chariot crews travelled on HMS *Alecto* to spend two months on Lunna Voe preparing for further operations against German shipping in the harbours and fjords of Norway. The war between the 30th (Norwegian) Flotilla and the German occupiers had by this time been raging for two years, with 'D' Class motor torpedo boats (known in naval parlance as 'dog boats') and motor gun boats (MGBs) making the long journey across the North Sea to carry out hit-and-run attacks on German coastal shipping. The normal procedure was for a pair of dog boats to make the crossing and then hide, well camouflaged, in one of the many available fjords while waiting for a target to appear. These were known as 'lurking' missions.

There had been some dramatic successes in the early days, but also some tragedies. By 1943, the Germans were wise to the Norwegian Flotilla's stratagems, and a poke with a stick by the plucky Norwegians operating from the Shetland Islands more often than not stirred up an angry, immediate and violent response. The Germans regarded those Norwegians continuing to fight them as terrorists or pirates who, when captured, could be murdered under the terms of the *Kommandobefehl* that had led to the death of Bob Evans a few months earlier. Such was the fate, for example, that befell MTB 345 in July 1943. After hiding for four days, the boat was observed from the air and attacked by a flotilla of German vessels. Following a fierce fight, the crew were captured and taken to Bergen for questioning. Next day they were handed over to the Gestapo; eight men were shot and their bodies thrown into the sea attached to depth charges.

A new plan was devised. This was to not conduct the attacks on German shipping while the enemy was at sea, but instead to deploy Chariots against them in their harbours. An MGB (escorted by two dog boats) would transport two Chariots on its back, hoisting them in and out of the water by means of davits. The target was German shipping in Askvoll, about 75 miles north of Bergen. The Norwegian-speaking commando Lieutenant Commander Patrick Dalzel-Job was to be dropped off on the island of Atleo; MGB 675 would move a few miles north to seek cover. Dalzel-Job would watch for shipping, and then radio up the Chariots from their hiding place, 10 miles away on Vaerø Island. After a difficult passage in heavy weather, the boat succeeded in dropping off Dalzel-Job, before reaching the lying-up point on the Norwegian coast, but was observed and attacked from the air by six Focke-Wulfs and Messerschmitts. In a hard-fought battle, MGB 675 barely escaped with its life. Well and truly shot up by repeated bullet and cannon-fire in an attack lasting three hours, it suffered thirteen wounded from a complement of fourteen, managing to limp back to the Firth of Forth seventy-two hours later on one engine and no compass. A second operation failed to find any appropriate targets and had to be aborted. Dalzel-Job was picked up several days later.

In the meantime a new and improved Chariot, the Mark II, had been designed. Butch Woollcott and his partner Tony Eldridge, together with another crew (Sub Lieutenant Steve Philp, RNVR and A/B Leslie Warner), were instructed to report to Fort Blockhouse, Gosport. Thinking that they were about to receive orders for an operation, they were instead introduced to the second iteration of the Chariot, the Mark II, which they nicknamed the 'Terry' after its designer, Commander Stan Terry. Painted red, it was considerably larger and longer than the Mark I and had two cockpits cut in to allow the crew to sit inside the machine. While crewman No. 1 faced forward, unusually the No. 2 faced the rear. The Mark II was faster, too, with a top speed of over 4 knots, and the warhead had nearly doubled in size, to 1,100 lb of Torpex high explosive. 'There was no superstructure at all, so it was just one long immense torpedo,' observed Woollcott, who was impressed with most aspects of the redesign.

When the four men returned, they joined 'Tiny' Fell on the *Titania* at Loch Corrie for training on this new device. At the time there were only four extant Chariot crews in British waters. The introduction of the new 'Terry' device paradoxically came at the same time as Claud Barry told Fell that he believed that, because of the dearth of suitable targets, 'the time for using Chariots and Wellman [*sic*] craft' in Europe had passed. 'This was really the death-knell for Chariots,' recalled Fell, at least in European waters, 'and it came as a bitter disappointment to us all. We clung to hopes that something would turn up and were told to continue training on a very reduced scale.'

The request to deploy Chariots as part of the Royal Norwegian Navy's continuing attacks on the Norwegian coast, which led to the operations with MGB 675 described above, and others, provided some respite. What Barry may well have told Fell, although it is not recorded in the latter's memoirs, is that Northways had for some time been advertising the capabilities of the midget submersibles, such as X-craft, Chariots and Welman craft, to the United States and Australia, in the hope that these specialist capabilities might be utilised in the Far East. Indeed, as early as 28 April 1942 – before a single British Chariot had been built – Max Horton was sublimely confident, not only that they would be successfully produced, but that planning needed to be undertaken even at this early stage to ensure that the British and Americans did not expend unnecessary energy duplicating each other's efforts.

He concluded that Chariots should be deployed in the Far East and the Mediterranean where they could be targeted against enemy capital ships and aircraft carriers. Chariots were duly sent to Malta later in 1942, but no interest was shown by those fighting the Japanese. In March 1943, a 'Hush Most Secret' memorandum was sent to the Australian Commonwealth Naval Board from the Admiralty strongly advocating the use of these weapons:

1. Our development of midget submarines and human torpedoes has reached a stage when they can shortly be put into operational use. The 3 main types are:
    a. X-craft – 3-man submarines
    b. Welmans – 1-man submarines
    c. Chariots – 2-man human torpedoes
2. 'Chariots' have penetrated enemy underwater defences and have achieved success in Mediterranean and the trials of the other 2 types have shown their potential value.
3. Owing to the comparatively static nature of the war in Home and Mediterranean waters few valuable targets can be found outside heavily defended and often inaccessible harbours. But it is thought that conditions far more suitable for successful employment of these craft may exist in S.W. Pacific among Japanese anchorages.
4. The major difficulty here to be anticipated is transport of the craft to within striking radius of the target. The following methods are being developed:
    a. X-craft. Can be towed at slow speeds, either on surface or submerged, by surface craft or by submarine on surface or submerged. The craft may be released from tow about 159 miles from its objective.
    b. Welman. Can be carried by parent submarine and released while submerged, or by M.T.B., destroyer or almost certainly by Sunderland [flying boat] aircraft. Recessing of craft into casing of submarine minimises

211

increase of silhouette and enables it to be carried on normal patrol. Distance from objective at which craft is launched depends on nature of operation.

c. Chariots. Can be carried in watertight containers by parent submarine or in M.T.B. or Sunderland. Up to now submarine has had to be on surface for launching but launching from submarine on bottom is under trial.

Specifications relating to the three craft were provided, followed by the plea: 'Request you bring these details before [the Commander South West Pacific] and endeavour to obtain his serious consideration of the great possibilities for the successful employment of these weapons that may exist in South West Pacific.' It added, almost as an afterthought: 'Trained crews would be supplied with the craft.'

Woollcott and his colleagues continued training in both Loch Corrie and Loch Cairnbawn in their new Mark II vessels in ignorance of the plans that were being made for their future. The new boat took some getting used to, and they concentrated on mastering its idiosyncrasies:

Their higher speed was quite noticeable, especially under the surface and although the extra was only two knots we found that once we had dived we couldn't travel in comfort at top speed, for we couldn't keep our heads still. The water pressure was so great that it felt as if someone were holding our heads and twisting them from side to side; so we had to knock down the speed a notch when we were dived.

I didn't go much on the back to back arrangement either. I always like to see where I'm heading, not where I've been. The worst part though, was getting in and out of those cockpits. They were such a tight fit that you had to lower yourself in such an exact way that it was like getting a ring over a prize at a hoop-la stall. The two oxygen bottles on our backs always seemed to get caught up somewhere. It amazed me how Tony managed to fold himself up into such a small space, however, that problem was solved in time. Instead of wearing the two bottles on the back, our breathing sets were modified so that we wore just one bottle hanging in the front below the bag, just like a D.S.E.A. set . . . After a few short preliminary dives just to get the feel of the new machines, we started on an intensive programme of five-hour runs. For these runs the machines were taken on board our trawler or on special wooden chocks fixed to the pressure hull of a T Class submarine, one each side of the conning tower. We were then taken out into Edrachillis Bay and released, to make our own way back into Loch Cairnbawn and stage a dummy attack on *Bonaventure*.

It was getting towards midsummer now, and with there being only about three hours darkness in those latitudes at that time of the year, combined with the fact that the clocks were advanced two hours as a wartime measure, it didn't get really dark until 1.00 a.m. So we used to start off our runs at midnight. It was a marvellous sight, watching the effect that the setting sun had on the mountains ahead of us: from green and purple they would gradually turn, just like glowing steel from a blacksmith's forge, then they would go back to purple again and just before they disappeared completely they would turn dead black. Then, before we had reached our target we would see the same process in reverse, as the sun rose again and peeped over the top of the mountains at us. By the time we had reached *Bonaventure* it would be full daylight again.

SIXTEEN

'For Padfoot, Unwell in Scarborough'

Following the return from Operation *Source* and the departure for the Pacific of HMS *Bonaventure* in February 1945, Loch Cairnbawn became the focus for the introduction into service of six new X-craft (*X20–25*) and six new training craft (*XT1–XT6*); the development of a new variant for service in tropical waters (the XE-craft); two offensive operations against Bergen, Norway (Operations *Guidance* and *Heckle*); as well as critical support for the Normandy invasion in June 1944. At the same time, and during this busy year, a long-term role for the X-craft in the Allied order of battle – especially in the Pacific – was also being pursued by the Admiralty. The British, pushed by Claud Barry, were strong believers in the concept and tried hard to persuade their less keen American allies of the virtues of this type of attack against Japanese anchorages.

In late 1943, Max Shean was appointed to command *X22*, with Joe Brooks and Ginger Coles as his crew. He was jubilant, not just at the prospect of independent command, but with his crewmates. 'I could not have asked for more,' he reflected. 'It gave me my first operational command, and brought Joe, Ginger and me together in one crew.'

The first task was to take delivery of their new vessel, which was being built in Chesterfield by the engineering company H. V. Markham and Son. The three men duly travelled to Chesterfield to take charge of their new baby. 'Does that look right?' asked the works manager, indicating the black, glistening vessel. 'We have never built a submarine before.' It was perfect, they thought, and were delighted with the quality of the work. *X22* was transported to Faslane by rail, hidden under tarpaulins, where it was lifted into the water by crane. The daughter of the company's managing director launched and named her. Sitting in his first command, Shean gave his first order as commanding officer. 'Engine clutch out, tail clutch in. Ready ahead, group down.' The weeks that followed allowed the crew to complete all of *X22*'s acceptance trials. Not a single defect was found in her.

A few weeks had passed before a series of penetration exercises designed to test the security of the Royal Navy's fleet anchorage at Scapa Flow on the Orkney Islands was scheduled to begin with *X24*, commanded by the bearded Australian 'Digger' McFarlane. *X24*, however, unlike *X22*, was beset with post-production problems, so much so that she was swapped with *X22* for the exercise against the three entrances to the Scapa anchorage. Now that the British had demonstrated the viability of the midget concept, there was nothing to stop the Germans attempting the same type of attack on British capital ships in their harbours, especially if they had managed to capture one of the X-craft lost in the attack on the *Tirpitz* and quickly copied the concept. Accordingly, McFarlane was instructed to swap his defective craft for *X22*, and proceed on the exercise, while Shean and his crew were forced to put up with, and attempt to repair, the defective *X24*.

Then tragedy struck. On 7 February 1944, HMS *Syrtis* was in the process of towing *X22* into Pentland Firth, the rough stretch of water between the tip of Scotland and the Orkneys, amidst a fierce storm. Lieutenant Charles Blythe, the officer of the watch on *Syrtis*, was washed overboard as the submarine rolled heavily, and lost. As HMS *Syrtis* turned around to attempt to recover him, it collided with *X22*, which promptly sank with all hands. Brian McFarlane and fellow Australian Lieutenant W. S. 'Jack' Marsden, together with ERA Cyril Ludbrooke and Able Seaman John Pretty, were lost. HHZ took the tragedy hard. To be killed while on operations against the enemy was one thing, and to be expected. To be sunk in an accident caused by your own side was something else altogether.

Shean was then instructed to take *X24* to Scapa to complete the exercise, this time carried on board HMS *Bonaventure*. The fleet at anchor were informed ahead of time that the test runs would be made, every spare man having his eyes peeled to spot the intruder. Three runs were completed:

> I had learned, from my days in *Bluebell*, the conditions which affected asdic and hydrophones adversely, and made the best of this experience then, keeping speed down, using auxiliary machinery sparingly, steering through the wake of other vessels, keeping close to the bottom, and other techniques. Once through, we would surface, signal by aldis [lamp] to our escort, and be led back to *Bonaventure*. I noticed as we passed [the battleship HMS] *Anson*, a growing number of officers accumulating at the quarterdeck guardrail to get a glimpse of this unusual craft flying the white ensign, conned by a solitary figure who seemed to be gliding on water. In heavy seas, the casing was frequently invisible.

To Shean's horror – and amusement – Joe Brooks took the opportunity of flashing by Aldis lamp the signal bridge on the battleship with the quick comment: 'My, what a big bastard you are.' Shean remained on tenterhooks for days lest he be reprimanded for insulting the admiral, but was relieved when, as time passed, nothing came of it. Ordinarily all signals to the ship were shown to the captain and admiral, but the signalling officer on that particular watch could take a joke, and deleted it from the record.

The tragic loss of *X22* was tempered in part by the publication in the *London Gazette* on 22 February 1944 of the award of the Victoria Cross to Godfrey Place and Donald Cameron for their successful attacks on the *Tirpitz*. The Admiralty had only discovered on 6 January 1944 the names of those who had survived the attack and who had been taken prisoner. By the end of the month, Claud Barry had received details of the attack through secret messages, inserted in seemingly innocuous letters, sent out of the men's prison camp in Germany. Barry quickly drafted a citation and on 14 February King George VI approved the award. It made the headlines over a week later, when all the major newspapers across Britain and the free world carried carefully scripted accounts of the X-craft, and the attack on the *Tirpitz*. As far afield as Harrisburg, Pennsylvania, for instance, the syndicated Associated Press article trumpeted this new and ingenious method of warfare: 'Midget Subs Used to Torpedo Tirpitz 40 Feet Long, Can Travel 2000 Miles':

Pictures released today in connection with the honors paid to the crews of British midget submarines which torpedoed the German battleship *Tirpitz* on Sept. 22, 1943 indicate that this new British naval weapon is about 40 feet long, with a deck beam of from five to six feet and a hull flare giving considerably more than ordinary width below the waterline.

The number of men winning medals for crippling the Nazis' mightiest battleship indicate that the craft, known to Navy personnel as 'Tiddlers,' carry crews of from three to four.

The cryptic official accounts of the performance of the midget submarine also hinted at a cruising range of up to 2000 miles, since they apparently made a voyage of about 1000 miles to reach the *Tirpitz* hideout.

Lieutenant Basil Charles Godfrey Place and Lieutenant Donald Cameron, commanders of the *X6* and *X7*, respectively, won the rarely-awarded Victoria Cross for helping to carry out the 'most daring and successful' attack on the *Tirpitz*. Both are now prisoners of the Germans. The Conspicuous Gallantry Medal was awarded to engine room artificer Edmund Goddard and the DSO to sub-Lieutenants Robert Aitken, Richard Haddon Kendal and John Thornton Lorimer for their part in the feat.

The citations accompanying the awards said: 'Whilst they were still inside the (anti-submarine and torpedo) nets a fierce enemy counter-attack by guns and depth charges developed which made withdrawal impossible. Lieutenants Cameron and Place therefore scuttled their craft to prevent them falling into the hands of the enemy. Before doing so they took every measure to ensure the safety of their crews, the majority of whom, together with themselves, were subsequently taken prisoner.'

Rear Admiral C. B. Barry, in a broadcast account today of the attack by the tiny submersibles, said that when the *Tirpitz* was hit from a range of only 200 yards there was an enormous explosion which 'lifted the huge bulk of the battleship several feet into the air. When she fell back into the water,' he added, 'she was crippled, so thoroughly crippled, that she was no longer a fighting ship.'

Meanwhile, in the famous Marlag und Milag Nord naval POW camp at Westertimke, north-east of Bremen, Place and Cameron got news of their awards by listening clandestinely to the BBC. Place, for one, was nonplussed. In the report he wrote when he returned to Britain the following year he observed that celebrations were muted because 'I was too busy feeling hungry and thirsty to care very much about the award.' But every serving X-craft crew member in HHZ and Port Bannatyne was buoyed immeasurably, not just by the news that Operation *Source* had been successful, and that at least some of the crews had survived, but because the nation's gratitude for the extraordinary effort – and sacrifice of the crews – extended to the award of two Victoria Crosses.

From the outset of the introduction into service of the six new X-craft in late 1943, they had been allocated a significant role in helping to prepare for the invasion of France – Operation *Overlord* – and more particularly the Allied landings on the beaches – Operation *Neptune* – which was given the codename 'Bigot'.

Following the success of small parties of men undertaking reconnaissance of enemy beaches in the Sicily landings, and reconnaissance of enemy shores more generally across the Mediterranean since 1941, the role of the Combined Operations Pilotage Parties (COPP), under the command of Lieutenant Commander Nigel Willmott, RN, had demonstrated their value in understanding the nature of enemy defences, together with the natural topography of the landing areas. The possibility of using X-craft to bring the COPP divers close to shore had been mooted during the year, and agreed.

An instruction from Claud Barry on 3 November 1943 allocated four of the six new X-craft to the role of supporting Operation *Overlord* (three on operational duty, with one in reserve). Once their work-up was completed, joint working was to begin with troops of the COPP in the Rothesay area under Willmott's command. The X-craft would be transferred to the command of the Fifth Submarine Flotilla at Portsmouth, to be based on Fort Blockhouse. 'It is hoped,' Barry concluded, 'that the first COPP unit will be available to commence working up with X-craft by 1st December 1943. In that case, *X20* will be transferred to Portsmouth about 15th December 1943. *X22* (and *X21* if available in time) will be transferred to Portsmouth about 7th January 1944.'

Shean and his fellow X-men put up with the newcomers reluctantly. Trials with members of the COPP personnel took place in Ettrick Bay, on the south side of Bute, at night. Shean recalled:

It took some time for the Army and Navy to get to know each other's requirement. Having put soldiers, dressed in lightweight waterproof suits, into the sea, off a featureless beach at night, it took time to locate them two hours later, especially when the sea was rough. They would want us to venture closer in than we considered safe. To save them a long swim, we risked running aground. On a falling tide, this could prove fatal.

But the biggest problem with utilising X-craft for this task was that of space. X-craft were cramped at the best of times, being designed for a maximum crew of four. Repeated ingress and egress of combat divers from an X-craft sitting on the seabed off an enemy beach for days on end in order to plot tides, secure sand samples and identify enemy defences had not been part of the original design specification, and the five men needed to operate the craft and conduct beach reconnaissance made a tight squeeze. The answer was to test the concept. Accordingly, on 10 December 1943 a further instruction from Northways allocated *X22* to a test run of the beaches allocated for Operation *Neptune*. This reconnaissance was to take place between 30 December and 4 January. *X22* would be towed to the target area, with cover operations undertaken to distract any watching observers.

The specific questions asked of Willmott were, in the area of the French coast between longitudes 0° 24′ and 0° 38′ to report on the type, nature and substrata of the beaches; the presence or otherwise of mines at high and low water (and if so, samples should be obtained); the extent of any minefields and identification of any gaps; the gradients of the beaches; and the presence or otherwise of 'Flame Warfare Devices'. The client for this information was General Montgomery's HQ 21st Army Group, which was building up the detailed plan for *Neptune*.

The C-in-C Portsmouth, however, was concerned lest the presence of an X-craft off the French coast be detected by the Germans and tip them off to its intent. He advocated instead that a surface vessel be used for collecting samples of the substrata of the beaches, at both Mean Water Line and Low Water Line* – the primary requirement of the reconnaissance according to the 21st Army Group. But Admiral Ramsay, the Allied Naval Commander of the Expeditionary Force and the man who had organised the Dunkirk

---

* The Mean Low Water Line was the average of several years of recordings, whereas the Low Water Line was the actual.

evacuation three years before, disagreed. He recognised that utilising X-craft entailed some risks of discovery, but argued that the rewards outweighed these. The Admiralty therefore authorised the use of X-craft, citing:

(a) The facts that longer periods can be spent on shore and that several sorties should be possible during each dark period

(b) It may be necessary to obtain information later in the year when nights are too short to enable this to be done by surface craft

(c) The chances that dark periods and periods of bad weather may coincide

(d) Military requirements as yet unstated, may call for more information than can be obtained by parties operating from surface craft

(e) The fact that valuable information may be obtained by watching certain parts of the French coast through a periscope during the day

It was agreed, however, that the first operation would be undertaken by surface vessel. If the results were satisfactory, a second would be undertaken by X-craft. This first reconnaissance by Major Logan Scott-Bowden and Sergeant Bruce Ogden-Smith successfully returned to England with the required samples on the night of New Year's Eve 1943 from the area west of Ver-sur-Mer, later known as Gold Beach. On 16 January 1944 they repeated this exercise in *X20* – commanded by Lieutenant Ken Hudspeth and Sub Lieutenant Bruce Enzer, RNVR – successfully surveying the area that would become Omaha Beach, near Vierville. Watching the shore by day through the periscope, the divers made visits by night to collect information and samples from the beach.

Both *X20* (Ken Hudspeth) and *X23* (Lieutenant George Honour, RNVR) played important roles in D-Day as it unfolded. Now that beach reconnaissance had been completed, the X-craft were required to act as way-markers in the sea for the invasion fleets bearing down on both Sword Beach (from Ouistreham to the Orne River estuary) and Juno Beach (from Courseulles-sur-Mer to Saint-Aubin-sur-Mer). Ensuring that the invasion fleet arrived at exactly the right place, where reconnaissance had already indicated that a successful landing was possible, was hugely important to the British planners for Operation *Neptune*, who were determined that no mistake would be made on the final approach for the hundreds of vessels carrying tens of thousands of assault troops. X-craft lit with green marker beacons positioned at either end of the invasion beaches provided the answer. Each craft was to have five men crammed into hulls designed for four – three X-men and two COPP personnel – although hopefully they would not find themselves confined for long.

With D-Day originally planned for 5 June 1944, both X-craft engaged on what was labelled Operation *Gambit* slipped away from HMS *Dolphin* in the gloomy half-light of the evening of Friday 2 June. They made their way in the pitching waters to their rendezvous with two armed trawlers, which would tow each vessel to a slipping point off the Normandy coast, after which *X20* and *X23* would make their way unseen to their marker points off the beaches. All the men were conscious that they were about to play a role in momentous events, leading the largest invasion fleet the world had ever seen, and being the vanguard of the entire assault force. The heavy seas off Spithead meant that the operation very nearly failed even to get under way, as Ken Hudspeth on *X20* struggled to secure the line from HMT *Darthema*. Her captain, Lieutenant Carl Brunning, described these difficult moments:

Securing the tow under these conditions was a slight fiasco. We had rehearsed it several times prior to D-Day but not in a rough sea . . . The procedure was that *X20* moved up near my stern. We then launched a sizable boat with four oarsmen, a coxs'n and hand. The towing cable was taken over the stem of DARTHEMA and the connecting tow-bar was put in the boat. This tow-bar was three to four feet long, heavy and had to be slid into an orifice in the snout of the submarine. My boats now got into position but both craft were pitching up and down, probably six to seven feet. They missed getting the tow-bar into the hole every time.

After about fifteen minutes of abortive attempts, Hudspeth crawled out into the bow of *X20* in an effort to grab the end of the tow-bar and guide it in to the aperture. In which he succeeded but not before he became like a drowned rat. One minute he was up in the air, the next wholly submerged. He had anticipated this and was clad only in shirt and pants. When the tow was fixed, they came alongside me and I think I fitted out Hudspeth with some dry clothes.

Meanwhile, George Honour in *X23* had no such difficulties:

Having secured the tow in which the 'phone cable had already parted we remained on the surface and then made our way under main engine at an average speed of three knots to a position half-way across the Channel and sixty miles from the French coast, where we slipped the tow. We were then on our own in mid-Channel. I remember feeling very lonely and thinking that *X23* was very, very small. Although we managed to keep company with *X20* until the dawn came up. At 5.21 a.m. we dived and we stayed submerged for seventeen hours and fifty-nine minutes. We did 'guff through' three times, that means we took in fresh air through the 'snortmast' without surfacing for we were over-manned, with five crew and full of extra equipment. There was no room to move and one could not, of course, smoke. All you could do was yarn or sleep fitfully in the increasingly foul atmosphere.

We arrived off SWORD Beach British sector at dawn on Sunday, 4th June. We all had French identities, in case we were captured or just drowned. I had the complete disguise outfit of a

French taxi driver. That would put the Hun off the scent if he got hold of our bodies, dead or alive. They would never think we were members of one of H.M. Submarines!

By the time they first observed the tranquil Calvados coast on Sunday morning – at a distance of three miles – the weather was calm and the scene peaceful. There was no indication that the people they could see on shore, walking to church, or the German soldiers slouching around, had the slightest idea that the invasion was expected, at least not in that particular place. Both crews had nothing to do but wait. When instructed, they would surface in the dark of the night, and turn to face the oncoming armada, providing a checkpoint by means of a green light.

They spent the day sleeping, playing games and chatting. When darkness fell, they cautiously surfaced, and breathed in the fresh sea air: only hours to go before they were to play their role in D-Day. But as they listened to the coded messages that followed the BBC News at 6 p.m., they were surprised to hear 'For Padfoot, Unwell in Scarborough'. This was the signal that the invasion had been delayed by twenty-four hours. It was certainly not the message that they were expecting. Sitting in the sunny calm of the Calvados beachhead, they could not understand what might have happened off the English coast to delay events. The following day, therefore, was spent again being cooped up in their tin coffin on the seabed off France. They could do nothing but wait, in their oxygen-starved environment, for another seventeen hours under the surface of the sea. That night the message relayed through the BBC was that the invasion was on.

By 5 a.m. the following morning, both X-craft surfaced in a heavy sea, their welcoming blinking green light – on an 18-foot mast – pointing out towards the invasion fleet. The first evidence of impending drama came with the endless flights of aircraft overhead, followed by the flashes of heavy explosions far inland. Then the naval bombardment began. The crashes of the unseen guns at sea were followed by the whirr of shells overhead as they arced in vast numbers towards the enemy ashore.

Still there was no sign of the seaborne armada, the host of landing craft of every description who were to drive the assault divisions of the Second British Army onto the Normandy beaches. Then, in the grey half-light of morning, through the bouncing swell, the massed ships of the invasion fleet appeared and grew rapidly larger as they approached. 'It was unbelievable,' recalled George Honour. 'Although I knew they were on our side it was still a frightening sight. One can only imagine what the enemy must have felt, waking up to this awesome spectacle and knowing that they were the targets.' Those standing on the casing of the heaving vessel cheered and yelled themselves hoarse as the ships piled on past them towards the beaches, a few helmeted soldiers waving at the strange sight of two men apparently standing on the water, the bulk of the X-craft of course hidden from sight, and the casing awash with the swirling seas.

From that point on, both *X20* and *X23*, having accurately marked the landing beaches for the D-Day fleet, were spectators in the extraordinary spectacle that followed, as 156,000 British, Canadian and American troops initiated the long-awaited Second Front. After having watched the first waves safely ashore they headed for home, threading their way through the busy seas until they were safely back with their towing trawlers, an enormous White Ensign flying from *X20*'s mast as an aid to identification in these crowded waters. That night the ten men were back in HMS *Dolphin*, toasting the remarkable success of the joint COPP and X-craft mission to provide the vanguard of the greatest seaborne invasion in history.

SEVENTEEN

Bergen

The final offensive X-craft operations in North West Europe prior to the move of HMS *Bonaventure* to the Pacific were both against Bergen, Norway. The first, Operation *Guidance*, was designed to destroy the floating dock in the Puddefjord, in an industrial area called Laksevaag, some two miles south of the city, where the Germans had built their concrete U-boat pens. This attack, in April 1944, sank the wrong target, so Operation *Heckle* was launched in September – two months after the invasion of Europe in Normandy – to repeat the performance. It succeeded spectacularly. Bergen was one of the most heavily defended areas on all of the German-controlled European coast. The town lies 40 miles inside a deep fjord that in 1944 was heavily mined and protected by E-boats, coastal artillery and observation posts along the approach banks, reflecting its importance to enemy coastal activity in northern waters, which included sanctuary for U-boats, who made extensive use of the floating dock. The dock itself was protected by anti-torpedo nets. After Operation *Source*, the alarm had been well and truly sounded and the German defenders were alert to any further attacks, but it was clear that the destruction of the dock would paralyse the enemy's ability to conduct extensive repairs to any of their vessels in Norway, and necessitate their hazardous removal to Germany, where they would be prey to prowling British submarines.

Having missed out on the chance to prosecute his attack on the *Tirpitz*, Max Shean and his crew began extensive training with *X24* against a mock target in Kames Bay during March. Shean spent a considerable amount of time with Tiny Fell and Willie Banks planning the attack. Bergen was a very busy port, even in wartime, and Shean's greatest concern was that a periscope-level approach – which would guarantee great accuracy – would nevertheless run the risk of detection and possibly collision. Although none of the *Tirpitz*-bound X-craft had returned, the plan was for *X24*'s towing submarine – HMS *Sceptre*, commanded by another Australian, Lieutenant Ian 'Mac' McIntosh – to wait for Shean's return, and tow it back to the Shetlands at the end of the mission. If that were not possible and the crew were forced to scuttle their craft, they were provided with rudimentary instructions about escaping to Sweden with the help of the resistance. Names of contacts were given to them to memorise should they need to escape by land. Because of the relatively short distance across the North Sea to Bergen, which would take three days, Shean planned that the attack crew would conduct most of the outward journey, and the passage crew would bring her back after the attack.

In addition to Shean, the attack crew comprised Sub Lieutenants Joe Brooks and Frank Ogden and ERA Vernon Coles. Sub Lieutenant John Britnell commanded the passage crew, together with ERA Syd Rudkin, 'Lofty' Ellement, and Stoker Bill Gillard.

HMS *Sceptre* and *X24* left HHZ at 9 a.m. on Sunday 9 April 1944. For the journey to the Shetlands they were escorted by HMS *Alecto* and the Royal Norwegian Navy's *Narvik*. The late afternoon of 10 April found them safely in Burra Firth in the Shetlands, and after repairing a broken manila tow rope, they departed for Norway at 12 noon on Tuesday 11th, with the attack crew commanded by Shean on board *X24*. On the whole the journey went as expected. Irritatingly, a surfaced U-boat was seen at 6.35 p.m. the following day but, as in Operation *Source*, attacking her was out of the question. Late on the evening of Thursday 13 April the slipping position was reached and, with final instructions and 'Good Luck' over the telephone, 'Mac' and Shean prepared to part company. If all went well they would meet again at the same spot the following evening.

Standing on the hull casing, with a tingle of excitement Shean unhooked the 600 yards of manila rope and *X24* motored under her own power at 5 knots towards the Norwegian coast as *Sceptre* slipped away below. 'We could have been anywhere for all I could see,' Shean remembered, the darkness complete,

> but I had no doubt that, at the estimated time, Fedje Horden Light would appear. The Germans had, upon occupation, extinguished all navigation lights showing to seaward, but the shoreward sectored lights continued to show. Right on time, the light appeared on our port beam. We ran on for two miles, then turned to starboard to run through Fejeosen to Hjelte Fjord, inside the outer row of islands toward West Byword twenty-five miles to the south. For the first time, we were in enemy defended waters.

Shean carried on, standing on the hull, as *X24* headed quietly and quickly into the fjord system, fixed lights showing on their right-hand side, 35 miles to go until their target.

It wasn't until 2.30 a.m., just before dawn, that Shean stopped the vessel, climbed in through the W&D compartment, and proceeded to submerge. Checking every hour through the periscope (which entailed rising from 40 to 10 feet), they turned left into Byfjord three hours later – entering a major minefield, but in party with a number of ships. Plotting the ship's route through a dogleg in the fjord allowed *X24* to follow the same course, but submerged at 40 feet, to avoid using the periscope and risking collision in the busy waterway.

When this plotted journey was complete, they surfaced to check the accuracy of their map work. 'As soon as the periscope broke surface, there, right ahead, was a black patrol boat,' recalled Shean. 'Clearly visible were the swastika flag and a crew member relieving himself over the stern.' They could see, at this point, the submarine pens at Laksevaag, but their dangerous situation was signalled at that point by the 'ping . . . ping . . . ping' of an echo detector on their hull. Had they been detected? Shean reduced speed and zigzagged forward, in the hope of losing the contact. More zigzags, and the pings disappeared. Another fifteen minutes elapsed, and at what should be a mile from their target they rose again to periscope depth to have a look around. Shean's report stated that:

All was clear in our immediate vicinity, though there was some haze over the dock area. Checking our course, we continued on, taking peeps frequently. At 8 a.m. I could see the dock 850 yards away, flooded down. To its right were two ships at coal berths. The one nearest to the dock had an old style counter stern which appeared to be overhanging the berth. It was difficult to be sure of the position of the end of the anti-torpedo net, so I estimated its position, reduced to one knot, set course to pass clear to the right, and ordered sixty feet.

At the expected time *X24* grounded gently. In the final approach, several propeller sounds had come and gone as the vessels passed overhead or close by. With rudder hard a'port, *X24* moved under reduced motor revolutions to enter the net protected area. An object darkened the top scuttle, then a second. No details were visible, but the draught could be that of either a dock flooded down or a ship. I could see the approximate bearing on which this second object lay, and it was the same as that of the dock, but it seemed to be too soon. The plot at this stage was not accurate because our speed fell to zero on touching bottom, and would take some time to pick up again. We continued on for about ten minutes without passing under anything else. I considered that we must have passed the dock, and ordered port rudder to retrace our track. Once again, the large shadow passed above. 'I am not sure if that shadow is the dock so we will go out to the middle of the harbour and take another bearing,' I said. This we did, at slow speed so as not to make noise. I was torn between two courses of action, one to take time to make sure we had the right target and two, to get on with it before we were sighted, or rammed, and after all, our information revealed that there could be only one object lying on that heading, and that was the dock.

Back in the middle of the harbour, we turned to point at the estimated position of the entrance, and stopped. I asked Joe to bring her up to ten feet, stopped. This is difficult to do, but was within Joe's capabilities. *X24* came up and stopped at periscope depth. Perfect. I took the bearing, ordered sixty feet, slow ahead. Ginge asked, 'What course?' I gave him the course calculated from the bearing. As before, *X24* grounded, course was altered to port, and at the same interval of time, a shadow appeared. We carried on past it with the same result as before, nothing else seen.

'That must be the dock,' I said. 'Port thirty. Steady on the recip-rocal course. We will attack.' I felt very dry in the mouth. As soon as the shadow reappeared, we altered course to port and went astern, sat on the seabed, set four hours delay on the first (port) side cargo, and released it. It peeled away without a hitch. Joe pumped her back to diving trim, and we went ahead, dead slow, bringing up suddenly on a hard bottom. Rock spalls were visible to starboard. This was as I had expected, being the short rock pier leading to the shore end of the dock. We stopped the motor, sat on the bottom and released the starboard cargo with the same clock setting. It also peeled away correctly. I ordered slow astern with rudder hard a'port. *X24* moved astern and round to port.

Shean crept calmly back out of the fjord system during the day that followed, working hard to avoid the two minefields that they had traversed when entering the day before, as well as the busy surface traffic. The men were elated, though Shean was careful not to celebrate until they had at least completed their rendezvous with the waiting *Sceptre*. But everything went well. 'It all seemed too easy to be true,' he thought. 'Here we were, still in enemy waters, having planted two-ton mines a few miles away, motoring quietly

230

toward the open sea, half the crew asleep, and no X-craft defects. There was some distance to go yet of course, but it seemed that the further we went, the less hazardous it should be. We were already twenty miles from Bergen.'

They carried on, submerged, until 8.55 p.m., when *X24* surfaced. Emerging from the hatch, Shean saw the dark shape of a vessel ahead, so they submerged again, and carried on their planned route, hoping to leave what must have been a German guard vessel far behind. The unmistakable ping of an echo detector gave them momentary cause for concern, but after an hour and a half Shean judged that they were well away.

The air-cleaning system was malfunctioning, which meant they had the need to surface. Eventually they were able to do so, and Shean was promptly sick over the side. The diesel engines were started and *X24* progressed out into the North Atlantic, Shean standing on the casing for the first hour. At 11 p.m. *Sceptre* was seen, and the two vessels flashed the proper codes using infrared torches. After following in *Sceptre*'s wake for a further hour, the passage crew were transferred, the manila rope attached, and Shean and his crew climbed wearily into the submarine.

Shean was convinced that he had dropped his dual two-ton charges underneath the floating dock. A signal to this effect was sent to Northways and at 6.35 a.m. on Tuesday 18 April both *Sceptre* and *X24* entered HHZ, the latter proudly flying the Skull and Crossbones. Shean's account followed:

As *Sceptre* moored, one of *Bonaventure*'s boats came and transferred us to the mother ship, while Willie cast off the tow and secured *X24* in a berth alongside. Joe and I went with Captain Fell to his cabin. He had welcomed us at the gangway with the warmth that was typical of him. He sat us down around a coffee table, with coffee as well, and listened carefully to our account of the operation and the tow each way. He was particularly interested in details of our final approach to the target. I went over every part a second time. After hearing us out, he said that aerial reconnaissance showed the dock still floating, and a German coal ship *Barenfels* sunk at her berth close by.

Intelligence from Bergen indicated that the explosion was devastating, blasting fragments of the ship far and wide. But it wasn't the floating dock that had been attacked. 'I broke the sad news to the rest of the crew,' reported Shean disconsolately. 'All of them had performed splendidly.'

'Tiny' Fell was gentle with Shean. A closely guarded enemy harbour had been penetrated, and an enemy ship destroyed. What is more, Shean had managed to extricate his X-craft and bring it home, a feat that had not been achieved when the *Tirpitz* had been attacked. 'The photos showed that the ferro-concrete jetty, alongside which *Barenfels* had been lying, had collapsed,' wrote Fell, 'and had spilled a vast coal dump into the fjord. Max Shean was livid with fury that he had missed his target, the dock, and demanded that he be allowed to go back and complete the job'. Though Shean was prevented from so doing, he was awarded a DSO for his efforts. Eleven were killed, and seven injured in the explosion.

The attack left the Germans baffled. Their suspicions of terrorism seemed to be reinforced when six days later, on Hitler's fifty-fifth birthday, the *Voorbode*, a requisitioned Dutch cargo vessel carrying 240,000 pounds of explosives, blew up in the harbour, killing perhaps 160, injuring 5,000 and laying much of the city centre to waste. The German supposition, given the date, was that it was the result of sabotage, although as it turned out it was entirely the result of an accident. But two mystifying 'attacks' in a week seemed to the Germans not to be accidental. Believing them both to be the work of the resistance, they rounded up a number of entirely innocent suspects.

The second attempt to sink the floating dock had to wait until September, when *X24* was launched again, but this time with a new crew. By coincidence, the towing submarine was again HMS

Sceptre. This second attack was considered to be doubly dangerous, as although the Germans would not necessarily have traced
the destruction of the *Barenfels* to a midget submarine, suspecting
perhaps walk-on sabotage by the Norwegian resistance, security
was certain to be tight.

HMS *Sceptre* and *X24* left the familiar Shetlands at noon on 7
September. The attack crew was commanded by the New Zealander
Lieutenant Herbert ('Pat') Westmacott, DSC, RN, Sub Lieutenant S.
H. Denning, RNVR, Sub Lieutenant Derek Purdy, a grocer by trade,
who was a member of the Royal New Zealand Navy's Volunteer
Reserve, and ERA B. C. Davison. The weather between Loch
Cairnbawn and the Shetlands had been appalling, and so it continued
into the North Sea. The day after they left the Shetlands they were in
the midst of a full-blown storm, and both vessels were forced to
submerge to 120 feet to ride out the worst of its effects. Despite this,
X24 continued to roll heavily. They surfaced that night to repair the
induction pipe that had been damaged by the stormy seas, and tragedy
struck. Derek Purdy was climbing into the W&D compartment, ready
to perform the repair, when he was swept out and lost to the sea.

Despite this loss, they pressed on. Late on the night of 10
September, still in heavy seas, Pat Westmacott slipped *X24*'s tow,
waved farewell to Ian Macintosh on the conning tower of HMS
Sceptre, and set course for Bergen. Rain squalls and poor visibility
characterised the several hours that followed, and Westmacott did
the first hour's duty clinging grimly to the induction trunk as the
vessel bounced its way through the darkness. It wasn't an easy
passage. The air compressor broke down, high levels of phosphorescence in the water worried Westmacott lest it betray the tiny
submarine to observers, the gyro compass broke down at 11 p.m.
for an hour and a half, and just as that was repaired, the main
engine stopped, to be restarted twenty minutes later. *X24* was
determined to live up to her problematic reputation. It wasn't until
3 a.m. that she finally dived to her cruising depth of 40 feet, entering the Byfjord two hours later.

Just like Shean, Westmacott found the shipping lane very busy, and had to join the rest of the traffic. This was a dangerous patch of water, and so as to prevent collision and to avoid the deep minefield, they were forced to proceed at periscope depth, hoping that ships' captains in the half-light of morning were content to watch the vessel ahead of them, not the patch of water in between. 'At last Puddefjord opened up in front of us, and we began to identify objects like the observatory – the cathedral – and other things,' Westmacott recalled. The time was 7.05 a.m. Westmacott's log records:

0712 Altered course 090 degrees, heard ship pass directly over-head. Proceeded to middle of Puddefjord, there to take stock of the harbour's all too adequate installations. Sea glassy calm, whilst the delightful prospect of Bergen hides demurely beneath a shroud of haze.

0730 Observed U-boat pens nearing completion.

0739 Nazi fleet minesweeper passed close astern.

0748 Object in reconnaissance photos taken after Max Shean's attack is a mast with a notice 'Langsam Fahren' (Go slow). Max's ship is not visible in this part of the harbour, which resembles a knacker's yard, with several ships lying aground.

0805 Dock regrettably empty. Lots of traffic. Periscope defective and can only be raised by hand with difficulty.

0810 Commenced run in for attack.

0820 Under dock.

0840 Released port charges, having bottomed in sixty feet under northern end of dock.

0850 Released starboard charge under southern end of dock in fifty feet of water. Withdrew at slow speed.

When a thousand yards had been put between themselves and the dropped charges, Westmacott wrote that he took one fix on his position at periscope depth and then 'tucked her head down, and went like a racehorse for the entrance of the West Byfjord'. It was a textbook operation, and after safely making her way out of the fjord system, *X24* rendezvoused with HMS *Sceptre* on the evening of 11 September. Two days later, she sailed triumphantly into the Shetlands for a second time after completing a mission against a German harbour, her Jolly Roger flying. 'Reconnaissance photographs and messages from Norway were not long coming in,' recalled Fell, 'and long before *X24* reached Shetland we knew that the dock had been blown to bits.' A signal was sent to HMS *Sceptre* with the good news, and the passage crew on *X24* duly hauled out the flag to fly on its return.

EIGHTEEN

Phuket

On 3 March 1943, the Director of Plans at the Admiralty, Captain Charles Lambe, RN, wrote a memorandum for the attention of naval commanders-in-chief which suggested that the most fruitful place for the future deployment of what were described as 'Special Service Craft' – namely X-craft, Welmans and Chariots – was the Far East. This was because, he argued, in both European and Mediterranean waters the use of these types of vessels entailed 'almost prohibitive risk, as naval warfare in these areas is static and the harbours used by the enemy are ones which he has had ample time fully to protect'. The Pacific, he suggested, was very different, because the enemy were using a large number of 'harbours and anchorages which are not, and never can be, fully defended against underwater attack'. Lambe noted, nevertheless, the reluctance of US commanders in the Pacific to deploy this type of unorthodox weapon, although he suggested that General MacArthur, in the south-west Pacific (an area which included Australia), might be interested, given that this region teemed with enemy anchorages.

While the British struggled to persuade the Americans of the merits of these submersibles during 1944, the Admiralty neverthe-less decided to deploy Chariots to the Far East – where the epicen-tre of operations was the island of Ceylon – and in July 1944 six Chariot Mark IIs and their crews under the command of the South African Lieutenant Commander John McCarter were loaded into a converted Canadian liner, HMS *Wolfe*. Their destination was the naval base at Trincomalee, on the north-eastern coast of the island. From here, operations were to be launched against Japanese anchorages, principally those on the Malay Peninsula 1,200 miles to the east on the far side of the Bay of Bengal. Trincomalee had been the base of the Royal Navy's Eastern Fleet since the loss of Singapore over two years before, and the 2nd Submarine Flotilla was to be the Chariots' new home.

The first task for Captain John ('Tod') Slaughter, simultaneously captain of the *Wolfe* and of the 2nd Submarine Flotilla, was to find suitable targets for attack by Chariots. A particular consideration that had to be borne in mind while planning for operations was the utter brutality of the Japanese to captured enemy servicemen. In some ways it wasn't vastly different to Gestapo treatment of British commandos captured in Europe after October 1942 – execution following interrogation – but the added dimension when fighting the Japanese was the cruelty they inflicted at the moment of capture, and the wanton neglect of those in their custody. The Japanese had a particular hatred of anyone they caught mounting commando-type raids, and there were many notorious examples of this, notably the fate of ten of the survivors of the abortive Operation *Rimau* raid by members of Force Z who, in Singapore shortly before the end of the war, were afforded what amounted to little more than a mock trial before being ceremonially beheaded.

There was already enough evidence to suggest that, on top of the substantial risks entailed in mounting a Chariot operation, those incurred by trying to survive off the land – on the run among native populations who might not be willing to take any risks themselves on behalf of Charioteers – or indeed by enduring a spell in Japanese captivity, were very high indeed. These factors, combined with the scarcity of both the Chariots and their highly trained crews, meant that any operation that was authorised needed to yield significant rewards. Certainly, if the chances of their crews escaping to safely were not considered high, Chariot operations were not progressed.

After arriving in Trincomalee on 19 August, the six crews settled into an intensive training routine, acclimatising to the tropical weather and preparing for an operation against the Japanese in a month or so. The water was beautifully warm, which was both an immediate delight for the Charioteers, and the source of various unexpected problems. 'Diving in that beautiful, warm, clear water was a wonderful experience,' recalled Woollcott. But in stripping off their heavy diving suits and practising in the Chariots wearing nothing but swimming trunks, they quickly fell victim to a range of conditions unheard of in colder climes: from ringworm to sunburn and a heat rash known colloquially as 'scot rot', but which, joking aside, was a painful affliction that could drive a man mad through the urge to scratch. Septic sores caused by cuts and scratches, tropical ulcers and salt loss also became a problem. A particular irritation was a mite that burrowed into their ears, causing a painful green discharge – sufficient to prevent a man from diving.

Daily swimming, diving, Chariot practice and weapons training with .38 Smith and Wesson revolvers and Lanchester sub-machine guns were complemented by a three-day survival course in the jungle, which built on the training already provided to RAF aircrew. They were taught jungle lore: how to use bamboo, how to navigate in the jungle and the best ways to deal with pests, such as leeches. These were a particular irritation 'in those wet, wild woods' remembered Butch Woollcott:

they abounded in their thousands; and though we all took the prescribed anti-leech measures, like rubbing soap on our boots, wearing special closely-woven cotton socks under our woollen ones and stuffing tobacco leaves in the tops of our socks, the little brown perishers still managed to climb up our legs and bodies. However, we had all been given a half lime fruit which we impaled on the pointed end of a thin stick with the cut face outwards. Thus, by stopping every couple of minutes, we were able to de-leech each other, by dabbing them with the limes. The acid in the fruit made them curl up and drop off.

They were also taught how to deal with some of the natural hazards common to these waters. Lieutenant Dennis Lilleyman, a member of Blondie Hasler's Small Operations Group, based at Hammenhiel on the Jaffna Peninsula, Ceylon, who trialled the Sleeping Beauty in tropical waters with Butch Woollcott and others, described the advice they were given:

In tropical waters one is liable to encounter various unneighbourly types of underwater denizens. I remember an instruction I read about the octopus (which I rather think must have been written with the tongue in the cheek): it said – 'As the octopus is a timid but curious creature, if one is caught by a tentacle, the thing to do is to remain motionless. The octopus, being curious, will probably feel you all over for perhaps a quarter of an hour, then it will get bored, and withdraw to its lair. If disturbed, it will get frightened and bring its tentacles into play. The thing to do then is to get as close into its body as possible. The octopus is very sensitive where the tentacle joins the body, try to tickle it under the armpits when it will convulse itself with laughter. The other method is to jab it in the eye with a knife.'

There were several alleged methods of frightening sharks. One was an evil-smelling grease to be smeared over the body, another was a perforated box of chemicals, or there was a packet of dye – presumably to be used as a smoke screen. They were all reputed to scare off sharks. On one occasion, however, when I was planning an operation in shark-infested waters, I asked advice as to the best methods of combating the brutes, and the reply I got from the authorities was: 'Before the operation, drop some dead horses into the area and the sharks will be fully occupied with those!'

Their equipment worked in different ways, too. In European waters, the protosorb canister, which extracted carbon dioxide from the diver's breath, became warm as the diver exhaled, and was then cooled by the water. The temperature of the inhaled oxygen, therefore, was one of pleasant coolness. In the tropics, however, the oxygen did not cool down: uncomfortably warm, it irritated many divers' mouths.

After the six crews had been in Trincomalee for a month, Northways decided that the value of the targets presented to the Chariot teams in South East Asia did not justify what they described as the risk of the men falling into the hands of an 'inhuman enemy'. Whilst their concern for the men's lives was applauded, not least by the men themselves, all the crews were adamant that they wanted an opportunity to 'have a crack' at the enemy, and the representations of Tod Slaughter and John McCarter were sufficient to allow one operation, at least, to go ahead. The Japanese coastal traffic along the Kra Isthmus and the Malay Peninsula down to Singapore, and around the coast of Sumatra, comprised relatively small vessels, with most battleships and larger ships over 10,000 tons operating in the Pacific rather than the Bay of Bengal or the seas around Malaya. This limited the number of targets for conventional submarines, which were now increasingly resorting to surfacing to sink Japanese vessels – which included large numbers of local junks – by gunfire rather than wasting torpedoes.

But the harbours still housed targets of value. On Phuket Island, for instance, on the Thai side of the entrance to the Malacca Strait, two 6,000-ton ex-Italian liners lay in harbour, the Lloyd Triestino company's 6,000-ton *Sumatra* and the 5,200-ton *Volpi*. Both had been scuttled by their Italian crews in December 1941,* but the

---

* They were caught in Phuket when Italy declared war. Italy (unlike Germany) did not warn its merchant fleet that war was to be declared, thus denying them the chance to get to neutral or friendly territory. In this case the Italian crews did not want their vessels to fall into the hands of the Japanese (who of course joined the war a year after Italy).

Japanese – desperately short of shipping following enormous losses in the Far East and Pacific – were working to raise them from their shallow graves, and to reuse them for the transport of troops. It was decided to send two Chariot crews against these targets, to sink the vessels at their moorings to prevent their use by the enemy once and for all. 'We were rather disappointed when we found out what the targets were,' recalled Woollcott. 'We had hoped for a couple of nice big battle wagons or maybe heavy cruisers, but all they turned out to be were a couple of old Italian merchantmen . . . and they weren't even in working order.'

Woollcott was to accompany Tony Eldridge in one Chariot (nicknamed 'Tiny'), while Petty Officer Bill Smith and Albert 'Buster' Brown would man the other (nicknamed 'Slasher'). Two full crews would accompany these teams as dressers and replacement crews. They were to be transported to Phuket on HMS *Trenchant*, which was captained by Arthur Hezlet, who had been part of Operation *Source* the previous year, when he had commanded HMS *Thrasher*, towing the ill-fated *X5*. Lieutenant Roland 'Lefty' Hindmarsh was in command of the two Chariot teams. The Chariots were placed on chocks welded to the *Trenchant*'s deck casing, one each side of the conning tower, and then tied securely to withstand their carriage across the 1,200 miles of the Bay of Bengal to their target.

On 22 October, *Trenchant* left Trincomalee, the men on *Wolfe* waving and cheering as the Charioteers departed for their long-awaited action. Little did they know that this would be the last Chariot operation of the war. The journey was uneventful, and *Trenchant* was able to travel for most of the five-day journey on the surface, a passage recalled almost lyrically by 'Lefty' Hindmarsh:

Two days later, I felt as if Trincomalee had ceased to exist. Our world was the submarine, the sea and the sky: nothing more. Hour after hour, day and night, we ploughed a furrow through an ocean without any swell: an endless deep blue like the summer

Mediterranean by day, and an intense blackness at night. Illuminated with phosphorescence as we stirred its surface into foam with our bow wave, and whirled up the water beneath us with our screws, leaving a sparkling wake that lived for a few seconds and then subsided into its dark somnolence once more.

Under the sun the blue waters of the Indian Ocean, sometimes as smooth as glass, at other times lightly stippled by some faint breeze, would suddenly be parted by a shimmering shoal of flying fish speeding above the waves as if on an imaginary roller coaster, then dropping as unexpectedly below the surface and vanishing utterly.

The cloudless sky above; the featureless blue sea and the submarine, throbbing eastwards without cease: these had a mesmeric effect upon me. Out here war did not exist, could not exist, should not exist. We had moved into an endless dimension of sea and space and sky. I spent as much time as I could up on the bridge. Ostensibly I was helping to keep watch, but the likelihood of any enemy activity so far west was minimal. The war was being fought far away in the Pacific; we were sailing through an unending zone of peace, magically created in this warm blueness of sea and sky.

'Baldy' Hezlet brought *Trenchant* to a point off Phuket on the night of 27 October. At dawn the next morning he dived, and cautiously approached the harbour to conduct a periscope reconnaissance of the two targets. The departure time for the Chariots had been set for 10.10 p.m. that night. Being able to see their targets through the periscope was a new experience for the men, and one they valued. Butch Woollcott recalled that both targets 'appeared to be quite close to the shore and not far away from each other. *Sumatra* was lying at anchor and *Volpi* was still submerged, with what looked like steel sheds built on her upper deck, to house lifting gear and there seemed to be some activity going on aboard her.' The weather was calm and clear, with the result that Hezlet wanted to take no risks with being seen, and took HMS *Trenchant* out to sea, surfacing at 7 p.m. that night off the tiny tree-covered island of Goh Dorkmai, south-east of Phuket in the Andaman Sea. Tony Eldridge remembered it as 'a perfect night with a brilliant moon. Chariot drivers then went on to the bridge and had another reconnaissance of the harbour entrance.'

The work of preparing for departure was painstaking. The personal equipment carried included escape equipment, designed to allow the men to evade the Japanese in the jungle, to live off the land and persuade native Malays and Chinese to help them. Each man carried a .38 Smith and Wesson revolver; a diver's knife; a Fairbairn–Sykes commando stiletto; and an all-purpose tool with a screwdriver, tin-opener, wire cutters and hacksaw. Survival rations of concentrated foods, condensed milk, first-aid and snake-bite equipment and two hundred pounds in Malay dollars were carefully packed in waterproof containers, together with twenty gold sovereigns for use in case the natives had no time for paper money. Every detail had been thought of, as Butch Woollcott described:

> We also carried a few short hacksaw blades encased in rubber, which we sewed into our clothes; two metal fly buttons which could be placed one on top of the other to make a compass; two or three other small compasses which could be stowed away somewhere in the clothing; and one other item, also encased in thin rubber, which I hoped very fervently that I would never have to use. This was a white tablet, about the size of an aspirin and was known as an 'L' tablet or suicide pill, to be used in the event of our wanting to escape torture. There were two watches included in the kit too. One was a pocket watch and the other a water and pressure proof one for wearing on the wrist . . .

It was a long and complex process to 'dress' for an operation. It was decidedly more complex in the confined space of a submarine, and especially so in the sweating heat of the tropics. Woollcott again:

At about nine thirty at night the chariot crews mustered in the fore-ends and our dressers began getting us into our gear. It was like an oven in there and when we'd had our rubber diving suits put on we were sweating like we were in a Turkish bath. However, the Torpedo Gunner's Mate, the C.P.O. in charge at that end of the boat, was a very thoughtful man and had prepared for this. He had cut some short lengths of hose which he ran from the louvres in the overhead air ducts down into our visors, which made conditions much more pleasant for us. My dresser was Walter ('Whacker') Payne and when he tested my breathing set he found that there was a leak in it, so he went and found another one for me.

One other thing they carried was what they called a 'Blood Chit'. It was a small piece of white silk on which was written, in a number of languages, the following:

I am a British Naval Officer who has been engaged in operations against the Japanese. If I am captured, I cannot continue to fight against the Japanese so I appeal to you to hide me and provide me with food until I can rejoin our forces. If you will help me by giving me food and hiding me in safety until our armies arrive in Malaya, you will earn the gratitude of my government who will give you a big reward and I am authorised to give you a chit to this effect.

Then they were ready to go. Tony Eldridge:

Zero hour, 10.10 p.m. 'Open fore-hatch – up divers.' By the time we were comfortably seated in our machines and the Captain was ready to trim down, our protosorb canisters were almost glowing with heat through breathing out of water. Our final instructions were from the Navigation Officer, who came down on to the saddle tanks and gave us our course – North 65 West for six and a half miles entering Phuket harbour, South 75 East for seven miles retreating from Phuket harbour. By 10.15 p.m. the launching had been completed without a hitch.

On 'Slasher', Bill Smith (known as Smithy to his mates) was initially dismayed to discover that he had a leak in his new rubber diving suit. This would mean that it would gradually fill with water and give him negative buoyancy. By the time he reached the target, he would have to ensure that he held on to the Chariot, or he would sink to the bottom with no means of saving himself. He quickly put this problem to the back of his mind, and allowed himself to be mesmerised by the still sea, brilliant moonlight and calmness of the night. There were no other vessels visible. Cutting through the water with only the phosphorescence caused by their wake to worry about, it appeared that they had 'the Andaman Sea to ourselves'. As they closed in on the harbour, they noted the absence of nets of any kind, and gently submerged 'Slasher', lining themselves up with the dark shape in the distance that was the *Volpi*.

Unbeknown to Smith and Brown as they cruised towards their target, Eldridge and Woollcott faced a serious problem of their own, described by Tony Eldridge:

I had been on my course for approximately ten minutes when I was signalled by my Number Two [Butch Woollcott] who told me he could get no oxygen from the machine and was only breathing from the one three-hour bottle attached to his bag. We then went alongside the submarine again and reported the distressing news, which, in the ordinary course of events, would have scrubbed out the attack. It was suggested to Petty Officer Woollcott that he should carry out the long run-in on air. This was immediately agreed to, which in my opinion was a most courageous decision, knowing that should we have to dive hurriedly he would have been drowned.

Getting under way again, 'Tiny' headed off towards Phuket harbour. They could see the blinking lighthouse on the island of Goh Tapou Noi, just off the Phuket beach, on their left-hand side. After about twenty minutes Woollcott managed to free whatever obstruction had been preventing oxygen getting into his bag, enabling them to slowly submerge to 18 feet. Eldridge:

The target became visible when about one and a half miles away. I started making long dives in second speed when about one and a half miles from the harbour entrance, because of the particularly bright moon. The water was very clear indeed, and I estimated the temperature as eighty-seven degrees Fahrenheit. We probably passed through a few freshwater patches as I continually found myself dropping suddenly from eighteen feet to thirty feet without any apparent reason. I dived for the final time on a compass course when five hundred yards from the target.

After what seemed to be a very long time, we finally passed under what we thought must be the bows, because of the narrow beam, and proceeded to go out on the other side and for some unknown reason dropped to thirty-five feet. I did not blow main ballast and, having regained a trim, started to come in on the port side at about twenty-two feet. When I was under the shadow of the target I blew main ballast, the time being half past midnight on the 29th. The jackstay protected us as we came up on to the bottom, and Number Two [Woollcott] got out and went forward. Finding the head not near enough to the bilge keel he signalled me to come forward slightly. As soon as I moved the main motor, the jackstay held in the barnacles and folded over backwards, leaving me cramped over to one side bearing off with my hands against the most shocking ship's bottom I have ever been on. However, under the circumstances I was really quite comfortable, seeing that I could at least breathe. To bring the head up so as to help Number Two affix it, I moved the battery aft. He then proceeded to fix the explosive head with two clips on to the bilge keel. Number Two worked incredibly fast, he had secured the head and set the clock by [0.45]. As soon as he had secured the head Number Two returned to the machine, we both shook hands over the cockpit, and proceeded to make our escape.

Number Two could not get into the machine until we were clear of the ship's bottom, but clung on to the side until we were about twenty-five yards away on our return course. Approximately forty yards from the target I received signal four, to surface, from my Number Two. Well knowing that there must be some very good reason to come up, I did so about fifty yards from the ship. I proceeded to leave the harbour on the surface at slow speed, trusting that I would not be seen, which fortunately was the case. A few minutes later my Number Two signalled me that he was OK and breathing comfortably once more. Without delay we dived away for approximately twenty-five minutes. (Apparently Number Two's complaint had been that, during the time he was working on the ship's bottom, one side of his oxygen bag had come adrift and his breathing became restricted owing to a kink in his breathing tube.) When well clear of the harbour entrance, we surfaced, blew main ballast, and proceeded in fourth speed steering for Goh Dorkmai. This was quite a comfortable trip, even though we had a slight ahead swell. I flashed the arranged signal three times on the way out and finally saw the welcome sight of a 'T' boat silhouette.

On coming alongside the submarine I was received with a fearful flashing of red lights, apparently because they thought we were going past. Petty Officer Smith on the second machine had just come back alongside and was being taken inboard. My Number Two and myself were then lugged inboard in a great hurry because of an Asdic report of an MTB in the vicinity. This prevented us from salving any gear, torches, etc., from the machine, or from removing the battery vent. Both machines' compensating tanks were flooded and main ballast was vented, thus sending them to the bottom for ever.

As the *Volpi* was sitting on the seabed, Buster Brown was forced to find an alternative place to place his charge than the underside of the hull. He managed to find an entrance to the engine room, where he attached the warhead, before making his way back to 'Slasher'. Shaking hands, Smith and Brown began heading back on the course they had been given to rendezvous with HMS *Trenchant*. It was Smith who then experienced problems:

A pin-prick hole appeared in my breathing tube and seawater seeped into the canister of Protosorb. It caused a chemical reaction which burnt my mouth, so I had to surface and put myself on to air. We returned to the rendezvous this way. Luck was with me. Nothing and nobody around; but even so I was pleased to see *Trenchant* again.

By remarkable coincidence, both 'Tiny' and 'Slasher' arrived back at *Trenchant* at exactly the same time. The submarine's Asdic operator had mistaken the oncoming Chariot engines for those of an enemy vessel – an MTB perhaps – so the two crews were bundled aboard without ceremony and told to scuttle their Chariots to allow *Trenchant* to escape. 'I swam away from the sinking Chariot,' Smith recalled, 'and then felt my "oppo" Brown cling on to my leg like grim death, which didn't please me at all. With my visor open, my swimming hampered in this way and Brown's suit full of water, I don't know what would have happened if someone on the submarine hadn't thrown me a line.' He couldn't understand why Brown was clutching hold of him. It was only when safely in the bowels of the submarine that Brown confessed that he was a non-swimmer. 'I could not believe it!' wrote Smith later. 'The mystery was that he'd managed to conceal the fact from everyone, during nearly three years of swimming and diving instruction.'

There was nothing now to do but to wait for the explosions. Woollcott thought about sleeping – he had been awake more than twenty-four hours – but he found that he was too excited to do anything but pace around in the cramped space of the submarine.

At about 5.30 a.m. I strolled along to the control room to see what was doing. The Captain was in there periodically raising the periscope and having a quick look at our targets while there seemed to be quite a lot of people clustered around him. Suddenly, at about 5.30 a.m. we heard the sound of an explosion. Unfortunately though, the periscope was lowered at the time and by the time it was raised again the full effect of the explosion had been missed, but apparently it was Smithy's target which had blown up.

The minutes ticked past . . . Then at 6.32 a.m. the Captain was looking through the periscope, when suddenly he said, 'There she goes!' Immediately there was a concerted rush for the periscope, while the Captain hurriedly backed away. Four people had had a peep, then had been brushed away, before the sound of the explosion hit the boat. I think I got in at about No. 8 but even so, there were still bits of wreckage descending and the ship had started to sink by the stern. I had another look later on and could see the bows sticking well out of the water, then later, just before *Trenchant* left Phuket Harbour, I had one last peep and all I could see was the tops of her masts above the surface.

The entire crew were jubilant at the success of the attack, and they had every right to be. 'Pity it wasn't a Jap battleship . . .' thought Bill Smith, 'but it was the best, in fact the only opportunity that had been presented to the Chariot Party in the Far East . . . Also, it was the last and fittingly the only Chariot operation that was completely successful – a textbook operation in fact.' Tony Eldridge also observed that the attack on Phuket had been the 'only completely successful British Chariot operation' of the war, because after destroying their targets the Chariots managed to recover to their parent submarine. Following the attack, HMS *Trenchant* continued on her patrol, engaging Japanese surface vessels with torpedoes and gunfire, and returned to Trincomalee, triumphant, on 21 November 1944.

NINETEEN

Cables

Captain Charles Lambe's recommendation to dispatch X-craft to the Pacific continued to fall on deaf ears in the US. For the eighteen months that followed his initial suggestion, a series of high-level representations were made to the American military authorities to deploy these weapons in their operational jurisdiction. On 23 October 1943, Claud Barry wrote again to the secretary of the Admiralty urging that measures be taken to promote the operational benefits of X-craft for use in Far Eastern and Pacific waters, in particular among their American allies. The attack on the *Tirpitz* 'proved without doubt the value of X-craft as offensive weapons', he argued. 'This offers great possibilities for the employment of X-craft in the Eastern war, for attacks against the Japanese fleets.'

It is considered that the majority of Japanese Home bases, though heavily defended, are open to attack by X-craft, and so are the Japanese advanced bases, such as Hong Kong, Truk, Jaluit, Palau, Manila, Singapore. All these are within range for attacks from United States Pacific bases, but not from bases in the British South-Eastern Asia area. It is therefore considered that, to commence operations as soon as possible, we should offer to put our X-craft and their depot ships at the disposal of the Commander-in-Chief, United States Pacific Fleet, to be based and operated as desired by him. It would be immaterial whether

251

the X-craft were towed to their scenes of action by British or United States submarines.

Barry followed this with a request for the immediate construction of eighteen X-craft modified for service in the Far East, together with a vessel similar to HMS *Bonaventure* to act as an additional depot ship there. If approved, Barry suggested that *Bonaventure* – carrying six XE-craft – could be ready for deployment to the Far East by mid-1944, with the second depot ship, carrying a further six XE-craft, in the Far East by the end of the year. On 12 November 1943 the British Admiralty Delegation (BAD) in Washington was asked to place the offer of X-craft before the US authorities, for use in the Pacific:

Operation SOURCE . . . proved beyond doubt the value of X-craft as an offensive weapon against an enemy major unit known to be in the habit of lying for considerable periods in the same harbour. Very minor improvements to the towing equipment and by providing the passage crews to effect a series of reliefs, X-craft towed by submarines could carry out very long passages. It would be immaterial whether towage were provided by British or American submarines. This offers great possibilities for employment against the Japanese main units at Truk or at their home bases. These places would be within range from United States Pacific bases but not from bases in the British S.E. Asia command; therefore towage would have to be provided by American submarines. We are willing to construct 6 X-craft now, suitable for service in the tropics, followed by 6 and possibly 12 others, all with trained crews. Also to put the depot ship HMS BONAVENTURE at the disposal of the Americans in order to attack the Japanese main units by the end of 1944. This depot ship can only operate six craft, so that it would be necessary for the Americans to provide a similar ship to carry six more craft, the further six being freighted out for use as replacements.

However, on 22 December 1943 BAD relayed a curt response from the Americans: Admiral Ernest King, the combative commander-in-chief, United States Fleet (COMINCH), while thanking the British for their kind offer, refused it, on the ground that it would take his own patrol submarines away from their primary duties. His attitude was understandable. In King's conception of things Japanese, 'main units' needed to be attacked and defeated, and the best place to do this was when they were at sea, by coordinated attack from sea and land-based aircraft, as well as by surface and sub-surface combat 'assets'.

There was a time when the Royal Navy would have entirely concurred with King's strategy for taking on and sinking each and every one of Japan's combat ships, but that was before Alexandria, December 1941. Now, the Admiralty believed passionately in taking every opportunity to destroy major enemy naval assets *before* they sailed, when the enemy believed they were safe in their harbours. They extended this to attacking and destroying strategic naval infrastructure in harbours, as was evidenced by Operation *Chariot*, the extraordinary Trojan Horse attack by British motor launches and an ancient destroyer packed with explosives, and commandos, in March 1942 against the German-held port of Saint-Nazaire.* But the Pacific was an American-led theatre of war, with naval operations helmed by King, a man who was concerned to preserve American naval prerogatives in the region, especially against the British, for whom he held a well-known disregard. The presence of the British Pacific Fleet was forced on King in 1945 against his will, and it may have been also the case that, well-intentioned though they were, efforts by the Admiralty to send X-craft into the region as well ignored the American determination to restrict the naval combat presence in the Pacific to American forces alone.

---

* See the author's *Into the Jaws of Death: The True Story of the Legendary Raid on Saint-Nazaire* (London: Quercus, 2013).

The Admiralty debated its options throughout 1944. In March it replied to BAD, believing that the stumbling block to its earlier proposal was the utilisation of US resources, ruling out any reliance on American naval assets:

It is disappointing that Admiral King is unwilling to provide American submarines for towage of X-craft. We are so convinced of the value of this form of attack that we are prepared to accept the reduction in normal submarine operations involved in detaching 7 submarines from Eastern Fleet for this purpose.

Request you will obtain Admiral King's concurrence to our sending BONAVENTURE with 6 X-craft to the Pacific. The operation would be mounted entirely by British resources and would, of course be under US operational control.

No clear commitment was ever received from King, so the Admiralty proceeded to plan for the suggested operations regardless, convinced of the X-craft's essential merits. If politics accounts for its ally's reluctance to welcome a Royal Navy contribution to the Pacific campaign, London seems never to have twigged. It was clear that with no solid role in the Pacific, the bulk of British X-craft would need to be scrapped. Barry was determined to give the craft one last shot, by sending *Bonaventure* directly to the Pacific.

'Tiny' Fell recalls that he was sent for by Claud Barry in London in December 1943 and instructed to take over HMS *Bonaventure*, ready to proceed to the Pacific. Carrying *XE1* to *XE6* in what was now constituted as the 14th Submarine Flotilla, HMS *Bonaventure* departed on 21 February 1945. Travelling via the Azores, Trinidad and the Panama Canal, she emerged into the Pacific on 20 March, before heading to Pearl Harbor. Unfortunately, the news Fell received when he arrived at the home of the US Pacific Fleet was bad. 'We were not wanted by the Americans in the Pacific,' he recorded disconsolately. 'They had no tasks for us and it appeared to the Admiral, who broke the news to me, that we might as well go back to the UK where the war was rapidly ending.'

Unaware of the politics behind their deployment, Fell ignored this setback and set himself energetically to canvas support for X-craft operations from whomsoever he could. It was a demoralising period for all, as *Bonaventure* travelled first to a remote Pacific Island – Funafuti in the Ellis Islands – before sailing to Brisbane, in search of an operational tasking. In a letter to his brother, Mick Magennis expressed the concern of all the X-craft crews about whether they still had a role to play in defeating the Japanese:

> Left here 14 May and proceeded to Townsville, small port north-east coast of Australia, left next day for the island of Cid on the Barrier Reef. Arrived following day. Commenced working up again, but nobody interested. Have got the impression that we have been dumped here till they consider what they will do with us. The skipper is flying all over the various areas pleading for targets, sort of hawking his wares.

In the chapter in his memoirs entitled 'The Struggle for a Job', Fell told how he left *Bonaventure* in Australia before travelling huge distances in uncomfortable military transport planes – from Australia to the Philippines, via Papua New Guinea – in an attempt to present his case to Rear Admiral James Fife, who commanded the submarines of the US Seventh Fleet. When, finally, Fell found himself in front of Fife, the American listened sympathetically, but ultimately could not help. He had no political reason for not using British midget submarines, but by this stage of the war, little enemy shipping of any worth was now found south of Shanghai: operations by X-craft appeared unlikely because there were simply no credible targets for them.

Disconsolate, Fell flew back to Townsville – where the X-craft and their crews were training in their new tropical environment – bearing the bad news that, with no remaining military rationale, the remaining X-craft would be scrapped, the 14th Flotilla wound up, and the men transferred to general service. It seemed that a brilliant idea had met a sad end without ever having been developed to its full potential; and arguably because of reasons entirely unrelated to the military capabilities of the equipment or the skills, training and experience of the crews.

Then, in the dying days of May 1945, out of the blue, came a request from the US Navy. Did Fell believe that X-craft could cut through submarine telegraph cables? 'Of course they could!' was Fell's response. The X-craft was designed to allow a diver to exit the vessel to penetrate protective barriers, and a cable – though thick – would be no different. While the Japanese military codes had long been broken, it was apparent they were continuing to use the pre-war civilian telegraph cables that lay between Hong Kong and Saigon and Singapore, together with one direct from Saigon to Singapore. If these were severed, the last effective (and secure) means of communication the Japanese enjoyed would be removed. In a matter of days, a plan was pulled together, and training begun to identify the best ways to find, and sever, these cables.

In order to grab the cable a simple grapnel was designed which, when dragged behind an XE-craft, was able to pull it from the seabed and the sand or mud sediment in which it had been lying. The pulling power of the vessel, however, meant that the grapnel could only penetrate to a depth of about six inches: if the cable was not lying on or just under the sea floor, it would be difficult to find. The diver would exit the W&D compartment and, using hydraulic cutters, cut through the cable.

The first task was to find the exact location of each of the respective cables. Shean recalled: 'By some miracle, *Bonaventure*'s Pilot [navigator] produced charts from his library showing the exact position of these cables at Saigon and Hong Kong.' Clearly, however, the cable would have to be found, and cut, in very shallow water, as diving for any length of time on pure oxygen below 30 feet, as all

X-men now knew, was dangerous. It would be possible to drag, and find, the cable at deeper depths, but it would need to be hauled into shallower waters for cutting. With *Bonaventure* in the Whitsunday Islands in Northern Queensland a wire hawser was laid across Cid harbour on which the XE-craft could practise. These trials successfully completed during May, *Bonaventure* moved south to conduct training on a real – though unused – telephone cable that entered the ocean at Hervey Bay, south of Bundaberg and close to Fraser Island.

It was here, however, that tragedy struck, and two experienced X-men – both members of Lieutenant Ian Fraser's *XE3* – lost their lives to Oxygen Pete. The problem did not stem from finding the cable – the grapnels did a good job; it arose because the energy expended by the diver in reaching and then cutting the grapnel threatened him with oxygen poisoning. Mick Magennis, one of *XE3*'s divers, recorded the trial off Hervey Bay:

Had a go at it myself, done it OK but realise how slow one must go. Working too hard on oxygen at over thirty feet is dangerous, liable to black out. Had another couple of goes at this found it OK. Lieutenant [David] Carey, RN, our first lieutenant and second diver very keen to have a go. These second divers are not properly coursed divers, are merely blokes who are very keen. Lieutenant Carey had done quite a lot of diving with me and was good. Twenty-third, Carey went out, was away at cable twenty minutes, when skipper saw him through periscope coming back, he swam into wet-and-dry compartment, gave thumbs down then seemed to tumble out again. Surfaced the craft and went down with other divers but found no trace of him. Presumed oxygen exhaustion. Next day Lieutenant [Bruce] Enzer [who had successfully reconnoitered Omaha Beach just before D-Day], another second diver done exactly same thing only he surfaced then sank, never found him. One more experienced diver bailed out and just made the surface, another blacked out in W & D.

Morale hit rock bottom following the loss of these two popular and experienced men, and Fell was tempted to abandon the mission altogether. However, during the week that followed, each diver was able to make a successful cut in the cable, and confidence returned. Oxygen Pete was not to be trifled with, however, and the significant threat posed to the safety of the divers by over-exertion at depths greater than 30 feet was on everyone's minds. The willingness of the divers to return to their dangerous work following the deaths of two of their friends spoke of discipline and courage of the highest order, especially since, with the war in Europe now over, they might have felt that they no longer had to exert themselves as before. But Fell, watching in admiration, saw no diminution of their commitment.

He felt able therefore to allow the mission to proceed, and he flew by a convoluted four-day route to Subic Bay in the Philippines to present his plans to Admiral Fife. The American accepted them without demur, then looked up over his spectacles and said to Fell: 'What about having a crack at the two ten-thousand-ton cruisers in Singapore while we are at the cables?' After all these weeks, this was precisely what he had been looking for, and exactly the work for which the vessels had been designed. Fell nearly collapsed in astonishment:

> The sheer delight at hearing these words was almost too much for me. I can only remember Jimmy Fife taking me off to the beautiful new mess that had just been completed and giving me an old-fashioned that nearly knocked my head off.

The two cruisers were the *Takao* and the *Myōkō*. They were berthed in shallow waters in the Johore Strait, and while they no longer provided a naval threat to the Allies – the *Takao* had been torpedoed by a US submarine and was undergoing repairs – with their 8-inch guns they presented a hazard to the British and Indian troops expected to advance on Singapore following the invasion of

Malaya – Operation *Zipper* – due to take place in September 1945. Travelling back to Australia as fast as he could – he later described the journey as a 'nightmare': 5,000 miles in forty-six hours in the back of seatless cargo planes – Fell rejoined *Bonaventure* and began making detailed plans for four separate missions against Japanese targets.

The plan at this stage was that D-Day for all four missions would be 31 July 1945. On 8 July the *Bonaventure* sailed for Subic Bay – a watchful voyage through a region still full of lurking dangers – arriving on 20 July. Fell briefed Admiral Fife on the final plans and received his blessing for the operation. It was here that *Bonaventure* met up with her four Royal Navy towing submarines – *Spark*, *Stygian*, *Selene* and *Spearhead* – which were supported by their depot ship, HMS *Maidstone*.

A second triumph for Fell came during this period in Subic Bay. Through his personal advocacy and the professionalism of the crews – and their self-evident pride in their XE-craft – he won over the commander of US submarines in the Pacific, Admiral Charles Lockwood, who became an enthusiastic X-craft convert after visiting *Bonaventure* and spending several hours under water in Max Shean's *XE4*. It was a remarkable turnaround in American policy, one driven by personal experience and engagement rather than politics. One wonders what might have happened if Lockwood's introduction to these remarkable machines and their skilled and dynamic crews had been made a year before: he now began energetically looking at opportunities to use them against the remnants of the Japanese fleet across the Pacific.

The tasks for the two missions were allocated by Fell as follows:

1. Attack on the *Myōkō* – *XE1*, commanded by Lieutenant John ('Jack') Smart, towed by HMS *Stygian*, from a launch site in Brunei Bay, on the island of Borneo
2. Attack on the *Takao* – *XE3*, commanded by Lieutenant Ian Fraser, towed by HMS *Spark* from a launch site in Brunei Bay

3. Cutting the Saigon cable – *XE4*, commanded by Max Shean, towed by HMS *Spearhead* from a launch site in Brunei Bay
4. Cutting the Hong Kong cable – *XE5*, commanded by Lieutenant Pat Westmacott, towed by HMS *Selene*, starting from Subic Bay

The operation was now completely 'joint' – that is, inter-Allied. Admiral Jimmy Fife took command of both ventures, and he and his ninety-strong staff joined HMS *Bonaventure* for the two-day journey to Brunei Bay, off the western coast of Borneo, from whence the operations against Singapore and Saigon were to begin. An emotional Fife gave an address to the crews of *XE1* and *XE3* before they sailed. According to Fell, he had completely endeared himself to the British crews.

Leaving Subic Bay after a hurricane on 23 July, the XE-crafts' depot ship and its two escorting US destroyers arrived off Muara, Brunei's port, on the morning of 26 July. With the minimum of fuss, both *XE1* and *XE3* began their tows on the 600-mile voyage to Singapore at 3 p.m. that day. At 5 a.m. next morning – 27 July – Max Shean began his journey to the southern coast of Vietnam, taking two divers in his five-man crew (Sub-Lieutenants A. K. 'Jock' Bergius and Ken Briggs, RANVR). Ginger Coles and B. A. N. Kelly were his other two crewmates. There were two cables to cut on this mission, one that headed for Hong Kong, and another that crossed the South China Sea to Singapore. The passage crew for the three-day tow was commanded by John Britnell, who had done the same task for Shean during the attack on Bergen in April the previous year.

Max Shean has left a vivid account of his journey:

At 4 a.m. on the fourth day, crews changed over by bringing *XE4* close astern of *Spearhead*, making fast with a short line and running the motor astern to prevent contact. We stepped from one to the other. Sea and swell were low, enabling the changeover to be completed quickly and easily. The engine was run for half an hour to ventilate, following which we dived, and towed at ten knots. The craft was in excellent condition. At 11 a.m. we surfaced to ventilate. I went up onto the casing to keep a lookout for aircraft as *Spearhead* had dived three hours earlier, and we were nearing Japanese held territory.

All that I saw of note was a sea snake quite close to port . . . We ventilated again at 4 p.m. At 7 p.m. *Spearhead* phoned to suggest that I might like to surface to have a look at Cape St Jacques lighthouse [near Saigon] to the east north east, seventeen miles away. This was to be our principal landmark for the task ahead, when accurate position finding would be essential. I surfaced, took a quick look, went below, and dived the craft. We surfaced finally at 9 p.m., and having said our farewells, slipped the tow, and proceeded at half speed on engine toward Cape St Jacques. The night was quite dark, the lighthouse was not operating, and I could not yet distinguish its outline as we closed the shore. The only other landmark was a range of mountains called Nui Baria, to the north . . .

The wind was rising while we were running in to make a landfall on the lighthouse, setting up a short sea in the comparatively shallow water over the Formosa Bank. Spray swept over the casing, misting up the binocular lenses till they were useless. Several times I had to go below to clean them. To get back up on the casing in a choppy sea, one had to open the hatch and quickly leap up to sit on the casing, swing legs out of the hatchway, and over the side, and shut the hatch before a wave broke over the casing and down the hatch.

One time I did all this just as a larger wave than usual broke over the craft and swept me into the water. *XE4* was going slow ahead on engine, and by the time I got my head above water, I was back level with the rudder. I took several swift strokes, and grabbed at the jumping wire which ran from the periscope guard to the rudder. At this speed of about two knots, it was not difficult to pull myself hand over hand, forward along the wire, and regain the casing, even with the binoculars hanging on their lanyard around my neck.

I had to go below again to clean the lenses and to inform the crew of my swim. They were not aware that anything was wrong. If I had missed that wire, which we had rigged for that very purpose, *XE4* would have continued on until maybe a quarter of an hour had passed before the crew noticed the absence of any communication from the upper deck. Then they would have discovered my absence and turned around to search, though a recovery would have been unlikely. But, I had caught the wire, after swimming the fastest few strokes of my life, so all was well. Next time on deck, I spotted the outline of the lighthouse.

Having established our position from our own observation and found, as expected, that it confirmed that given to us by *Spearhead* we stopped, and commenced standing charge of air and batteries. I rigged the grapnel in readiness for the day's work . . .

Shean then began the long, slow process to trawl for and find the correct cable, something that he knew would not be easy, because a number of abandoned cables lay off the shore. As it transpired they also had to contend with heavy traffic by junks in the waters overhead, and he was forced to stay still on the seabed for the first few hours after arrival. Their presence would have been reported to the Japanese had they been spotted. The first run was a disappointment, failing to connect with a cable, and *XE4* turned to repeat the process from the opposite direction. It was nerve-racking. Every member of the five-strong crew was desperate for their mission to succeed. Shean continues:

The next run was started after turning to starboard and setting course to cross the cable's recorded position in slightly deeper water. There was nothing for the divers and me to do but to have patience. Ben was keeping depth as best he could with the ever changing pull of the rig, while Ginge was keeping her on course. I lay for a few minutes on the small bunk next to the chart table, feeling depressed. I knew that we could not expect to contact the cable first time. All the same, after all our trials, preparation and the activity of the previous twenty-four hours with little sleep, we had arrived at an anti-climax. What if we could not find the cable? How deep was it in the alluvial deposit from the Mekong River, the mouths being just a short distance away? On the other hand, all was well with *XE4*. This was only the second run on the first morning. There was no deadline, we could carry on dragging for a long time yet. There did not seem to be any Japanese patrol vessels around, though among the junks there could be sympathetic or opportunistic observers, ready to report anything suspicious. We must not break surface, however difficult it was to control the craft's depth while pulling a sea plough.

At 10 a.m., I came to periscope depth and took bearing on the lighthouse and mountains. We had passed the line of the cable for the second time. The Cable and Wireless company engineer had assured us that the positions as shown on the chart would be accurate to within fifty feet. We had ploughed across it twice, so it must be too deep in the sand. The next run must be in deeper water, where finer sand, or silt, could be expected. I turned to port and set course for run number three. The depth now exceeded forty feet. At 10.27 a.m. the craft suddenly stopped. I increased motor speed. We remained in position until full speed, then moved forward. I turned to re-cross the same position, at reduced speed. She stopped again. This could be it, though there was a doubt. During trials, when a cable was caught, the grapnel did not let go. But the only way to be sure was to have a look. The motor was stopped, and water pumped into the compensating tank to hold the craft in position on the seabed. Water was flowing past the scuttles at about half a knot.

Ken Briggs dressed and went through the W&D. Depth showing on the gauge was forty feet, indicating a bottom depth of fifty feet. Ken must not remain there for more than fifteen minutes. The understanding between us was that the diver should attach himself to the cutter hose. Then, if he were overdue, we would surface, pull him aboard, dive immediately, revive him, and await any reaction from the Japanese. But nothing went wrong, except that Ken returned within five minutes to report there was no cable, only a patch of hard clay. We continued the third run, feeling rather disappointed.

However, only ten minutes later – at 12.05 p.m. – in 44 feet of water, *XE4* suddenly stopped, held fast by the grapnel. Ken Briggs climbed out of the W&D compartment and within minutes had found the grapnel locked onto the Saigon–Singapore cable. The hydraulic cutter sliced through it with ease, Briggs returning in triumph to the submarine with a section of the cable as evidence. The crew were delighted, and Shean now shifted track to look for the Hong Kong cable. At 1.26 p.m. *XE4* was again brought up short. The second diver, Sub Lieutenant Bergius, RNVR, exited the craft and after two attempts he returned with a foot of cable as evidence of his achievement. Operation *Sabre*, the name of the mission, had been a complete success. All that was now required was to rendez-vous with HMS *Spearhead*.

The main aim of Operation *Sabre* had been achieved: that is, assuming that they were the correct cables, which was not really in doubt, as bearings on the lighthouse had confirmed. A secondary task for *XE4* was to attack enemy ships harbouring in the Mekong delta, for which the vessel carried a cargo of limpet mines. However, on meeting HMS *Spearhead* at 11.40 p.m. that night they were told that there were no Japanese ships taking refuge there, and they were to return to Brunei under tow. The XE-craft was hooked up, passage crew transferred by rubber dinghy, and the return journey got under way. They reached *Bonaventure* in Muara in less than three days.

Pat Westmacott's *XE5* also found and damaged the Hong Kong–Saigon cable in a dramatic operation, but the crew did not know of their success at the time. The first – and almost catastrophic – difficulty *XE5* faced was the breaking of their towing cable, some thirty-six hours after leaving Subic Bay, in very heavy weather, on 30 July 1945. The 600-mile journey to Hong Kong began on Friday 27 July, and for the first day and a half all went well. *XE5* settled to a good trim at between 110 and 140 feet, surfacing every six hours to 'guff through'. Westmacott enjoyed 'looking forward through the night periscope (only about two inches above the casing), one saw the little spots of phosphorescence stirred up by the vibrating tow ahead flying towards one, as if the watcher at the periscope was in some space craft shooting through space; a glorious sight which I never tired of watching'. Then, on 30 July, the tow parted. The first indication Westmacott had that anything was wrong was the depth indicator slowly dropping to 240 feet. For some reason, the telephone with HMS *Selene* was not working, but he assumed that the towing submarine had also dived, and so gently recovered his trim to 130 feet. But something was not right.

At 2.20 a.m. he surfaced. His log reported:

0220 Surfaced. No sign of SELENE. Tow hanging down in the water at a steep angle. Estimated that it was about 54 miles, 325 degrees to the slipping position. Slipped the tow and proceeded. Course 325 degrees. Rendezvous with SELENE seemed unlikely. I intended to proceed with the operation, assuming that SELENE would await me at the pre-arranged recovery position.

0245 Sighted green flare bearing 070 degrees. Altered course towards. Burnt one flare. Forty minutes later, no more flares having been seen, I resumed my course for Hong Kong.

It was then, at 5 a.m., that *Selene* made contact and came alongside. After establishing another tow line, they proceeded towards Hong Kong two hours later.

At 7.50 a.m. next day *XE5* said farewell to HMS *Selene* and proceeded the remaining 25 miles to Lamma Island, on the southwest coast of Hong Kong Island. The large number of native junks on the sea convinced Westmacott that the area was relatively mine-free. They waited on the seabed until nightfall allowed them to surface to recharge their batteries and prepare the grapnel. Cable and Wireless Ltd, who had laid and owned the cables, had explained precisely where the cable to Singapore was to be found, in the East Lamma Passage at a depth of about 40 feet. Westmacott described the first trawl of the drag the following morning:

At 9.53 a.m. the grapnel fouled something and at 10.27 the diver, S/Lt. Clark, left the craft. The bottom was soft white mud, into which *XE5* sank about four feet. The visibility was barely 2 feet. After about 20 minutes, we heard the cutter working and four minutes afterwards Clark re-appeared at the W and D hatch and entered hurriedly. It was clear that he was in some distress. We pumped down and opened up. What had happened was that Nobby Clark had caught his finger in the cutter's blade and had badly cut it and fractured the bone. In addition, his body had been stung all over by the barbed tentacles of Portuguese men-of-war [venomous cnidarians].

When Westmacott told him to lie down on the battery compartment so he could receive an injection of morphia he exclaimed: 'God! If it isn't one thing it's another!' The second diver, Lieutenant D. V. M. Jarvis, could not free the grapnel from whatever it had become embedded in, and they had to abandon it.

That night, the injured Clark was transferred to HMS *Selene*, after which *XE5* returned to Lamma Island. A further day in the sticky mud and murky water failed to find either the original impediment or a new target. After three days of continuous but seemingly fruitless dragging – seventeen passes were made in total – Westmacott came to the view that they would never find the cable, and regretfully headed back to the rendezvous with HMS *Selene* for the journey back to Subic Bay, their tails between their legs. Some weeks later, however, when the British reoccupied Hong Kong, they discovered that *XE5* had indeed damaged the cable, sufficiently so for it to cease operating – the Japanese being forced to rely on the use of radio traffic alone for the last few weeks of the war.

When Admiral Lockwood received news of the efforts of Westmacott and *XE5* to find the cable he sent a signal of admiration: 'Well tried, the little guys with a lotta guts!' It was a good summing up of what Fell described as one of 'the most daring, dangerous and tenacious operations of the war'. Pat Westmacott and Max Shean's separate successes entirely vindicated the use of XE-craft in this venture, and demonstrated not just the versatility of these craft but the commitment and professionalism of the crews, especially the divers. Knowing the substantial risks they faced by breathing pure oxygen at depth, they repeatedly scorned death to achieve their mission, despite the loss of David Carey and Bruce Enzer just weeks before.

TWENTY

Takao and *Myōkō*

The X-craft's swansong in the Second World War also proved to be one of its most spectacular missions. Leaving the sanctuary of *Bonaventure* and the tiny Bruneian port of Muara in the late afternoon of 26 July 1945, *XE1* and *XE3* headed out across the South China Sea for Singapore at the outset of Operation *Struggle*. The attack crew of *XE3*, commanded by Lieutenant Ian ('Tich') Fraser, with the very experienced Leading Seaman Mick Magennis as diver, ERA Charlie Reed and New Zealander Sub Lieutenant Lanyon 'Kiwi' Smith (who had taken the place of the unfortunate David Carey) at the controls, boarded the submarine by dinghy – exchanging places with the passage crew – at first light on 30 July, off the famous Horsburgh Lighthouse on Pedra Branca island 34 miles east of Singapore. They waited on the seabed until 11 p.m. that night to make their way into Singapore harbour, the darkness permitting a surface approach for much of the night.

The first problem facing both crews was navigating in the dark (it was cloudy, with no moon) without lights and unaided by any of the navigational buoys that marked out these treacherous waters in peacetime. The deep-water channels flowing into the harbour were now impossible to identify, and frequent shallow water posed a significant threat of grounding. That, together with the presence of minefields, made access to the harbour a very dangerous proposition. On both craft the commanding officers stood on the casing, roped to the stanchion, passing instructions down the voice tube to the crew. A fast 5 knots was maintained until half-past midnight.

Fraser's log on *XE3* demonstrates the careful attention to compass-based navigation during the night leading through to D-Day, 31 July. In a testament to Fell's organisational and planning ability, the date for the attack of *XE1* and *XE3* was exactly as he had originally planned:

> 11 p.m. 30 July to 0.34 a.m. 31 July – 240 degrees at 5 knots on diesel engine
>
> 0.34 a.m. to 1.28 a.m. 31 July – 260 degrees at 5 knots on diesel engine
>
> 1.28 a.m. to 1.38 a.m. – 224 degrees at 5 knots on diesel engine
>
> 1.38 a.m. to 2.17 a.m. – 279 degrees at 5 knots on diesel engine
>
> 2.17 a.m. to 2.47 a.m. – 279 degrees on battery power
>
> 2.47 a.m. to 4.00 a.m. – 280 degrees at 4.5 knots on diesel engine

The reason for switching to battery power alone was the suspected presence of a Japanese hydrophone listening post at the outer entrance to the harbour.

A fishing boat was sighted at 3 a.m. and two further larger vessels at 4.20 a.m., which forced Fraser to dive. At a depth of 30 feet he continued into the Johore Strait, again using compass-point navigation. Now and then he was able to secure fixes from known waypoints, such as Johore Hill, which confirmed his position. It was exhausting work, and they struggled to stay alert in the hot and humid environment of the vessel, despite taking Benzedrine tablets to keep them awake.

The first major challenge in the daylight was passing through the anti-shipping boom at the entrance to the inner harbour. Keeping just under the surface, at 10.30 a.m. they finally approached the boom, and were astonished to find it wide open. An anchored trawler guarded it, so Fraser took *XE3* through on battery power in case the guards were alert with their hydrophones. Once inside the inner harbour, the surface was as still as a millpond, and forced Fraser to use his periscope sparingly: in these waters the periscope wash was a dangerous giveaway for a vigilant watcher.

At 12.50 p.m. the *Takao* was spotted through the periscope by Fraser, whose excitement at finding the great grey target exactly where he expected it to be was shared by the crew. Here, at last, was the opportunity for which they had waited so long. The cruiser lay in water so shallow that it rested on the bottom at low tide. They had to time their approach to match high tide: even then there would only be inches to spare as they sneaked under the enemy hull.

The first attack run began just after 2 p.m., when Fraser brought *XE3* slowly onto the seabed – a depth of about 22 feet – and slid her beneath the *Takao*. For this operation both *XE1* and *XE3* were armed with limpet mines in addition to the two explosive cargoes weighing two tons each. An attack would require Magennis to exit the craft through the W&D compartment, extract the limpet mines one by one from the containers on both side of the X-craft, and fix them individually to the hull of the *Takao*. Fraser had been briefed that the Japanese cruiser lay across a depression in the seabed, where the high-tide depth at bow and stern was very shallow, but a deeper water pocket lay in the middle of the vessel. He had expressed some reservations to Fell about finding this deeper water and being able to manoeuvre under the enemy warship, but the sight of the massive vessel – some 630 feet long – looming through his periscope dissolved his concerns: he had to get beneath it.

Fraser asserted:

Each of the crew must have been by now feeling the strain of nineteen hours without real sleep and nine hours breathing in the confines of a midget submarine. But now had come the supreme moment, which could have been their last. They knew they must concentrate harder than ever before if they were to make a success of our allotted task. And concentrate they did.

270

The water was calm and clear. The huge armaments looked for-midable:

> Her three for'ard turrets stood out distinctly like Olympic winners
> on a rostrum, the centre one above the other two, and all three
> close together. The guns in 'C' turret pointed aft, unlike any other
> cruiser constructed at that time. Her massive bridge-work was
> easily discernible, with the thick black-topped funnel raking astern
> of it. I could see the second funnel, smaller, and somewhat insig-
> nificant, stuck vertically upwards between the two tripod trellis-
> work masts, and on 'B' and 'X' turrets a sort of tripod framework.

They swooped towards their target at a depth of 40 feet, popping
up regularly to 10 feet for a look through the periscope. The clear-
ness of the water gave Fraser some concern: he could only hope
that no one on board the cruiser looked down. If they did, they
were bound to see the approaching submarine. At 12.08 p.m. they
were 2,000 yards off her port bow, and rapidly closed in on their
prey. When they were 400 yards from the target, Fraser raised the
periscope and was spurred to a sudden dive when he found himself
a stone's throw from a passing cutter, full of sailors. As luck would
have it, none of the men were looking down, and did not see the
trespasser below them. They were so close they could see the men's
faces, their lips moving in chatter, one of them casually trailing his
hand in the water.

At 200 yards they gently bottomed at a depth of 30 feet, and then
bumped and scraped their way forward, at some points the depth
gauge showing only 15 feet. Gradually the water – seen through
Fraser's periscope – darkened, and they knew they were coming
under the shadow of the enemy ship. With a crash they then hit its
side. In dread that the noise of the impact had alerted the enemy,
they stood there and sweated in the darkness.

The depth gauge now showed only 13 feet. Fraser judged that
they were too far forward, and had missed the deeper depression

that lay under the centre of the vast ship, so he attempted to pull back, but *XE3* refused to budge. Somehow they had become jammed between the *Takao* and the seabed. Ten minutes of struggle were required – a time of 'severe strain' in Fraser's recollection, in which a considerable amount of dark mud was stirred up – before they broke loose.

Aiming to hit *Takao* amidships, at 3.03 p.m. they approached again from a distance of 1,000 yards. This time they did locate the depression under the vessel. Sliding across the seabed at a depth of 13 feet, they slipped into it without striking her hull. They were underneath! The depth gauge showed 20 feet. They were resting on the seabed now, with only a foot between them and the bottom of *Takao*'s dirty, barnacle-encrusted hull. Magennis strapped on his breathing apparatus and clambered carefully into the Wet and Dry compartment. His instructions were to fit as many of the six limpet mines in the attached container as quickly and silently as he could. On the XE craft the W&D had an observation window, and Fraser could see the water slowly rising around the seated Magennis, who was breathing calmly into his DSEA.

Through the night periscope, Fraser could see out into the inky darkness outside, the keel of the *Takao* clearly visible for about 15 yards in both directions. It seemed to Fraser, with the sunlight shining down to the outer edges of their shallow depression, that they were in a cave. By now he could see that the W&D was full of water, but that Magennis was having difficulty getting out: it appeared that the hatch could not be opened fully because it was jammed against the *Takao*'s hull. It was with a sense of relief that he saw Magennis's feet finally disappear from view, as he managed to get out.

Magennis had had to remove his DSEA, take a deep breath and extricate himself from the compartment before putting the breathing hose and equipment back on when he was outside. He looked towards the periscope and gave Fraser a thumbs-up sign, but Fraser noticed with concern a dribble of bubbles emerging from his suit: there must be a leak in one of the valves, and this was a dangerous problem, as bubbles could be easily spotted by someone on deck above. Inside the boat there was nothing that the men could now do but wait patiently and trust that Magennis would complete his gruelling task before the tide began to drain away, leaving them stranded.

Magennis found himself engaged on the most difficult job of his entire naval career. The immediate problem, apart from safely extricating himself from the submarine, lay in attaching the six limpet mines to the heavily encrusted hull of the enemy cruiser. It proved to be exhausting work, as he had somehow to hold on to each mine while scraping at barnacles and weed with his diving knife. All the while the slow leak from his DSEA valve was a reminder that he had limited time in store, and any sharp-eyed lookout above could not fail to notice the steady flow of bubbles on the surface. The limpets, despite their neutral buoyancy, were large and ungainly devices, and even when a big enough patch of barnacles had been scraped away, the magnetic holdfasts did not always do what they were meant to. On several occasions he found himself chasing limpets that had failed to stick, and restarting the process. It was exhausting work. He managed nevertheless to plant six mines, in two groups of three, each group about 60 yards in either direction of *XE3*. When at last the job was completed, he made his way back to the X-craft, took off his breathing hose again, and squeezed inside.

Inside the submarine, the wait for Magennis's return was agonising, and tested Fraser's patience almost to breaking point. They could hear him every time he came back to the container to take out each limpet, and thought that he could move faster, having no idea of the strife he was enduring in the dark waters outside. Fraser judged that the time it took to do this was thirty minutes, but it felt an eternity. 'I cursed every little sound he made,' Fraser recalled, 'for every little sound was magnified a thousand times by my nerves. It was a long wait.' With the engines off, the air-

273

conditioning was not operating, making the inside of the boat stifling hot. The sweat streamed from them all, dripping copiously onto the deck and mingling with the condensation pouring off the inside of the hull.

Then, abruptly, Magennis was back – clambering into the W&D, closing the hatch and sitting there while the water drained out. Fraser was intensely relieved. When he learned the full story of Magennis's achievement, it amazed him. 'Looking back on the limpet-placing part of the operation, I see how wonderfully well Magennis did his work,' he was to write. 'He was the first frogman to work against an enemy from a midget submarine in the manner designed: he was the first and only frogman during the whole X-craft operations ever to leave a boat under an enemy ship and to attach limpet mines: in fact, he was the only frogman to operate from an X-craft in harbour against enemy shipping.'

They had to get out quickly, as time was ebbing away with the tide. Fraser ordered the two side charges now to be released. They were set to explode in six hours' time. The procedure to release them was simple: an internal wheel was turned which unscrewed first to allow water into the charge, and then pushed it off the side of the X-craft. Simple. Even before Magennis was out of the compartment, Fraser was unscrewing the containers. But on this occasion things went awry, as Fraser would write later:

The port charge fell away – we heard it bump down our side, but we hung on for Magennis to re-enter the craft before finally letting the starboard limpet-carrier go. As a result of this delay, it became too heavy and would not release or slide away. Such an emergency had already been thought of by the designers of XE-craft, and an additional wheel had been provided. This operated a pusher to push the side cargo off, and between us we wound the wheel out to its limit, but with no effect. The bottom of the cargo swung out from the ship's side, but the top was still held fast. By now I felt sure that the pins at the top were holding, but I thought to myself that the movement of the craft might shake it loose. We certainly couldn't make headway very far with two tons of dead weight fast to our side.

To their horror, they found themselves stuck fast. Fraser strove to shift the vessel, moving forwards and sideways, trying to shake off the errant charge, but nothing seemed able to budge *XE3* from her position underneath the *Takao*. He considered evacuating the vessel while they had the chance – every second with the falling tide was bringing the 10,000 tons of enemy warship down on the roof of the XE-craft, and soon they would not have the opportunity to escape – and hiding in the swamps until the British arrived in the next few months.

They tried every trick in the book to shake themselves free, moving ballast from front to rear and trying to waggle the vessel from side to side. Then just when it appeared that they would have to consign her to a watery grave, *XE3* began to move. Fraser reckoned them to be about 30 feet on the left-hand side of the cruiser, at a depth of 17 feet, but although the port charge had dropped into the depression successfully the right-hand charge was still attached. They would need to remove it manually. Although exhausted by his exertions, Magennis at once volunteered to go back out and see what he could do. He climbed into the W&D compartment for the second time. Armed with a large spanner, he hammered away at the charge container, trying to wrench it from the submarine. It was a nerve-racking five minutes before he managed it, all the while with bubbles ascending to the surface from the faulty valve on his breathing apparatus. The water, to make it worse, was clear. Had any of the Japanese on board been observant they would have seen the air bubbles – and indeed the XE-craft – below them. Five minutes later – it seemed to Fraser, Reid and 'Kiwi' Smith an agonising age – Magennis was back, sliding into the W&D compartment, looking at them with his thumbs up again.

'Starboard twenty steer 090 degrees half ahead group up,' I ordered all in one breath.

'Aye, aye, sir.'

'Twelve hundred revolutions.'

'Aye, aye, sir.'

'O.K.,' I said. 'Home, James, and don't spare the horses.' I think we all managed a smile at that moment.

XE3 managed, under Fraser's careful control, to make her escape from Singapore harbour by the skin of her teeth. 'Happily we steamed on,' Mick Magennis remembered later. 'Lieutenant Fraser lashed himself to the induction trunk on the casing. At 11.50 p.m. we picked up our parent submarine HMS *Stygian*. She was using an infra-red lamp as a signal. It could only be seen by us wearing special goggles. Hours later we transferred to *Stygian* and the tow crew took over. We had been fifty-two hours without sleep except for the doze I had before the attack.' In a subsequent letter to his brother he described the escape succinctly: 'Clear of boom and out 9.30 p.m. 10 p.m. till 11 p.m. loud explosions and clouds of shit. Joy in our hearts.'

> We felt happy. There were tots of rum all round, big eats and lots of sleep. Later we learned we had blown a sixty feet by thirty feet hole in the *Takao* and put her guns out of action. One man inspired us all on that mission: Lieutenant Fraser. He was cool, real cool.

Lieutenant Jack Smart's *XE1* had a more difficult journey into Singapore, and because of a number of delays came through the inner boom ninety minutes after *XE3*. The time that they would have required to reach the *Myōkō*, place their limpets and lay their charges, and then get out back past the boom before the tide fell or the boom was closed, persuaded Smart that he had no choice but to lay her two main charges alongside the *Takao* as well. He achieved this successfully. His biggest risk, when coming to this decision, was not knowing either where *XE3* was, or the state of any charges or limpets she might have already dropped. In Fell's words, her arrival to lay her own charges alongside the enemy cruiser brought the risk of disturbing the 'fuse of *XE3*'s charge and blowing him to pieces'.

Smart managed to escape from Singapore and meet up with his towing submarine, HMS *Spark*, the following night. They arrived safely back in Brunei three days later to join in the celebrations. The explosions they caused removed a considerable expanse of *Takao*'s hull and settled her on the bottom of the harbour, nothing more now than a metal hulk. This – together with the cable-cutting operations – had been a staggering success, not just for Fell and the crews of *XE1*, *XE3*, *XE4* and *XE5*, but also for the entire X-craft concept. Through no fault of their own they had come too late in the Pacific to achieve the successes that Rear Admiral Claud Barry in London had always asserted would be her due, but vindication of sorts had at last been received, in what nobody knew at the time were the dying days of the war against Japan.

Epilogue

It is reasonable to argue that both Chariots and X-craft in British service did not reach the potential envisaged for them in the Second World War by their designers and advocates. Yet what they did achieve remains significant. Taking their lead from the shock delivered by the *Maiali* of the *Regia Marina* in 1941, Fell and Sladen turned their wooden log into an effective weapon of war within six months: only massively bad luck prevented the extraordinarily brave Norwegians and Charioteers on Operation *Title* from crippling the *Tirpitz* in her Trondheimsfjord lair. This was left to an equally extraordinary weapon – the X-craft – which took an idea that had been prevalent in submarine circles since before the start of the First World War, and created a fighting device of tremendous potential.

Operation *Source* demonstrated unequivocally to an Admiralty traditionally sceptical of this type of innovation that X-craft had a role in threatening enemy capital ships in their harbours. Only the unwillingness of the United States Navy to accept a role for the Royal Navy in any guise in the Pacific prevented the full flowering of the X-craft in the war against Japan. This was a significant missed opportunity. Such methods of warfare are often as important for the psychological threat that they pose as for what they can deliver in terms of combat capability. X-craft could have played a vital role in locking Japanese capital vessels in their harbours, as Northways so loudly and persistently argued. It was not to be, however, and the possibilities offered by these brave men in their 30-ton submersibles must remain one of the 'What If's of the Second World War. What is clear, however, is that only Britain managed to design, build and deploy midget submarines with consistent effect in the war. The Japanese mini-submarines that raided Sydney in 1942 were one-shot suicide weapons, and fit an entirely different category of warfare.

What undoubtedly sets apart the Chariots and X-craft is the remarkable quality of the men who operated them. Many heroic deeds were undertaken in the war, but the sheer guts, perseverance and death-defying courage of the crews who attacked enemy vessels in the Trondheimsfjord, Altafjord, Bergen, Palermo, Tripoli, La Maddalena, La Spezia, Phuket and Singapore set the men of the Special Service craft apart from the ordinary run of mortals. That this is so is demonstrated by the stunning array of gallantry medals awarded to the relatively small number of men associated with this branch of naval service. No more than a couple of hundred men served in these two types of craft during the war, but sixty-eight awards were given, including four Victoria Crosses; eleven Distinguished Service Orders; seventeen Distinguished Service Crosses; six Conspicuous Gallantry Medals and twelve Distinguished Service Medals. It was a truly incredible haul, and pays witness to the courage of the men who operated these dangerous craft, and the physical, mental and emotional demands made on them. It is hard to point to any similar field of service in Britain's military past that has seen so shining a panoply of the highest awards for gallantry. These men – their heroism heart-stoppingly authentic – were truly the *real* X-Men, vastly more exciting and attractive than anything created in cartoons about the heroes of another, unreal, world.

Bravery, of course, was not limited to the British. The courage of the men of the Decima Flottiglia, who struck the first of these blows against the Royal Navy in Alexandria in December 1941, did much to repair the military reputation of the Italian armed forces at the time, at least in British eyes. It was an act that removed any vestiges of complacency or arrogance in the minds of those who properly understood the risks that the mission entailed, and the courage required to mount so audacious a venture. In an unprecedented ceremony in March 1945 Luigi de la Penne was summoned to receive the *Medaglia d'Oro* – Italy's highest decoration for bravery, the equivalent of Britain's Victoria Cross – from none other than King Victor Emmanuel III. Also in attendance was the Royal Navy's Vice Admiral Sir Charles Morgan, who was, at the time, Senior Allied Naval Representative to Italy. When the moment came for the award to be pinned on de la Penne's chest, the king turned to Morgan, and suggested that he do the honour. Laughing, Morgan agreed, and in one of the most unusual medal presentations of all time, congratulated the Italian charioteer for the extraordinary courage he had displayed in sinking HMS *Valiant*, the ship in which he – Morgan – had been captain – over three years before.

Acknowledgements and Remarks

This book could not have been written without the support and collaboration of many people. In particular several families have allowed me to quote liberally from the records, diaries and memoirs – published and unpublished – of their X-craft and Chariot fore-bears. I am especially grateful to Teresa Woollcott of Canberra, Australia, who painstakingly scanned her father Butch Woollcott's amazing memoirs for me. His record, together with his oral account in the Imperial War Museum in London, remains an arrestingly powerful memorial to an era now long lost to history. Woollcott's memoirs are so remarkable in their descriptive energy that I have quoted extensively from them, and I am grateful to Teresa for permission to do so. I am also profoundly in the debt of those veterans who wrote of their experiences, such as Ian Fraser, Max Shean, George Honour, Ken Hudspeth, 'Tiny' Fell, David Howarth, George Simpson and C. E. T. Benson, among others.

Pamela Mitchell's detailed interrogations of the subject of both Chariots and X-craft were also enormously helpful. Robert Hobson's interest in all things Chariot proved of enormous help, and I am grateful to him for his willingness to assist in this project. George Malcolmson, curator of the Royal Navy's Submarine Museum in Gosport, made available the entire suite of his material on the subject, and I am very thankful to him for his knowledge and helpfulness. I was also considerably helped by a number of experts who have written in this field, not least of all the late

281

Richard Compton-Hall, Robert Hobson and Paul Kemp. A number of excellent books proved of real worth in my research, such as those by Paul Watkins (on Godfrey Place, VC), Léonce Peillard (on the *Tirpitz*) and George Fleming (on Mick Magennis, VC).

I have relied very heavily on accounts that are held in various archives, in the United Kingdom and Australia. I am especially grateful to the Imperial War Museum for permission to use some of the vast store of material in its care, especially in the sound archives, and to the individual copyright holders who have kindly granted me permission to use their material in this account. In addition I wish to record my thanks once more to the curators and librarians of the Churchill Archive Centre, Cambridge; the National Archives, Kew; the Royal Naval Museum, and the Australian War Memorial, Canberra.

I am grateful, again, for the support of my wonderful family during the long absences they experienced while I wrote this book. My agent, Charlie Viney, continues to be a tower of strength, and Richard Milner, Josh Ireland and the quite superb team at Quercus have made the publication of this story an enjoyable experience.

I have followed the practice – requested by several readers – to convert the 24-hour clock into a.m. and p.m., throughout. I have, likewise, converted port and starboard in most instances, and the various spellings of place names have been unified using modern proper nouns. I have also continued my practice of not directly referencing the text, on the basis that masses of endnotes are unnecessary when accompanied by a detailed list of sources and merely create what Max Hastings has memorably described as an author's 'peacock display'. All the material used in the research for this book has been cited in the Sources below.

I have also exercised judgement when conflicts have appeared between sources. This problem occurs often when using original manuscripts, such as diaries, letters and reports. Historians writing of these matters before 1976 did not have the benefit of official files, which were only opened thirty years after the war, and errors of fact are to be expected as a consequence. Equally, veterans' memories have been proven – to me at least – to become less precise with age. Where two accounts exist, often by the same person, I have always taken the earlier one, on the basis that it was recorded closest to the event. Likewise, a feature of this book is the considerable amount of material provided by the participants. Not all accounts, even of the same operation, coincide, so a degree of weaving of sometimes contradictory accounts has been undertaken, in order to provide a coherent narrative. It is possible, therefore, that some errors in detail or judgement may exist. In any work of history relying substantially on oral and written memories this is inevitable, but where these have occurred as a result of my own failings I apologise, and any that are brought to my attention will be remedied in later editions.

Operations in Norway, 1942-44

0   200 miles
0   500 km

N

Kåfjord
Operation *Source*

Trodheimsfjord
Operation *Title*

Shetland Islands

Bergen
Operations *Barbara,
Guidance and Heckle*

NORWEGIAN SEA

SWEDEN

FINLAND

NORWAY

Oslo

Bergen

ESTONIA

RUSSIA

LATVIA

LITHUANIA

DENMARK

UNITED
KINGDOM

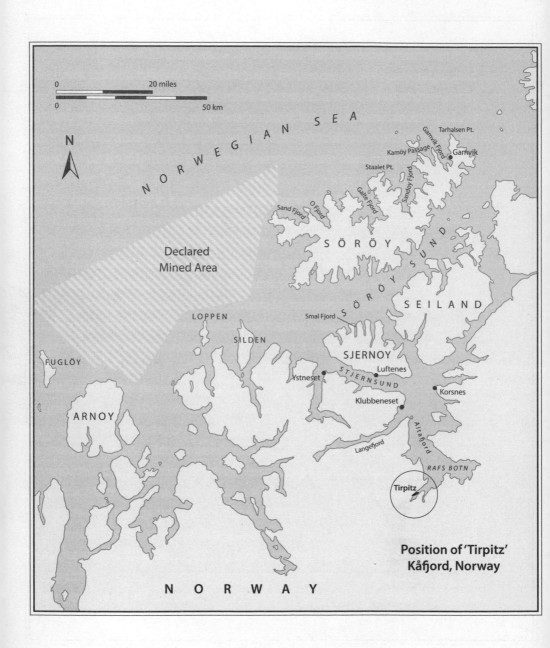

20 miles

50 km

N

NORWEGIAN SEA

Tarhalsen Pt.

Gamvik Fjord

Kamöy Passage

Gamvik

Staalet Pt.

Sandøy Fjord

Sand Fjord

O Fjord

Galte Fjord

SÖRÖY

SÖRÖY SUND

SEILAND

Declared
Mined Area

LOPPEN

Smal Fjord

SILDEN

SJERNOY

Luftenes

FUGLÖY

Ystneset

STJERNSUND

Korsnes

Klubbeneset

ARNOY

Langefjord

Altafjord

RAFS BOTN

Tirpitz

**Position of 'Tirpitz'
Kåfjord, Norway**

NORWAY

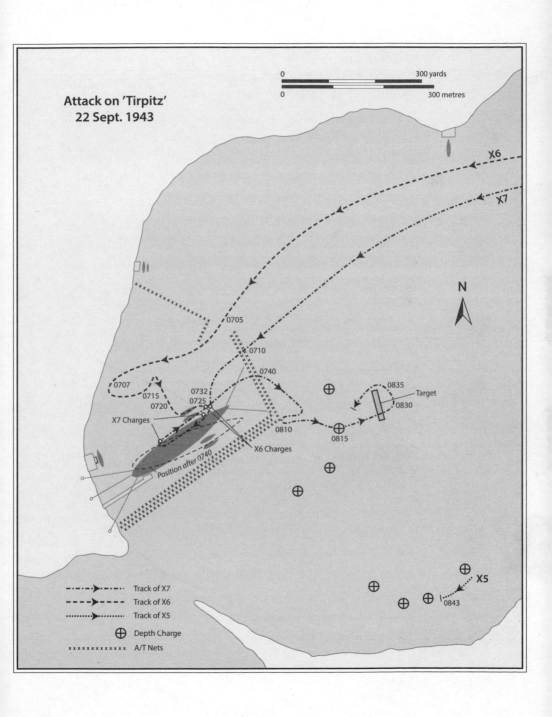

Attack on 'Tirpitz'
22 Sept. 1943

| 0 | | | 300 yards |
| 0 | | | 300 metres |

X6
X7

N

0705
0710
0740
0835
Target
0830
0707
0715
0732
0725
0720
X7 Charges
0810
0815
X6 Charges
Position after 0740
X5
0843

Track of X7
Track of X6
Track of X5
Depth Charge
A/T Nets

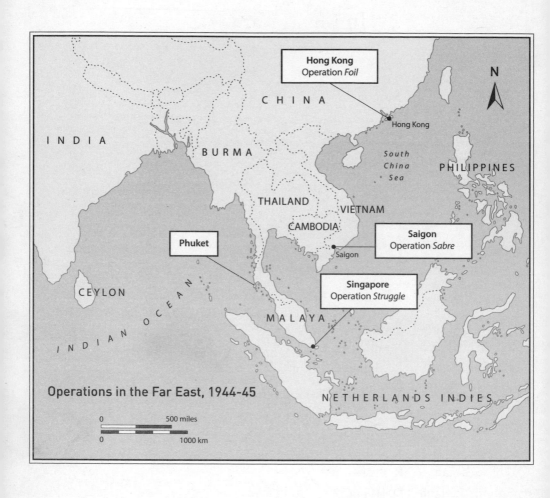

Hong Kong
Operation *Foil*

C H I N A

Hong Kong

INDIA

BURMA

South
China
Sea

PHILIPPINES

N

THAILAND

VIETNAM

CAMBODIA

Saigon
Operation *Sabre*

Phuket

Saigon

CEYLON

INDIAN OCEAN

Singapore
Operation *Struggle*

MALAYA

Operations in the Far East, 1944-45

NETHERLANDS INDIES

0   500 miles

0   1000 km

Appendix 1

In Memoriam

Rank	Name	Service	Type	Date
Lieutenant	P. C. A. Browning	RNVR	Chariots	May 1942
Sub Lieutenant	J. E. Grogan	SANF (V)	Chariots	Oct. 1942
Sub Lieutenant	I. M. Thomas	RNVR	X-craft	Dec. 1942
Lieutenant	C. E. Bonnell, DSC	RCNVR	Chariots	Dec. 1942
Lieutenant	S. F. Stretton-Smith	RNVR	Chariots	Dec. 1942
Sub Lieutenant	J. Sargent	RNVR	Chariots	Dec. 1942
Sub Lieutenant	G. G. Goss	RNVR	Chariots	Dec. 1942
Second Lieutenant	J. Kerr	Highland Light Infantry	Chariots	Dec. 1942
Leading Seaman	B. Trevethian	RN	Chariots	Dec. 1942
Leading Seaman	M. Rickwood	RN	Chariots	Dec. 1942
Able Seaman	R. Maplebeck	RN	Chariots	Dec. 1942
Ordinary Seaman	R. Anderson	RNR	Chariots	Dec. 1942
Stoker	R. W. Pridham	RN	Chariots	Dec. 1942
Lieutenant	H. F. Cook	RNVR	Chariots	Jan. 1943
Able Seaman	W. Simpson	RN	Chariots	Jan. 1943
Able Seaman	R. Evans	RN	Chariots	Jan. 1943
Sub Lieutenant	D. H. Locke	RNVR	X-craft	May 1943
Lieutenant	H. Henty-Creer	RNVR	X-craft	Sep. 1943
Lieutenant	L. B. Whittam	RNVR	X-craft	Sep. 1943
Sub Lieutenant	E. Kearon	RNVR	X-craft	Sep. 1943
Sub Lieutenant	A. D. Malcolm	RNVR	X-craft	Sep. 1943

Sub Lieutenant	T. J. Nelson	RNVR	X-craft	Sep. 1943
ERA	R. Mortiboys	E.R.A.	X-craft	Sep.1943
ERA	W. M. Whitley	E.R.A.	X-craft	Sep. 1943
Ordinary Seaman	A. H. Harte	RN	X-craft	Sep. 1943
Stoker	G. H. Hollett	Stoker	X-craft	Sep. 1943
Lieutenant	B. M. McFarlane	RAN	X-craft	Feb.1944
Lieutenant	W. J. Marsden	RANVR	X-craft	Feb.1944
ERA	C. Ludbrook	RN	X-craft	Feb.1944
Able Seaman	J. Pretty	RN	X-craft	Feb.1944
Sub Lieutenant	P. J. Hunt	RNVR	X-craft	April 1944
Sub Lieutenant	K. V. F. Harris	RNVR	Chariots	July 1944
Sub Lieutenant	D. N. Purdy	RNZNVR	X-craft	Sep. 1944
Leading Stoker	A. J. Brammer	RN	X-craft	Sep. 1944
Lieutenant	A. Staples	SANF (V)	X-craft	March 1945
Able Seaman	J. J. Carroll	RN	X-craft	March 1945
Stoker	E. W. Higgins	RN	X-craft	March 1945
Lieutenant	D. Carey	RN	X-craft	July 1945
Lieutenant	B. Enzer	RNVR	X-craft	July 1945

Appendix 2

Victoria Cross Citations

Lieutenant Charles Place and Lieutenant Donald Cameron (unusually, a joint citation)

The King has approved the award of the Victoria Cross for valour to Lieutenant Basil Charles Godfrey Place, DSC, RN, and Lieutenant Donald Cameron, RNR, the Commanding Officers of two of His Majesty's Midget Submarines X6 and X7, which on 22 September 1943 carried out a most daring and successful attack on the German battleship Tirpitz, moored in the protected anchorage of Kåfjord, North Norway.

To reach the anchorage necessitated the penetration of an enemy minefield and a passage of fifty miles up the fjord, known to be vigilantly patrolled by the enemy, and to be guarded by nets, gun defences and listening posts, this, after a passage of at least a thousand miles from base.

Having successfully eluded all these hazards and entered the fleet anchorage, Lieutenants Cameron and Place, with complete disregard for danger, worked their small craft past the close anti-submarine and torpedo nets surrounding the Tirpitz and from a position inside these nets, carried out a cool and determined attack.

Whilst they were still inside the nets, a fierce enemy counter attack by guns and depth charges developed which made their withdrawal impossible. Lieutenants Place and Cameron, there-fore, scuttled their craft to prevent them from falling into the hands of the enemy. Before doing so, they took every measure to ensure the safety of their crews, the majority of whom, together with themselves, were subsequently taken prisoner.

In the course of this operation, these very small craft pressed home their attack to the full, in doing so accepting all the dangers inherent in such vessels, and facing every possible hazard which ingenuity could devise for the protection, in harbour, of vitally important fleet units. The courage, endurance, and utter contempt for danger in the immediate face of the enemy shown by Lieutenants Cameron and Place during this determined and successful attack were supreme.

Leading Seaman James Joseph ('Mick') Magennis

Leading Seaman Magennis served as Diver in His Majesty's Midget Submarine XE-3 for her attack on 31st July, 1945, on a Japanese cruiser of the Atago class. Owing to the fact that XE-3 was tightly jammed under the target the diver's hatch could not be fully opened, and Magennis had to squeeze himself through the narrow space available.

He experienced great difficulty in placing his limpets on the bottom of the cruiser owing both to the foul state of the bottom and to the pronounced slope upon which the limpets would not hold. Before a limpet could be placed therefore Magennis had thoroughly to scrape the area clear of barnacles, and in order to secure the limpets he had to tie them in pairs by a line passing under the cruiser keel. This was very tiring work for a diver, and he was moreover handicapped by a steady leakage of oxygen which was ascending in bubbles to the surface. A lesser man would have been content to place a few limpets and then to return to the craft. Magennis, however, persisted until he had placed his full outfit before returning to the craft in an exhausted condition. Shortly after withdrawing Lieutenant Fraser endeavoured to jetti-son his limpet carriers, but one of these would not release itself and fall clear of the craft. Despite his exhaustion, his oxygen leak and the fact that there was every probability of his being sighted, Magennis at once volunteered to leave the craft and free the carrier rather than allow a less experienced diver to undertake the job. After seven minutes of nerve-racking work he succeeded in releasing the carrier. Magennis displayed very great courage and devotion to duty and complete disregard for his own safety.

Lieutenant Ian Edward Fraser

Lieutenant Fraser commanded His Majesty's Midget Submarine XE-3 in a successful attack on a Japanese heavy cruiser of the Atago class at her moorings in Johore Strait, Singapore, on 31st July, 1945. During the long approach up the Singapore Straits XE-3 deliberately left the believed safe channel and entered mined waters to avoid suspected hydrophone posts. The target was aground, or nearly aground, both fore and aft, and only under the midship portion was there just sufficient water for XE-3 to place herself under the cruiser. For forty minutes XE-3 pushed her way along the seabed until finally Lieutenant Fraser managed to force her right under the centre of the cruiser. Here he placed the limpets and dropped his main side charge. Great difficulty was experienced in extricating the craft after the attack had been completed, but finally XE-3 was clear, and commenced her long return journey out to sea. The courage and determination of Lieutenant Fraser are beyond all praise. Any man not possessed of his relentless determination to achieve his object in full, regardless of all consequences, would have dropped his side charge alongside the target instead of persisting until he had forced his submarine right under the cruiser. The approach and withdrawal entailed a passage of 80 miles through water which had been mined by both the enemy and ourselves, past hydrophone positions, over loops and controlled minefields, and through an anti-submarine boom.

Sources

Churchill Archives Centre, Cambridge
GBR/0014/FELL – Papers of Captain William Richmond Fell
GBR/0014/GDFY – Papers of Admiral John Henry Godfrey
RN Submarine Museum, Gosport
The list that follows is a sample of the material available
A1940/012 – Brief details of *X3* and *X4*
A1940/037 – Report on X-craft 1909–1945
A1942/003 – *X7*
A1942/004 – XE-Craft Handbook
A1944/028 – Patrol reports HMS *Sceptre*
A1944/048 – Patrol report on attack on Bergen
A1945/023 – Final report on Operation *Source*
A1980/091 – Beach marking on Normandy by Commander George Honour
A1981/001 – Material and articles by Compton-Hall
A1984/019 – Accounts by Cameron VC and others
A1984/082 – Letters from Ken Hudspeth
A1986/067 – Duties for passage crews by Able Seaman E Whitaker
A1987/040 – Correspondence between J Bowman and Gus Britton
A1987/043 – Recollections of Lieutenant Commander EK Forbes
A1988/037 – Correspondence between E Whitaker and Gus Britton
A1988/073 – X-craft operations details in WW2
A1989/108 – Letters concerning escape from an X-craft
A1991/169 – Report on attacks on Tirpitz
A1992/126 – Operation *Gambit* by Commander George Honour
A1995/165 – Letter by Magennis to his brother
A1995/181 – Memoirs of Petty Officer AS Gower

A1995/215 – Midget Submarines on D-Day

A1995/347 – Midget Submarines

A1995/403 – Recollections by Commander ET Stanley

A2000/006 – Various documents from Sub Lt Beadon Dening

A2003/179 – Reports on attack on Singapore

A2207/402 – Scrapbook by Sub Lt F Ainslie

TNA, Kew

- ADM1/12207   X-craft co-operation with the USA
- ADM1/12614   X-craft
- ADM1/12880   12th Submarine Flotilla training
- ADM1/12929   Simulated attack by X-craft on HMS Bonaventure
- ADM1/13686   Harbour defences against X-craft
- ADM1/14789   Report on captured Italian torpedoes
- ADM1/14810   Operation Source
- ADM1/14811   Trials of X-craft side charges
- ADM1/14824   Operation Source
- ADM1/16411   Sunderland Flying Boats
- ADM1/16490   Human torpedo trials in Gibraltar
- ADM1/18651   X-craft
- ADM1/18654   HMS Bonaventure
- ADM1/20026   Operation Source
- ADM1/25845   X-craft Training
- ADM136/10   HMS Queen Elizabeth
- ADM179/342   Exercise Pirate
- ADM199/888   Operation Source
- ADM204/1250   X-craft
- ADM204/1253   XE-craft
- ADM223/580   Italian Maiale
- ADM223/596   Italian 10th Flotilla
- ADM223/600   Italian 10th Flotilla
- ADM226/49-50   X-craft
- ADM234/347-8   Operation Source
- ADM234/480   HMS Queen Elizabeth
- ADM249/780   X-craft
- ADM280/4-5,13   Underwater explosion trials against X-craft
- ADM280/16-17   X-craft

- ADM358/1373   Enquiries into missing personnel
- Air2/9875   Operation Source
- CAB80/73/24   Operation Source
- DEFE2/1059   X-craft
- HS2/179   SOE (Operation Frodesley)
- HS2/206   SOE (Operation Source)
- HS7/175   SOE Norwegian Section
- HS7/280-2   SOE Scandinavia
- MR1/1015/10-14 Operation Source
- PREM 3/191/1   Tirpitz

Royal Naval Museum
- 1987/319(3) Diaries of Midshipman Barrie Kent, HMS *Valiant*
Australian War Memorial
- Woollcott, Sidney PR86/198
Imperial War Museum
Sound
- Sidney Woollcott 11911
- Anthony Eldridge 11259
- Vernon Coles 13422
- Max Shean 28642
- Claud Barry 02440
- Godfrey Place 2441
Documents
- Colonel J S Wilson CMG OBE 16849

Select Bibliography

Borghese, J. Valerio, *Sea Devils: Italian Navy Commandos in World War Two* (Annapolis, Maryland: Naval Institute Press, 1995)

Boyce, Frederick, and Douglas Everett, *SOE: The Scientific Secrets* (Stroud: Sutton Publishing, 2003)

Bragadin, Marc Antonio, *The Italian Navy in World War II* (Annapolis: United States Naval Institute, 1957)

Chalmers, W. S., *Max Horton and the Western Approaches* (London: Hodder and Stoughton, 1954)

Chatterton, E. Keble, *Amazing Adventure: A Thrilling Naval Biography* (London: Hurst & Blackett Ltd, 1935)

Clayton, Tim, *Sea Wolves: The Extraordinary Story of Britain's WW2 Submarines* (London: Little, Brown, 2011)

Cocchia, Aldo, *Submarines Attacking: Adventures of Italian Naval Forces* (London: William Kimber and Co. Ltd, 1956)

Compton-Hall, R. R., *Submarine Warfare: Monsters & Midgets* (Poole: Blandford Press, 1985)

Dalzel-Job, Patrick, *From Arctic Snow to Dust of Normandy* (Plockton: Nead-an Eoin Publishing, 1991)

De la Penne, Luigi, 'The Italian Attack on the Alexandria Naval Base', in *The United States Naval Institute Proceedings*, vol. 82, no. 2, February 1956

Eldridge, A. W. C., *Just Out of Sight* (London: Minerva Press, 1988)

Fell, W. R., *The Sea Our Shield* (London: Cassell, 1966)

Fleming, George, *Magennis VC* (Dublin: History Ireland, 1998)

Greene, Jack, and Alessandro Massignani, *The Naval War in the Mediterranean 1940–1943* (London: Chatham Publishing, 1998)

—, *The Black Prince and the Sea Devils: The Story of Valerio Borghese and the Elite Units of the Decima Mas* (Cambridge, Mass.: Da Capo Press, 2004)

Hobson, Robert, *Chariots of War* (Church Stretton: Ulric Publishing, 2004)

Howarth, David, *The Shetland Bus* (London: Thomas Nelson, 1956)

Kemp, Paul, *Underwater Warriors* (London: Cassell, 1996)

Mitchell, Pamela, *The Tip of the Spear: The Midget Submarines* (Huddersfield: Richard Netherwood, 1993)

—, *Chariots of the Sea: The Story of Britain's Human Torpedoes during the Second World War* (Huddersfield: Richard Netherwood, 1998)

Peillard, Léonce, *Sink the Tirpitz!* (London: Jonathan Cape, 1968)

Roskill, S. W., *The War at Sea 1939–1945* (London: Her Majesty's Stationery Office, 1954)

Sadkovich, James, *The Italian Navy in World War II* (Westport: Greenwood Press, 1994)

Saelen, Frithjof, *None But the Brave: Story of 'Shetlands' Larsen* (London: Souvenir Press, 1955)

Schofield, William, P. J. Carisella and Adolph Caso, *Frogmen: First Battles* (Boston: Branden Books, 1987)

Shean, Max, *Corvette and Submarine* (Claremont, Western Australia: Self-Published, 1992)

Simpson, George, *Periscope View: A Memoir of the 10th Submarine Flotilla at Malta, 1941–1943* (Barnsley: Seaforth Publishing, 2010)

Strutton, Bill, and Michael Pearson, *The Secret Invaders* (London: Hodder and Stoughton, 1958)

Waldron, Tom, and James Gleeson, *The Frogmen* (London: Evans Brothers, 1950)

Watkins, Paul, *Midget Submarine Commander: The Life of Godfrey Place VC* (Barnsley: Pen & Sword, 2012)

INDEX

Index